Postmodern American Poetry

Jerome Mazzaro

Postmodern American Poetry

University of Illinois Press

Urbana Chicago London

For my mother and in memory of my father

© 1980 by the Board of Trustees of the University of Illinois
Manufactured in the United States of America

Library of Congress Cataloging in Publication Data

Mazzaro, Jerome.
  Postmodern American poetry.

  Includes bibliographical references and index.
  1. American poetry—20th century—History and
criticism.   I. Title.
PS323.5.M39   811'.5'409   79-11119
ISBN 0-252-00759-X

Contents

Preface

Postmodern American Poetry is not an attempt to define or detail a movement in contemporary letters so much as it is an attempt to isolate recurrent patterns and influences in the work and reputations of seven poets. These patterns were first applied by critics to the work of W. H. Auden and later assumed or applied by a group of poets as diverse as Randall Jarrell, Theodore Roethke, David Ignatow, John Berryman, Sylvia Plath, and Elizabeth Bishop. The inclusion of Sylvia Plath in the group may at first seem strange, given her date of birth; but *Ariel* was completed a year before the publications of Roethke's *The Far Field* (1964) and Berryman's *77 Dream Songs* (1964) and thirteen years before Elizabeth Bishop's *Geography III* (1976). Similarly Ignatow's age and responses to "greatness" place him more in this group than with the younger poets who "discovered" him. I make no attempt to justify the exclusion of other poets, some of whom I have written on elsewhere and others on whom I plan to write, except to say that the book was never intended to be an extended all-inclusive overview. Robert Lowell, who might otherwise have been included, is the subject of my *The Poetic Themes of Robert Lowell* (1965) and is the focus of another full-length study currently underway. Richard Wilbur's formalism and "common style" present quite another approach to the individualism I treat here. Nor is it my intent to present these poets necessarily as "arguments." I have chosen, instead, devices of extended elaboration, hoping that a freedom from rigid pattern may allow the poets room to define their own cases, preoccupations, and messages. Yet even as moderator I impose style and perspective and whatever organization may be inferred.

Randall Jarrell first used the term *postmodern* in regard to American poetry in his famous review of Robert Lowell's *Lord Weary's Castle* (1946) to characterize the movement of which Lowell's verse was a part. Two years later John Berryman used the same term in "Waiting for the End, Boys," citing Jarrell as its source. It was not until the early fifties that Charles Olson used the term in another context and presumably toward another end. Joseph N. Riddel's *The Inverted Bell* (1974), which treats the "counterpoetics" of William Carlos Williams in the context of Olson's statement, persuades me that Olson's position as interpreted along the lines of Heidegger as explained by certain French structuralists is not markedly different from what I perceive as Jarrell's meaning. Without the technical language of the structuralists, the formulation of the essential differences between "modernism" and "postmodernism" becomes: in conceiving of language as a fall from unity, modernism seeks to restore the original state often by proposing silence or the destruction of language; postmodernism accepts the division and uses language and self-definition—much as Descartes interpreted thinking—as the basis of identity. Modernism tends, as a consequence, to be more mystical in the traditional senses of that word whereas postmodernism, for all its seeming mysticism, is irrevocably worldly and social. Rather than T. S. Eliot's belief that poetry "is not the expression of personality, but an escape from personality," postmodernists propose the opposite. The focus of this book as a description of the impact of W. H. Auden and the concepts of Freud, Marx, and Darwin on the poetry of the forties and fifties thus seems to bring the Jarrell and Olson positions into some accord without resolving their crucial distinctions of identity as form and identity as energy or the role of stylization in perception.

The demands of American poets, both in their tendencies to work out of different personal worlds and to appear independent of one another, account for disjunctions that may appear from the treatment of their individual poetics. These poetics come to stand for the guiding principles shaping and coloring the works, and it often pays the reader to remain as close as possible to the poet's formulations of these principles if a correlation of the two is one's aim. This has been my particular approach in contrast to the equally valid approach of correlating the poetry with principles imposed *ab exteriore* by the critic. Being in essence interpretations of an interpretation (the poem), both approaches fail equally to duplicate origins—the poem, and behind that the impulse that the poem misprizes; yet either misprision may be useful to a reader for an understanding of his role in interpreting life. In addition one can see in the individual bodies of poetry something of the diminishing energy that attends beliefs when they become commonplace. This is most notable in regard to Freud, who changes from *the* way of life to a comfortable literary prop. In no instance do I question the validity of the Cambridge anthropologists whose view of an origin of art in ritual shades the structuralist view of the origin of language in "mystical" oneness. Gilbert Murray's theory of the origin of Greek tragedy in ritual, for example, was answered as early as 1927 by Arthur W. Pickard-Cambridge in *Dithyramb Tragedy and Comedy*, and psycholinguists have been speculating for some time that the impulse to language and the discernment of meaning in syntax are genetic and have little to do with a "fall" from some privileged position. Instead the use of language, like so many biological traits, comes as a normal process of maturation. The seven poets considered in this book do accept the view of language and art advanced by the Cambridge group.

Other disjunctions lie in the value that postmodernists place on the long poem. All considered it necessary to the "great poet," though differences occurred as to whether the "long poem" should be sustained narrative, a lyrical sequence, or a "poem" at all. Auden wrote several long poems; Roethke thought of *Praise to the End!* (1951) as a lyrical sequence; Ignatow has described *Tread the Dark* (1978) as one poem; and Berryman's *Homage to Mistress Bradstreet* (1956) and *Dream Songs* (1969) are intended as long poems. On the other hand Jarrell, Plath, and Bishop remain faithful to the short poem, assuming that, if a long poem occurs, it occurs, as Eliot says of Shakespeare and his work, as "one significant, consistent, and developing personality." This ambiguity toward the long poem, especially in the case of Jarrell, is tied to a fear of strong personalities. Politically the personality cults of Winston Churchill and Franklin Delano Roosevelt were matched by those of Josef Stalin, Adolf Hitler, and Benito Mussolini; and in English literature Eliot reigned supreme. At times, as in the cases of Roethke and Berryman, the efforts at long poems came as rivalries with members of the modernist generation, as if the only way to assert personality was to "kill off" the parent in Freudian fashion. This drive toward "succession" was tempered by a sense of "simultaneity." Unlike science new discoveries did not invalidate the old. Instead great art could and did coexist, and long poems served as an initiation to these realms.

The book began as a series of book reviews that I published about the time I was completing *Transformations in the Renaissance English Lyric* (1970), and it shares with this earlier study a preoccupation with poetic form as a device for self-definition. Poets define self by changing convention. *Transformations* dealt with the phenomenon of self-definition as part of a separation of words and music. *Postmodern American Poetry* emphasizes the incorporation by its subjects of narrowly defined psychological and psychoanalytical and social principles, and I suspect that if a model exists for its effect, rather than divorce and ongoing existence with different partners, the model is a bouquet or the angelic choir of Dante's *Paradiso*—a unity that does not connote uniformity. In executing this model, I have tried to provide many of the references within the text. The abbreviations for these references together with the references for the remaining quotations can be found at the end of each chapter.

A number of colleagues, students, and friends aided me in the book's completion and I should like to give them thanks. They include Lionel Abel, Marcia Aronoff, Robert Boyers, Diane Christian, Jan Gordon, William Heyen, Marco Portinales, and John and Ruth Reed. I owe gratitude especially to Bruno Arcudi, Angus Fletcher, and Robert Edwards for putting up with me in moments when nothing seemed to go well and to Karl Gay and the staff of the poetry room of the Lockwood Memorial Library for their patience in my periodic raids on their holdings. I have been aided as well in the work's completion by grants from the Research Foundation of the State University of New York.

Versions of many of the chapters have appeared in forms different from those given here. The opening chapter was the basis of a lecture that I gave at Bennington College in May 1974. Chapters

2, 4, and 7 appeared in *Salmagundi* as "Between Two Worlds: The Post-Modernism of Randall Jarrell," 17 (fall 1971): 93–113; "Circumscriptions: The Poetry of David Ignatow," 22–23 (spring–summer 1973): 164–96; and "Elizabeth Bishop and the Poetics of Impediment," 27 (fall 1974): 118–44. To the Jarrell chapter I added material that appeared in "Arnoldian Echoes in the Poetry of Randall Jarrell," *Western Humanities Review* 23 (1969): 314–18, and "The Old Masters Disagree," *Nation* 214 (1972): 474–75. To the Bishop chapter I have added material that appeared in "Elizabeth Bishop's Particulars," *World Literature Today* 51 (winter 1977): 46–49, and "The Recent Poems of Elizabeth Bishop, *South Carolina Review* 10 (November 1977): 99–115. Chapter 3 of the book appeared as "Theodore Roethke and the Failures of Language," *Modern Poetry Studies* 1 (1970): 73–96, and chapter 5 as "John Berryman and the Yeatsian Mask," *Review of Existential Psychology and Psychiatry* 12 (1973): 141–62. It, too, includes material that appeared before in "Berryman's Dream World," *Kenyon Review* 31 (1969): 259–63. Chapter 6 was the basis of a lecture I delivered at the University of California, Riverside, in May 1974. It has since been included in Gary Lane's *Sylvia Plath without Tears* (Baltimore: Johns Hopkins University Press, 1978). I should like to thank the editors of all these publications for their permissions to reprint and the institutions for having let me try out my ideas on their students.

Jerome Mazzaro

Bennington, Vermont

1

The Genesis of Postmodernism: W. H. Auden

In 1935, when American writers embraced W. H. Auden as the leader of a new style of poetry that was to replace the "modernism" of the twenties, they did so because they felt that the poetry his work was to supplant was "untraditional" and that his style might serve as a corrective. John Crowe Ransom in "Poets without Laurels" (1935) expresses some of the readers' general discontent. He scores the "modernist" poets for rejecting identification "with public issues" and seeing instead "the possibility that an aesthetic effect may exist by itself, independent of morality or any other useful set of ideas."[1] The poets did so by insisting on a style whose purism precluded larger statements (Wallace Stevens) or whose confusing welters of detail obscured what meaning might be there (Allen Tate). In retrospect, cultural historians such as Robert M. Crunden in *From Self to Society, 1919–1941* (1972) are willing to attribute part of the discontent to an awareness of social injustice that crystalized with the executions of Sacco and Vanzetti in 1927. The executions greatly disturbed intellectuals yet seemed not to have troubled other segments of American society. The decision of the Tennessee supreme court in the same year upholding the constitutionality of the state's anti-evolution law struck a second embarrassing blow to liberals. Learning that they were powerless by themselves, many of these intellectuals began to resume their traditional roles as "keepers of the public conscience" and "men of public importance" by encouraging the working classes to act. The stock-market crash in 1929 confirmed a sense that something was crucially wrong with the structure of American society and that reconsideration of issues besides social injustice was needed.

Critics like I. A. Richards promised to isolate the content of poetry still further from public issues by institutionalizing a distinction between scientific and poetic language. As early as Morton D. Zabel's "A Dawn in Britain" (1931) Auden's own engagement with public issues was viewed as a response to Richards's *Science and Poetry* (1926). The sequence that Richards outlines of the demise of a magical view of the world and then of poetry was seen as counteracted by Auden's courage in revitalizing "the immediate and actual experience without denying the existence of the reason, or of the reality which reason has discovered." Embraced under these conditions, Auden, as Theodore Maynard and others supposed in 1935, seems to have understood no better than most readers that a spiritual bent lay behind the engagement in social issues or that he would soon be moving into the church.[2] For the moment, Auden was content to capture enough of the energies of the unbelieving young by writing of the ills of postwar England to direct their verse into reconceiving economics during and following the depression years. He was also able to redirect the technique of free association in T. S. Eliot's poetry toward a Freudian substructure as well as to infuse verse with a new Darwinism. These accomplishments matched a growing acceptance of Freud, Marx, and Darwin that became more visible with each new review of the poet's work until by the middle of the thirties Auden was the center about which critics framed a concept of poetry that Randall Jarrell was later to call "post- or anti-modern."

Since J. H. Plumb's *The Death of the Past* (1969) it has seemed appropriate to look upon this acceptance of Auden as reflective of a "crisis in history," a time when two discrete ontologies were competing for popular approval. The first, the traditional creation of man by God, demanded an allegiance to spirit; the second, the evolution of man from nature, demanded an equally firm commitment to technology. The optimism which Auden's poetry offered to the thirties by embracing evolution and the attitudes of an industrial society directed one toward "change rather than conservation" and an "exploitation and consumption" whose sanctions did not lie in a past.[3] Its psychological equivalents in industry would be an equation of the worker with the machine (Henry Ford) and a linking of the output of that "machine" with Alfred Sloan's belief that the way to attract people to repeated purchases is to make incessant improvements and changes. In poetry the attitudes would create a sense not only that every poet must be new but that each new book by any poet must also be different. Only the jading of "experiment" during the late forties and the fifties accompanied by failing social values, new concerns for environment, and the popularization of entropy and the laws of thermodynamics seems to have acted as any brake. By the time Auden himself realized what was happening and adopted a "past" with a return to Anglicanism in 1940, the image of a daring forward-looking spokesman that had emerged over the years and that perfectly suited an industrial imagination was so strong that it could withstand the disappointment that some admirers felt at his earlier desertion from communism. As critics have come to perceive, if Auden did not have the answers, he more than any other young poet seemed to know what the questions were.

Most students of Auden contend that the figure of the "visionary" poet implied and presented by American critics during the thirties is distorted and unfair to the currently dominant interpretation of the writing—Auden as maker. Nevertheless the image does offer another, equally valid "truth" in what American writers of the thirties and forties needed to embrace in order to create their own individual poetries. By imitating Auden, these writers hoped to reestablish a role which parallels that taken by industry and which critics have consistently assigned American poetry: a tendency to turn away from what is known toward what may be conjectured and tested by personal experience. Oscar Williams in his *The New Pocket Anthology of American Verse* (1955) allies this tendency of American thought to a "territorial imperative" that an absence of boundaries nourishes. In an amusing misuse of language, he christens the trait an "overfulsomeness, a kind of biting off of more than could be chewed." Earlier William Carlos Williams had opposed the trait in *In the American Grain* (1925) to a second Puritan strain in American culture; and, in a less biological context, Hyatt Waggoner in *American Poets* (1968) sees the characteristic as resulting from an insecurity that accompanies America's lack of a stable society with preestablished place, position, class, and creed. This insecurity turns one "naturally" from "inherited poetic forms and traditional genres" toward what Emerson in "The Poet" (1844) characterizes as "the metre-making argument." Accordingly Waggoner affirms Selden Rodman's contention in *A New Anthology of Modern Poetry* (1938) that—much as Auden had been presented—American poets have tended to see themselves as "complete" men talking to "partial" men, visionaries rather than craftsmen, who show by their breaks with the past the authenticity of their visions and by their abilities to create fresh language that "they have used, and not been used by words."[4]

Other definitions of the tendency, including Auden's own in "The Anglo-American Difference" (1957), associate the conjectural nature of the poetry with the ability of Americans "to move on and make a fresh start"; and Auden in his move to the United States in 1939 does seem to realize this intent. A. Alvarez in *The Shaping Spirit* (1958) sees the trait physically—as a response to "the strange, untouched, inhuman remoteness of the landscape" that the poet would have to acclimate to after his arrival. In concepts that are identical to those which G. S. Fraser in his *Vision and Rhetoric* (1959) will apply to Auden's pre-American work, Alvarez argues that, if the American poet wanted a moral world complex enough to satisfy him, he has always had to build it for himself and that this building has resulted in an extreme inwardness. The creation of these isolated, imaginary personal moral worlds has produced, in turn, what Marius Bewley defines in *The Complex Fate* (1955) as the practice of American poetry to become exercises in will, evincing, in the poet's "ability to see-saw from cynicism into optimism and enthusiasm, and a moment later, rigorous conviction," an impatience and satisfaction with one's own being. The poetry has had "to put into moving substantial form the artist's own moral tensions" by embodying a language which permits discovery, statement, and eventual resolution, just as if these "moral tensions" might have been devised to fit marketing considerations. Any difficulty that exists in understanding such a poetry occurs not so much in the referents or intricate syntax as in discovering the direction of "its tentative, exploratory independence from all traditions."[5] Once discovered, the direction removes much of what appears obscure and restores the poet to an innovative status.

The earliest American reviews of Auden's work and the poet's own comments on industrial society make the neglect of the industrial imagination by critics and Auden's eventual "visionary" status appear the more remarkable by contrast. Zabel in reviewing *Poems* (1930) considers the volume modernist, "hardly more than a prospectus" for "a reconstruction of emotional values, personal and social," and he cites as the book's "greatest value" the certainty of the poet's "gift." Zabel is generally as consoled by Auden's "traditional topics" as he is moved by the style. Auden's "response" to Richards carries with it the common "ideals of affection, sympathy, and honor," and presumably the style affords his difference from the poetry that Richards considers outmoded. Dudley Fitts in his review in the *Hound and Horn* (1931) sounds a similar but less positive note. Fitts concentrates on the "extreme inwardness" of the poet's vision, attacking principally the book's "symbology" by claiming that too often the poet "fails to achieve anything but a prosaic iteration of incoherencies." Fitts goes on to observe, in language suggestive of French symbolism and in terms taken from Imagism and Eliot's idea of an "objective correlative," that "the imagery is not precise, the emotion only partially released. It is curious to observe that this is nearly always the result not of slipshod composition, but of composition too sedulously disordered—too refinedly chaotic." Fitts is willing to connect the result to Ransom's criticism of one aspect of "modernism"—obscurity for the sake of obscurity—comparing Auden finally to his "poetic" antecedent, the "modernist" Gerard Manley Hopkins.[6]

It is clear from both reviews that, whatever the precise crisis in history was that occurred during the thirties, an awareness of that crisis had not yet surfaced. In *The Orators* (1932) Auden works to consolidate some of the gains against Richards and to clarify the incoherency that Fitts objected to. By the book's completion Auden had become a communist, and he was being claimed by Michael Roberts in *The New Country* (1933) as a spokesman for anticapitalist views. The "bleak industrial civilizations" that Zabel found depicted in *Paid on Both Sides* were turned immediately from the inwardness of personal sentiment to the expression of

Marxist ideology. Still, in light of the poet's realization that the "Lawrentian doctrine of obedience to passion" could be regarded as a "rediscovery" of the Greek and Catholic doctrines of "nature," Henry Bamford Parkes in his review of the volume (1933) properly asks "whether artistic honesty and the organic growth of the individual, with which Mr. Auden is chiefly concerned, can be reconciled with [communism's] present intolerance." For Parkes, despite a surface similarity, Auden like many of the American Marxist writers was too individualistic to accept an ideology that went against personally felt experience. However much he was intent on showing that "the individual needs an appropriate environment in which to exercise his powers" and that one "cannot achieve harmony and integration except in a regenerated society," Auden was fated to defect.[7]

In "A Poet of Courage" (1933) John Gould Fletcher remarks on the private/public dichotomy, complaining again in concepts which are finally rhetorical and stylistic that one difficulty in following the poet is "that he seems to be perpetually mixing up two levels of experience, private and public." The "mix up," one assumes, results because Auden has not found an adequate correlative to his emotions: "Publicly he tries to persuade us that the world is a farce, privately we feel that he regards it largely as a tragedy." Fletcher again pinpoints obscurity and ambiguity as the major problems of the poetry, but he makes no mention of Marx. Instead he finds in Auden a kind of fanaticism, and he hopes that "perhaps in a few years' time [Auden] will have assimilated better what he has learned." In the course of these comments Fletcher sounds the first strains of a cultural imperialism by branding this fanaticism "puritan," and thus he places the poet squarely in an American tradition. Generally, however, the tone of the reviews, based entirely on English editions, lies away from such appropriation, indicating, at least initially, a resistance by Americans to accepting Auden's ideas as an answer to any of their needs.[8]

The poems selected by these early reviewers for citation are also telling. They are not those poems now regarded as especially ideological. Both Zabel and Fitts consider "Petition" (xxx), the sonnet which closes *Poems*. Zabel includes sections of "The Questioner Who Sits So Sly" (i) and Fitts the closing stanzas of *Paid on Both Sides*. Both xxx and i suggest the break with the past that coevally will preserve man's station with God (xxx) and his ability to respond humanly (1), despite "a change of heart" and no consolation in accepting "cushions from / Women." Even the sections from *Paid on Both Sides* conclude with an optimistic vision of the future with "Big fruit, eagles above the streams." If the mothers of the play and the women of the poems are destructive, there is no mention of this fact in either review, and certainly the social and biological impersonalism that various poems attack is a safe enough subject. One suspects that the location of the poems in the volume is a deciding factor in their being quoted and that the reviewers may have been reacting as much to the excitement Auden had created in England as they were to their own bafflement. Parkes, in turn, does not quote from the poetry of *The Orators*. He summarizes the work, feeling perhaps that quotations from the poetry might not be understandable out of context; and the only lines of poetry that Fletcher quotes in his review are an instance of Auden's "alliterative measures" and his debt to William Langland. Even the vision of the work which so impressed Parkes as Marxist is ambiguous enough to be seen by Fraser as "the politics of a romantic radical of the Right." Fraser interprets the chumminess of *The Orators* in terms of one's "being initiated into the group of young braves of the tribe." The vision comes to represent for him later something nearer the isolated "extreme inwardness" of American art: "the fantasies of power and the daydreams of violent social change which . . . solidarity can evoke, in periods of decay, among gifted and discontented young men." [9]

The first American edition of Auden's *Poems* and the first hints of a change in attitude toward the poet occurred in 1934. James Burnham in his review in the *Nation* presents Auden less skeptically and impressionistically, though not necessarily more accurately, than had Zabel and Fitts. The article comes at what Willard Thorp in *American Writing in the Twentieth Century* (1960) places as the "high point" of "the leftist interlude in American writing." A few years later, Americans would be convinced by a series of events in Russia that the U.S. would never experience a similar revolution. Thorp characterizes the first defections from this peak of leftist activity as resulting from "the trials of the 'old Bolsheviks' (1936–1938)," after which there was a brief revival of faith in the Russian "experiment." This revival was brought about by "Rus-

sia's intervention on the Loyalist side of the Spanish Civil War,"
but Stalin's signing of the Russo-German pact with Hitler in 1940
completed the disaffection. For the moment, though, Burnham is
willing to interpret the implied vision which earlier critics presumed was given faulty expression in terms of two serious and perhaps even contradictory impulses—Marxism and psychology.[10]

Neither the impulse to Marx nor to psychology receives profound treatment, but the over-all care with which Burnham approaches the poetry carries over into other reviews of the book.
Reviewers generally are intrigued enough by the poet to have read
beforehand C. Day Lewis's remarks in *A Hope for Poetry* (1934).
They cite his assurances of the poetry's politics and psychology as
well as of the poet's literary forebears—Hopkins, Wilfred Owen,
and Eliot. "Yeats, the last in the aristocratic tradition of poets, remains," according to Day Lewis, "the most admired of living
writers: none of us can touch his later work, and it is too personal
in idiom, too insulated to allow an easy communication of its
powers." By this date, too, Auden's stature is such that A.J.M.
Smith in "Old Games, New Rules" (1935) can begin: "What remains to be said about the poetry of W. H. Auden?"; and, in a
letter to the young Theodore Roethke, Rolfe Humphries can propose the English poet as a model for solving some of the rough-
nesses of Roethke's style.[11]

Yet this acceptance does not prevent further and new refine-
ments. The Marxism which had contributed in part to Auden's
appeal was on the wane; and, as Parkes had indicated, the poet
would be leaving it. New ideological underpinnings were needed
if one wished to continue to support a relevance to public issues.
While alluding to the poet's apostasy from communism, Day
Lewis in "Paging Mankind" (1937) questions what was to become
for Americans the new major prop; he notes not the vague "psychology" of his earlier essay but a more precise "Freudian bent"
in *Look, Stranger!* (1936). The next year, T. C. Wilson in "Plenty
of News" enlarges the public/private dichotomy into a triple range
of invention that in "New Year Letter" (1941) Jarrell will simplify
into "Darwin, Marx, Freud and Co." Wilson sees Auden's value in
his having explored for poetry "such hitherto largely untouched
fields as economics, biology, and psychoanalysis," and he excuses
occasional personal indulgences as "Last Will and Testament," on

8

which Auden and Louis MacNeice collaborated. The poem may be "a hodge-podge of private allusions and pointless innuendoes that will be meaningless to all except the initiate," but that seems less objectionable to Wilson than it was to Fitts and Ransom and less important, too, than the reflections "on one's past and one's culture from the outside" that occur coevally. Although unemployment is mentioned as a concern, Wilson does not see it as part of an emerging crisis.[12]

Long detailed studies also appear in the *Sewanee* and the *Virginia Quarterly* reviews but share none of Day Lewis's fear that Auden's "putting all his eggs in one basket" might bind "the survival-value of his poetry . . . up inextricably with the survival-value of Freud's teachings." The first, James G. Southworth's "Wystan Hugh Auden" (1938), isolates the chief themes of the poet's work as variations on Burnham's dualism. Southworth connects Marxism with the poet's public postures and psychology with his private feelings and points out, perhaps for the first time publicly in America, that the private feelings owe much to the poet's homosexuality. This "wound," "the suffering from which increased his sensibility," broadens Auden's "sympathy toward an understanding of others" and contributes vitally to the general alienation from tradition that is present in the poetry. Hence Southworth thinks that psychoanalysis rather than politics offers the more important entry into the work.[13]

F. Cudworth Flint in "New Leaders in English Poetry" (1938) likewise goes to psychoanalytic theory to reply to Fitts's charge of incoherence. Flint emphasizes that many of the "incoherencies" derive from a stance of "betweenness" that the poet assumes. He begins the essay by wondering "how a group of the younger poets of England can regard as in some sense their leader that one among them who at first inspection may seem the most elusive," and then he proceeds to characterize the intent of the "sedulous disorder" as a style which is "antirhetorical" or "declarative." "The basis of the style is the forthright statement, in which words are in general used denotatively. . . . In this precise matrix are sometimes imbedded statements which are . . . positively flat. . . . The epithets and metaphors employed by Auden are not decorative or suggestive; they are—often surprisingly—definitive." The settings for these statements lie usually "*between* the imagined and the actual." The details composing their expression "are drawn from the actual world, but are invested with a peculiar vividness, a peculiar air of being about to change into something different and probably more terrifying." The main part of these details derives from "industrial English Midland counties," a generalized "frontier between the known and unknown" and psychiatry. Flint does not elaborate on the significance of the Midland details, and he concludes with a commonplace of psychoanalysis as popular as Southworth's: "The world constructed of such material is obviously the world of dreams," and "the symbols in our fantasies and dreams are, as any psychiatrist knows, often (perhaps always) ambivalent." [14]

Thus, while not negating the essence of earlier charges or even of an acceptance of Auden based on Marxism, Southworth and Flint take the poet out of an Imagist-modernist past and place him in a new context which, however negligent it is of an industrial imagination, still views as advantages what earlier critics had considered "faults." That the new context should be so overtly Freudian follows from predispositions in both the poetry and the times. *Look, Stranger!* demands a familiarity with Freud, and long before the thirties American poetry and criticism had been responding to such a demand. Auden's own interest in psychology dates back, according to Stephen Spender in *World within World* (1951), to Oxford and 1928; and the interest was no doubt reinforced by Auden's year in Berlin (1928–29) and his meetings with John Layard. In particular Auden seems interested in the control of the body by the mind and in psychosomatic explanations of illness, and as early as "Art and Psychology" (1935) he is publicly confounding the two disciplines. He announces there: "The task of psychology, or art for that matter, is not to tell people how to behave, but by drawing their attention to what the impersonal unconscious is trying to tell them, and by increasing their knowledge of good and evil, to render them better able to choose, to become increasingly morally responsible for their destiny." This "impersonal unconscious" is Georg Groddeck's notion of the "it" which subsequently influenced Freud's notion of the "id," and the belief that the task of art is "educational" rather than simply mimetic seems to derive from R. G. Collingwood and the view his *The Principles of Art* (1938) would present as art, the "bringing of

emotions to consciousness." As recently as "Sigmund Freud"
(1952) the poet was still praising Freud for insisting that the goal
of therapy is to make the patient better able to handle his personal
choices rather than to explain mechanistically why a patient reacts
as he does.[15]

The Freudian dream theory that critics of Auden would ally his
work to had already been used to give a new dimension to the neo-
medieval dream poem that poets had carried over from the nineteenth century as well as to support a surrealist poetry that had
blossomed in America after André Breton's *Surrealist Manifesto*
(1924). Even earlier the theory had affected American criticism.
Since World War I discussions of art had gone increasingly to
motivation and "psychic meaning" to exemplify yet another occasion in American culture when nonprofessionals adopted and pro-
moted a doctrine before the doctrine found professional sanction.
Moreover the internal as well as international nature of Freudian
theory would work in Auden's favor; one would not have to explain his Englishness or alter the forms of one's government in
order to embrace Auden or the universality of Freud's teachings.
What would be affected by the new formulation of mental processes is an attitude toward life and not life itself. Consequently
critics like Southworth and Flint, who accept Freudian premises,
are not obliged necessarily to accept Darwin, Marx, or the decadent conditions of the English social system. In the mid-thirties
when the theory of divine creation was still taught in schools,
when literary Marxism had begun its decline, and when English
life was still inaccessible, the very conservative nature of the psychoanalytic revolution widened its appeal to those who wanted
change but not a radical alteration in what was.

The early acceptance by Americans of Freud placed an emphasis
on the personal, sensational, optimistic, and wish-fulfilling characteristics of psychoanalysis. In poetry the acceptance manifested
itself in the uses of emotive language, overtly sexual matter, and
special typographies to represent surface and latent content as well
as in narrative bridges based on associative leaps rather than tran-
sitions. In criticism the most frequent uses of Freud had been in the
area of biography where, as in Southworth's essay, the author's
life shed light on his work or the work provided insight into the
life. The conclusions most critics reached were that artists suffered

from various "wounds"—usually Oedipus complexes—and that literature, as Flint proposed, was a substitute reality. The body of psychoanalytic criticism explaining audience reaction to serious drama and illustrating how drama portrayed "universal themes of the unconscious," which also appeared in the decade following World War I, seemed inappropriate to poetry. Except for the "affective" emphasis on audience reaction in some of the drama criticism and an occasional article like K. Weiss's "Rhyme and Refrain: A Contribution to the Psychogenesis of the Poetic Means of Expression" (1919) which accounted for rhyme in the infantile pleasure of repetition, most critics stressed content rather than form, past rather than future, and individual rather than collective response.

Yet, just as poetry was responding to a still undefined crisis in history during the thirties, so too was psychoanalysis. Freud had produced his *Civilization and its Discontents* (1929) in which he rejected the industrialist tendency toward "exploitation and consumption" for a bleak outlook; and in reaction to his pessimism a number of younger analysts like Karen Horney, Erich Fromm, and Henry Stack Sullivan began to reexamine both the doctor's theories and the individual's relation to society. Each of these analysts began publishing independently his opposing visions of a future less determined by the past. To different degrees Horney and Fromm were influenced by Wilhelm Reich's "Freudo-Marxist" movement, but Sullivan arrived at his conclusions free of any Reichian bias. He did so through work mainly with patients at St. Elizabeth's hospital. Of the three Horney's political and anthropological orientation seemed best suited to the progressive character of an industrial society, and her *The Neurotic Personality of our Time* (1937) was a bestseller and something of a cult book before World War II for people suffering from anxiety. She began by objecting to Freud's image of the detached analyst and moved to oppose his work in feminine psychology and his concept of the death instinct. She emerged from these considerations with a Rousseauistic view of man in which destructive impulses were created by cultural conditions. Her belief that the individual could change his character under proper environments clashed with the orthodox belief of an irreversible biological determinism which saw political action as sentimental and irrelevant, and her posing the future as a solution to man's problems challenged an emphasis on the individual past as the area for discovering the sources of choice.

Almost from the beginning Freud had perceived that America would welcome flattering views like Horney's and his own theories only insofar as they could be distorted into reassurances that, however much the present was imperfect, the paradise on earth envisioned by America's founding fathers was still possible. Joseph Adelson in "Freud and America: Some Observations" (1954) proposes that the motivation for this distortion is America's "idea of man's perfectibility"—the belief in man's ability to remake himself that is so much a part of the industrial imagination as well as of romantic art and thought. The belief is perhaps best preserved by the nation's politicians, sociologists, and educators who are obliged by their positions to take optimistic stances to what one writer calls "the confusion and sadness and incoherence of the human condition." Freud's vision of a permanent biological temper whose dynamics cannot change of their own accord requires that the removal of one repressive tendency will only give way to a second not, as Horney and others propose, to new freedom. Nevertheless Ernest W. Burgess in "The Influence of Sigmund Freud upon Sociology in the United States" (1939) shows how prevalent certain psychological concepts had become even in a basically deindividualized area. He lists among terms common in recent sociological studies such expressions as *inferiority complex*, *mental conflict*, *rationalization*, *repression*, *sublimation*, *transference*, *resistance*, and *Oedipus complex*; and he praises the work of Horney and other revisionists for having brought Freud and the social sciences into closer agreement.[16]

Much as Freud had envisioned the direction that Americans might take in accepting his theories, he had no premonition of the particular distortions that the critics would make in correlating his vision with an acceptance of Auden. David Daiches, Delmore Schwartz, and Jarrell were willing to go beyond Southworth's and Flint's simple uses of psychoanalytic terms and, in their separate appeals to novelty, superimpose Freud's basically therapeutic system on a traditional formalist aesthetics where time itself would be meaningless. Nor had Freud envisioned any more clearly Lionel Trilling's proposal in *Sincerity and Authenticity* (1972) that the decline of psychoanalysis among intellectuals during the forties and fifties is somehow related to the decline of narrative and that, in a yet more serious way, both declines reflect a collapse of history. Trilling attributes the rejection of the past which causes the collapse to the objections Jean-Paul Sartre's *Being and Nothingness* (1943) raised against psychoanalysis and the emphasis that work gave to eliminating "bad faith." Trilling concludes by showing that the social emphases of Freud's more popular successors— R. D. Laing, Herbert Marcuse, and Norman O. Brown—complete the emergence of the industrial imagination that began in the thirties.[17] One suspects that, in place of these literary reconstructions, Freud might have preferred revaluations based on the overwhelming weight of scientific evidence supporting the intensive effects of environment on character that Nazi concentration-camp records provide or the view that advances in technology make it possible for man to create new environments so quickly that the symbols of the past on which psychoanalysis relies have been greatly diminished.

One might also see, as Auden did, that the bidirectional thrusts of Freud (past) and Marx (future) presuppose that any effort to merge the ideologies demands a belief in linear history (Christianity). The placing of the systems into any other larger dialectic of private and public obligation would require, as Schwartz was to assert, an intelligence greater than Auden possessed. Although conceived along independent biological and economic lines, both systems present views of progressive stages of development that insist equally on observable, scientific, verifiable data. Both also claim to penetrate through a facade of seemingly chance irregularities to hidden but consistent patterns. Nonetheless the chiliastic character of Marx's vision stands opposed to Freud's basic view that man's instincts remain constant. The destruction of private property will for Freud not end aggression but will channel aggressive instincts in another direction. The constancy of these inborn instincts as Ransom in "Poetry: II. The Final Cause" (1947) implies, has much in common with the effects of original sin. The optimism of Marx, on the other hand, did suit the optimism of the Darwinians who saw a progressive evolution of the species without having to resort to the beliefs of religion that Richards had made part of his attack on poetry's capacity for magic. Some poets

hoped that the changes brought about by evolution might provide
an answer to Freud's opposition. The conflicts which he termed
biological and that he thought irresolvable by social change might
be resolved by evolutionary biological change. To manage such
possibilities while, at the same time, remaining true to the "realities" of Richards and the spirit of all three thinkers became the role
of the ideal "postmodern" poet for which critics were casting a
then still "unrepentant" Auden.

In the light both of the popular acceptances of Freud and of the
irreconcilability of Freudian and Marxist ideologies without a
Christian history, what lay ahead in Daiches's "W. H. Auden: The
Search for a Public" (1939), Schwartz's "The Two Audens"
(1939), and the essay by Randall Jarrell (of which John Berryman
said that it understood the poet's mind "better than anyone
ought to be allowed to understand anyone else's, especially anyone so pleasant and destructive as Jarrell" [18]) was a completion of
the cultural annexing of Auden that provided him with a larger
dialectic. The critics did so by blurring his attachment to the industrial imagination into the American view of poetry as conjecture and by ignoring the particular past which produced his poetry
to translate these personal responses into collective and formal
terms. Daiches's British nature keeps him, perhaps, from the "extreme inflations of art" present in the Schwartz and Jarrell pieces;
but the thrust of his work is still narrowly professional. He begins
with an interest similar to that with which Southworth began. He
too wishes to define the poet's alienation; but rather than suggest,
as Southworth did, that the alienation has something to do with
the poet's own homosexuality or even, as had Day Lewis's *Starting
Point* (1937), that it may have to do with defects in the social
and educational systems that the general strike of 1926 revealed,
Daiches proposes that the alienation results from a larger, vaguer
"modern poet's dilemma."

Daiches presents Auden's need to reject traditional substance
and technique for new subjects and for new ways of expression as
a variation of Sloan's reasoning behind having to restyle industrial
products. The possibilities and interests in the current model are
minimal. The early poems consequently "give the impression of a
man of genuine poetic gifts and possessing to a quite uncanny
extent the power to do new things with words, who is not quite

sure what he wants to say, and who is even less decided about whom he wants to speak to." His first desire is to write "for a larger group in terms intelligible only to a smaller group." Later he moves to an audience epitomized by the ideal schoolboy and begins addressing, like a consummate business manager, "those who will make the future, the alert youngster who observes his environment and is dissatisfied and requires more information about the present and direction for the future if he is able to do anything effective about it." Thus Auden is made to stand as a symbol of innovation and the leader in a generational conflict in letters whose psychological equivalent is the totemic ritual of killing one's father. This "killer" image, implicit in Auden's own work, is one that followers like Karl Shapiro eventually make pro forma. Shapiro in "The Death of Randall Jarrell" (1965) depicts Auden as having shot at a target constructed by Eliot and "modernism" and missed; and completing the industrial/psychological comparison in Daiches, Shapiro states that, in turn, "it became necessary for everyone my own age to attack Auden." [19]

Just as one may describe Daiches's position as an "affective" psychologizing of literary succession along industrial lines, one can see Schwartz's essay as an "inherent" psychologizing of Auden's subjects in language that is less industrial than implicit in Auden's "Art and Psychology." Schwartz identifies the poet's public Marxism as ego and his personal voice as id, stating, as Jarrell would echo, that the id, in the case of Auden, "is far ahead of the Ego, which is merely clever and ingenious," but upon which "the business of understanding depends." The presumption behind the psychologizing, in this instance, is the Eliotic notion that the whole of a writer's work comprises a single evolving personality and that somehow, in platonic fashion, this personality derived from the canon is an image of the mind defined in Freudian tension. Later, Ransom in his two-part "Poetry" (1947) will carry the breakdown of this image further by seeing individual works as models of the Freudian mind and interpreting "texture" and "structure" in each work of art as id and ego respectively. Schwartz, however, is content to remain tied to broader terms and to praise the early Auden, in which "most of the writing issues from the voice of the Id" and the obsessions which the poetry records often reflect, as in Yeats's poetry, more collective emotions than the precise social programs which set in after *The Orators*. Schwartz advises that "only a sharp break with the public poet which had been fashioned by a conscious will, and a return to the rôle of obedience to the passive, subconscious self would, it seems, free Auden from [a] perilous and immediate relationship" with passing issues.[20]

Jarrell in "Changes of Attitude and Rhetoric in Auden's Poetry" (1941) summarizes in the initial section many of the points that previous critics had made. He begins with an inventory of the various social and personal causes that might produce the concerns of Auden's poetry and shows how these concerns lead to a divided warring world of They and Me. "Auden wants a total war, a total victory," and for these reasons, Jarrell maintains, he never aligns himself with any ideology so completely that he can assume its liabilities. "They" comprises what is "economically unsound, morally corrupt, intellectually bankrupt," the old order, whereas "We" represents, in good industrial thinking, the future and change. Jarrell then goes on to catalogue twenty-six characteristics of Auden's rhetoric which constitute the arsenal for his attack and to demonstrate how they function in the early and later poems. Jarrell notes that "many of the early poems seem produced by Auden's whole being" whereas in the later poems a consciousness interposes between what the poet feels and what he expresses so that the result seems manipulated. Jarrell concludes that this manipulation is a product of Auden's institutionalizing his rhetoric. All the same the eclecticism of Auden's ideas emerges as an advantage over the typical solution to accessibility in the twenties and to the mass conformist solutions of political poetry in the thirties. Jarrell characterizes these two solutions respectively: "modern poetry is necessarily obscure; if the reader can't get it, let him eat Browning" and "poetry must be made available to the People or it is decadent escapism."

Jarrell recommends to readers three lyrics from Auden's first American volume (1934) as models of antimodernist technique. Two of the three lyrics—xxv and ix—are replacements for lyrics in the 1930 edition. Poem xxv ("Who will endure"), Jarrell notes, is "entirely non-Marxist" in its depiction of commerce in a Welsh community. He cites Auden's own wish to be a mining engineer and his love of machines rather than any concern for industrial matters as prompting the sense of waste in the unused machinery and the railway and pier. One is not conscious of any overt ideology, although the effect of the poem is certainly an attack on capitalism. One suspects that Jarrell's interest in singling out the poem is the value that personal experience adds, as later in his review of Elizabeth Bishop's *North & South* (1946) he will praise her work for having "written underneath, *I have seen it*." Poem IV ("Watch any day"), which appeared in the 1930 volume, is described, on the other hand, as an account of evolution and an example of the poet's blending science and Marxist ideology "in an unexpected but perfectly orthodox way." The subject of the poem is the epitome of evolution and capitalism; he is a perfectly useless man whose life is finding "the longest way to the intrinsic peace." Poem IX ("It's no use raising a shout") becomes a second "coalition of Marxism and biology," distinguished by Jarrell as "probably the prettiest" of such coalitions.[21] Thus one can see that the uses of Freud, Marx, and Darwin in which a postmodernist poet is to engage are to be integral to his vision. They should appear as subsurface attributes deriving from personal experience and reflective, subsequently, of man's evolution into a social being. A poetry of this kind requires for its own importance that the poet be at the center of significant social experience, and this itself demands an unusually fortuitous coalescing of poet and event.

At the same time that Daiches, Schwartz, and Jarrell were trying to accept Auden on the basis of his embodying aspects of Freud's biological vision, world political conditions were forcing Auden to submerge these interests to Freud's sociological theories and to revise what had been a concern for the industrial imagination into a concern for religion. Often this religious concern is masked under a guise of problems in regimentation and individual choice. Essay after essay in the late thirties begins with the suppositions that "Fascism is what happens to an industrial society when disorder is accepted as inevitable but has reached a point where it is felt as intolerable" and that in order to forestall the advent of fascism a new metaphysics rather than an inflated view of literature is needed. The causes of the disorder are outlined in lectures such as "Mimesis and Allegory" (1940), in which art is also presented as a deceptive alternative to action. Auden believes that "if past events cannot be altered, our attitude toward them can"; and he opposes art as a means for this alteration because, "when we say that art is beyond good and evil, what we really mean is that 'good' and 'evil' are terms which can only be applied to our own conscious choices, but not to the past, because it cannot be un-done, or to the world outside ourselves, because it is not our own property." For Auden Protestantism and romanticism have wrong-ly overexaggerated individualism and "the importance of art as a guide to life, and, within art itself, . . . the unconscious, the child-ish, and the irrational in the hope that in these lie human unity." To pursue these directions "without a sense of the Unconditional" and conscious "walking in fear of the Lord" is to invite, as he maintains in "Tract for the Times" (1941), the unconscious to see that one "has something else, airplanes or secret police, to walk in fear of." Instead what was needed were internal and subjective checks—an individualism which would be opposed by a system of commonly held, viable symbols and a metaphysics that would re-late the concrete phenomenal world to abstract concepts.

Underscoring this newly articulated attitude toward choice and communally held symbols are the writings of Søren Kierkegaard and a conviction on Auden's part that man belongs "to two orders of being, the natural and the historical." Kierkegaard provided categories of the aesthetic, ethical, and religious that would help one order priorities. As the poet notes in "A Preface to Kierke-gaard" (1944), the power by which man is "able to choose is re-ligious faith: without that faith, he must either despair, i.e., be unable to act, or become an idolator, i.e., invent an illusion of absolute certainty out of the individual passion of his immediate moods (the Esthetic) or the universal abstractions of his intellect (the Ethical)." This ability to choose would involve, moreover, a sense of the historical and oppose the "cyclical and reversible changes of Nature" by suggesting an irreversible realm both "of unique and novel events and of monuments." Auden depicts Freud as "actually thinking historically" when he is trying to retain "bio-logical notions of development," and in "The Greatness of Freud" (1953) he praises the doctor "for the revolutionary step" of decid-ing "to treat psychological facts as belonging, not to the natural order, to be investigated according to the methodologies of chem-

istry and biology, but to the historical order."[22] Auden's own reinterpretation of Freud consequently involves a reorientation of
personal as well as cultural standards.

In *The Poetic Art of W. H. Auden* (1965) John Blair argues that
the reorientation concerns the fabric of the poetry as well. He
maintains that the poet's particular emphasis on art as a corrective
mirror and on its communal rather than self-expressive character
leads in turn not to the evolving personality of Eliot's "John Ford"
(1932) and Schwartz's essay but to an "escape from personality"
like that which Eliot favored in "Tradition and the Individual
Talent" (1917) and which is present in Yeats's notion of antithetical selves. Like Auden's interest in psychology, this attitude toward impersonality goes back to his undergraduate days. Spender
reports that at Oxford Auden was already considering a poet "a
kind of chemist who mixed his poems out of words, while remaining detached from his own feelings. Feelings and emotional experiences were only the occasion which precipitated into his mind the
idea of a poem." This view of impersonality, according to Blair,
now prompts the poet to think of the work of art as "a performance for the sake of the audience." Any autobiographical details
that may be present are meaningless unless a reader feels them as
reflections of his own personal life. Thus implicit in the impersonality is a serious qualification of personal experience as the ultimate proof of abstraction and an insinuation instead of an antithetical mode of writing similar to Yeats's in which personally felt
experience finds expression in commonly accepted channels. With
this modification Auden anticipates both the concept of "lived
myth" that Thomas Mann develops in "Freud and the Future"
(1936) and the "autonymous" thinking David Riesman will eventually characterize in *The Lonely Crowd* (1950). As Blair notes,
Auden's "habitual attack on a subject is to distinguish two equal
but opposing extremes that are relevant, and, employing his pun-
gent wit, to describe them in their most extreme forms." In decid-
ing that "neither extreme is satisfactory," Auden supports a view
of the unimportance of art as a source of Truth except as it may be
a vehicle of conjecture upon which one may then make choices.[23]

Both the call for abstract communal symbols and the debase-
ment of art as personal expression draw attacks from Jarrell, who
in "Freud to Paul: The Stages of Auden's Ideology" (1946) exam-

ines the evolution of Auden's themes. Jarrell depicts how early preoccupations with "anxiety, guilt, isolation, sexuality, and authority" change from deeply felt, unexamined emotions akin to those that produce dreams, fairy tales, and myths to a self-conscious acceptance of Christianity because, as Auden states elsewhere, he had "come to realize that what is true . . . is implicit in the Christian doctrine of the nature of man, and that what is not Christian is not true." At the onset, according to Jarrell, "true development and genuinely moral behavior have nothing to do with the systematic, disinterested abstraction of the moralist; they are what you yourself are mixed up in, puzzle out, and work at all your life, failing or succeeding only to fail." One then moved with the poetry into a period when one is "free to choose," "choices are meaningful," and "the right choice is predestined to success," and where "everything important happens in the Realm of Logical Necessity." Finally one reached a point where "everything that is important happens in the Realm of Grace" and one's ultimate duty and "accomplishment is sitting still." At this point, too, Auden's suitability as a model for American postmodern poetry would end, for the very concepts of evolutionary will and personal experience which are so much a part of the vision would have disappeared.

Jarrell amplifies his objections in a review of *The Age of Anxiety* (1947). There he accuses "the man who, during the thirties, was one of the five or six best poets in the world" of having become "a rhetoric-mill." Anything and everything are purportedly "one more chance for rhetoric," and Jarrell expresses special anger at the poet's view that "all art is so essentially frivolous" its nature degrades those beliefs one thinks true and one prefers, as a result, that it embody beliefs that are false. The origin of this view can be seen as early as "New Year Letter" (1941) and lines such as "Art is not life and cannot be / A midwife to society" and "No words men write can stop the war." *For the Time Being* (1944) makes this notion of art as a "midwife" for life more remote, and the view is reaffirmed in such essays as "Squares and Oblongs" (1948) and "Henry James and the Artist in America" (1948). Still Jarrell's equating such a view to a dissociation of poetry and belief runs counter to Auden's many statements over the same period about belief in poetry and his own famous practice of pruning discarded ideologies from his work. What Jarrell seems to lament is not "belief" as "ideology" as much as "belief" as "emotional commitment." He sees a loss of energy resulting from a lack of personally felt experience. Such "belief" which Auden would associate with Protestantism had been used by poets like John Donne to make his lyrics sound more intense and dramatic. Jarrell mainly seems to object to the "distancing" that occurs when one divorces emotion from content and the loss of personality in art that results.

Joseph Warren Beach in *The Making of the Auden Canon* (1957) proposes that, despite their differences, Jarrell's first analysis of Auden's rhetoric may well have influenced what Auden decided to cut from the *Collected Poems* (1945). Beach conjectures that Jarrell's admiration of the fusion of evolutionary and Marxist perspectives in Poem IX of *Poems* (1934) may account for Auden's removing it. In 1945 Auden regarded neither ideology as true and he did not wish to have his readers suppose that he did. The same explanation is not the case, however, for the seven stanzas Auden removed from Poem XVII of *Look, Sranger!*. Here the section suits the poet's current views, but it contains many of the examples of abstract diction that Jarrell characterizes as sometimes degenerating "into the flatness and vagueness, the essayistic deadness, of bad prose." It seems clear from both instances that, whatever regard Auden may have had for Jarrell as a critic, he was not going to allow himself to become spokesman for an art whose ideology anyone other than he controlled or which he ultimately found "disquieting" in its imposed "literary conformity" and its assumptions of a "proper and authorized way to write poetry."[24] Instead he might occasionally defer to Jarrell's taste, but a poetry written to conform to outside mechanisms and not in response to inner symbols would fall into a fascism on a literary level comparable to the one that he detested on a political plane.

The particular need that Jarrell's attitude toward Auden reveals of American poetry in general becomes more evident when it is viewed against statements that Jarrell makes in "A Note on Poetry" (1940) and "The End of the Line" (1942) as well as in his eventual praise of Robert Lowell in "Poetry in War and Peace" (1945) and "From the Kingdom of Necessity" (1947) and in his support of Elizabeth Bishop in "The Poet and His Public" (1946). The essays offer a context which softens the sting that the two Auden essays might leave by indicating Jarrell's own belief that the analyses and enumerations were intended not as a control imposed from the outside but as a way poetry might become open to individual and therefore organically whole structures. The evaluations of Auden in these pieces were to be instructive mainly insofar as they informed young poets of the necessity of personally felt experience and only secondarily as they catalogued the techniques for conveying the sense that the poet "has used, and not been used" by language. In this regard Jarrell shares the interest of the New Criticism in practical rather than ideological issues; but he does not divorce, as they tend to, technique from feeling. Without any direct mention of Auden in "A Note on Poetry" he asserts the commonly felt sense that modernism had reached a dead end and that the kind of poetry that his own *The Rage for the Lost Penny* offers might be an adequate replacement. Such a poetry would be concerned with both personal and public issues and not with the irresponsible egotism of the twenties or the programmed system of Marxism. In "The End of the Line" he repeats this belief that modernism is dead, but uses as its hope for continuance Auden, whose "poetry is the most successful and novel reaction against modernist romanticism." Jarrell expresses reservations about the adequacy of Auden's poetry as a wholly acceptable model, for "though moving in the direction of a solution," Auden "soon goes past it into didacticism and abstraction."

American poetry would have to wait for another figure to see it through the failings of "modernism" and the thirties, and in "Poetry in War and Peace" Jarrell proposes Lowell as that figure. Lowell is cast, moreover, consciously in the manner of Sloan to compete with early Auden: "A few years ago he would have supported neither Franco nor the Loyalists; one sees him sending a couple of clippers full of converted minute-men to wipe out the whole bunch —human and hence deserving." In "From the Kingdom of Necessity" Jarrell continues the depiction in regard to Lowell's concept of Christ: "It is interesting to compare the figure of the Uncle in early Auden, who sanctifies rebellion by his authority; the authority of Mr. Lowell's Christ is sanctified by his rebellion or liberation." It is a Lowell, too, who seems as much constructed, as Auden had been, from needs rather than facts and one subject to a danger also of becoming programmatic. For this reason, perhaps, Jarrell provides himself with an alternate in Elizabeth Bishop. Much as he in

"Freud to Paul" had discussed Auden's problems of extenuating other people's wickedness, in reviewing *North & South* he states: "She understands so well that the wickedness and confusion of the age can explain and extenuate other people's wickedness and confusion, but not for you, your own." Thus the particular need for a personal activist poetry that brought into being Jarrell's various distortions of Auden's work are still urgent enough to bring about a perception of other poets along similar lines.

Much later Jarrell in reviewing *The Shield of Achilles* (1955) would try to come to terms with both these distortions and Auden's later work. Jarrell proposes that, although the poet in some ways is still wasting his talent, he has come through the false moralizing rhetoric of the forties poems splendidly: he has given up didacticism. Jarrell quotes from Auden's "Vespers" to the effect that "in my Eden each observes his compulsive rituals and superstitious taboos but we have no morals" and reasserts his own view of poetry's essential seriousness: "If Auden thought a little worse of himself, and a little better of poetry, how different Auden and his poetry would be." Knowing that no one "wastes powers if he can keep from wasting them," Jarrell decides to accept the passivity of these recent works by "the last of the great English eccentrics." "In many of these last poems," he notes, "the Conscious and Moral Auden is, quite consciously and immorally, coming to terms with the Unconscious Auden by going along with it, letting it have its way. . . . In some of the best . . . he accepts himself for whatever he is, the world for whatever it is, with experienced calm." Rather than condemn this "sitting still" as he had ten years before, Jarrell now suggests that "the poet is a man of the world, and his religion is of so high an order, his morality so decidedly a meta-morality, that they are more a way of understanding everyone than of making specific demands on anybody." He also confesses that he has never ceased being a compulsive reader of Auden and notes of the later Auden that he "has got over the shady side of so much, has become so convincingly old, so irrevocably, inexorably middle-aged, that we wouldn't resent his telling us that he is the Wandering Jew." Nevertheless Jarrell makes it clear that he prefers the early bewildered Auden to this wise old man and that he has not given up his view of poetry as proof of a Freudian view of self.[25]

Even before these admissions, Jarrell had come to reject the direction that other postmodernists had taken. Many young poets, feeling as he did that modernism was dead, appropriated the machinery that he described in the Auden essays without acquiring the necessary collateral personal feeling. The result was a body of poetry fashioned, as Shapiro suggests, often to "attack" Auden but which, as Jarrell complained in a number of reviews, mistook mechanical competence and eccentricity for individuality and avoided risk. By the beginning of the fifties this poetry appeared wholly manipulative and lifeless. The worst fear that Ransom and others had expressed about Richards's divorcing the language of poetry from that of life had come about, and it had come about years after scientists had begun to think of statements of science as conjectural. As Schwartz had foreseen in "The Isolation of Modern Poetry" (1941), the relegation of poetry to "pseudostatement" ended by the poet's being "engaged in following the minutest movements, tones, and distinctions of his own being as a poetic man. . . . The common language of daily life, its syntax, habitual sequences, and processes of association, are precisely the opposite of what he needs, if he is to make poetry from what absorbs him as a poet, his own sensibility."[26] Ezra Pound's view of the poet in *How to Read* (1929) as the guardian of civilization by being the guardian of language is thus counteracted by there being two languages. In no way would the purifying of the one effect the use of the same words in the second.

Under these conditions what critics were now impressed by was a kind of tolerant and formalistically inclined conformity. The poetry seemed less experimental, more regular, and less dogmatically insistent than at any previous time. In complete disregard of the industrial principle of continuous improvement, John Ciardi in the foreword to *Mid-Century American Poets* (1950) argues that experimentation is dead: poets now had an adequately rich and varied stock of techniques. As Richards proposes in "The Interaction of Words" (1942), the techniques, deriving from prior techniques, evolve into a sequence of "poetic misprisions" that Louise Bogan in *The Achievement in American Poetry* (1951) sees as misleading. "Very nearly all the members of this poetic generation functioned, to a greater or less degree, within the pervasive influence of the composite modern style—a style which was steadily returning, by degrees, to 'form.' This style often served to cloak poverty of thought and immaturity of feeling. Thus certain poets, by manipulating surfaces with skill, seemed more gifted than they actually were: they proved to be more fixated at childish emotional levels than a superficial examination of their writing had seemed to indicate." Earlier Auden had seen in "In Praise of the Brothers Grimm" (1944) the conformity as a "poverty of symbols, so that not only do we fail to relate one experience to another but also we have to entrust our whole emotional life to the few symbols we do have."[27] The alternative of further fragmentation again raises the specters of imposed order and fascism.

In 1948 the lag in innovation had been a topic of a *Partisan Review* symposium on modern writing. In that symposium Clement Greenberg counters the Richardsian separation of art and life by arguing that "the avantgarde has been allowed to freeze itself into such a standardized repertory of attitudes because of the absence of new challenges to itself within the field of experience," and Ransom joins in, arguing, in turn, that the "existing environment seems to the American artist too harsh for the responses of gentleness and beauty." He delineates the two kinds of artists that he honors in this circumstance: the "incomplete artist who must attack" and the withdrawn artist who means "to work out a stable living and to have an art for the complement and affirmation of the life." The first he locates in places like New York City "where life is lived grimly, at least by the literary colony, in the sight of ruined Europe." The second he places in "'regions' . . . (like the politically 'backward' South), where a normal and successful life goes on after the local fashion, and there is no compulsive consciousness that these times are only an interim, in which one enlists in some revolution in order that happiness may be possible again." Wallace Stevens concurs with Ransom that "our present experience of life is too violent to be congenial to experiment," and intimations of this violence exist in the statements of Berryman and R. P. Blackmur as well. In fact Blackmur cites the depressing nature of such current titles as Lowell's *Lord Weary's Castle*, Jarrell's *The Losses*, and Berryman's *The Dispossessed* as evidence of an "inadequate relation between culture and society." Both Leslie Fiedler and Lionel Trilling were willing to view the lack of experi-

mentation more sociologically, Fiedler as the consequence of legiti-
mizing a tradition by the university and Trilling as the result of
poets' having become university professors.[28]

Still, if American poetry did seem to have become less experimental, it also seemed to remain, at least superficially, concerned
with social issues. Marius Bewley notes that "American poets have
come through the War with an emboldened sense of function and
responsibility." Southworth adds that, unlike the young men of
the twenties, the postmodernist poets "went into war with their
eyes open and they matured during the war years. Their work is
affirmative in that they have had the ability and courage resolutely
to face facts." Ciardi parallels these statements with his own belief
that the postwar poets "*want* to be understood," and, in a revision
of his 1938 introduction, Rodman asserts that "the new poets,
whether concerned with the state, the war, with feeling or with
God, seem guided by a sense of responsibility toward their readers
and a taking-for-granted of the immediacy of poetry to contemporary speech that sets them apart from their predecessors." Thorp
also sees the postwar poets as socially concerned but as writing
"more simply and directly than their elders" and not wishing "to
escape from emotion."[29]

Alvarez, however, is more cautious about what these writers
present as the poets' "sense of responsibility." He senses that,
despite the social concerns, the poetry has remained highly individualistic. "Poetry in America may now have many social perquis-
ites, but it is not yet a particularly social act. It is self-responsible
and self-complete, and demands of the reader not so much his co-
operation than his complete surrender." Mark Strand in *The Contemporary American Poets* (1969) goes even farther. He notes in
the preface that "many of today's poets have made, if not a cult,
at least a lifetime's work of the self, a self defined usually by circumstances that would tend to set it apart. In their energetic pursuit of an individual manner that would reflect a sense of self-
definition, they have used what they wanted from various literary
traditions." Earlier M. L. Rosenthal in *The New Poets* (1967) had
seen these separate concerns for social matters and self as part of a
single dialectic in which the "political and cultural" world "centers on the individual as *victim*" and forces him to respond, much

as Jarrell proposes, "as a symbolic embodiment of national and cultural crisis. Hence the idiom of the poetry can be at once private and public, lyrical and rhetorical."[30]

Almost at the same time that Jarrell came to terms with late Auden, Donald Hall in "The New Poetry" (1955) framed new models for a new generation under four general heads: (1) Robert Lowell, (2) a group of individual but less important writers, (3) the "Wurlitzer Wits" or imitators of John Donne, and (4) the "School of Elegance" or imitators of Alexander Pope. Hall's selection of Lowell as a separate category and the forerunner of the generation results not so much from Jarrell's having chosen Lowell as Auden's successor in 1945 as from Lowell's being important in much the same way that Auden had been important twenty years before: Lowell managed to embody personally the tenor of America's postwar interests. As the nation was turning on its isolationist political past and becoming part of western culture, he was turning on his Puritan ancestors to accept many tenets of western culture in his Roman Catholicism. He became the recognized "heir" of modernists like Eliot, Pound, and Williams, of the New Criticism, of the advances in transportation and communication, and of apologists for Christian culture who surfaced in the thirties and continued to flourish in the sixties. He was also a member of two of America's foremost families and, therefore, subject to the coverage that magazines like *Time* and *Life* afforded to surveys into the continuing national heritage. Moreover, as Bewley points out, he had even amid "evidence of a crushing disillusionment . . . joyful and unexpected reversals" that assured readers that man can change for the better and that paradise on earth is only a few steps away from collective sincere conversion.[31] No other postwar American poet seemed to challenge his singularity by personifying in as many areas those pleasantly fortuitous coalescings of poet and significant event that made Auden so significant for the thirties.

One can see, in addition, the emergence of Lowell as the leader of "confessional poetry" in the late fifties as the consequence of a continuation of incessant changes and the dissolving of this coalition of poet and significant event that the precepts of postmodernism encouraged. Stephen Stepanchev argues in *American Poetry since 1945* (1965) that the disintegration is part of a general "fragmentation of modern life," which has left the poet "feeling secure only when dealing with personally tested facts." These poets "permit no veil of 'objective correlatives' to hang between them and their readers; they distrust the 'aesthetic distance' and 'anonymity' that were once prized by poets and critics." [32] They, in short, move into what Riesman would call "inner-directedness," Sartre "the authentic," and Auden "runaway individualism"; and they redirect postmodernism from conformity and social concern to idiosyncrasy and personal experience. Here, too, Lowell's having been so much a part of the forties works to give his own disintegration a relevance beyond that registered by the fragmentations of most of his contemporaries. Other poets of the generation remained less fortunate in their backgrounds or in the accidental modishness of their personal problems. Nor could many of them pretend problems as popular as those which Lowell experienced. Instead, pushed away from the centrality that he seemed to command, they had to choose—often in the politically "backward" regions that Ransom described—their own ways of coming to grips with their crafts, their problems, and their natures and to propose their own competing visions of the real.

Notes

1. John Crowe Ransom, "Poets without Laurels," *Yale Review* 24 (1935):505.
2. Morton D. Zabel, "A Dawn in Britain," *Poetry* 38 (1931):104; Theodore Maynard, "When the Pie Was Opened," *Commonweal* 22 (1935):339–41.
3. J. H. Plumb, *The Death of the Past* (Boston: Houghton Mifflin, 1970), p. 14.
4. Oscar Williams, Preface to *The New Pocket Anthology of American Verse* (New York: World Publishing Co., 1955), p. 16; Hyatt H. Waggoner, Preface to *American Poets: From the Puritans to the Present* (Boston: Houghton Mifflin, 1968), p. xvi; Selden Rodman, Introduction to *A New Anthology of Modern Poetry* (New York: Random House, 1938), pp. 42–43; Waggoner, p. xvi.
5. W. H. Auden, "The Anglo-American Difference," *American Literary Essays*, ed. Lewis Leary (New York: Thomas Y. Crowell, 1960), p. 211; A. Alvarez, *The Shaping Spirit* (London: Chatto and Windus, 1958), p. 177; G. S. Fraser, *Vision and Rhetoric* (London: Faber and Faber, 1959), pp. 149–55; Marius Bewley, *The Complex Fate* (London: Chatto and Windus, 1955), p. 155; Alvarez, pp. 182, 163.
6. Zabel, pp. 102–3; Dudley Fitts, "To Karthage Then I Came . . . ," *Hound and Horn* 4 (1931):629.
7. Henry Bamford Parkes, "The Orators," *Symposium* 4 (1933):248.
8. John Gould Fletcher, "A Poet of Courage," *Poetry* 42 (1933):111, 113.
9. Fraser, pp. 150–51, 152.

10. James Burnham, "W. H. Auden," *Nation* 139 (1934):164–65; Willard Thorp, *American Writing in the Twentieth Century* (Cambridge: Harvard University Press, 1960), p. 296.

11. C. Day Lewis, *A Hope for Poetry* (Oxford: Basil Blackwell, 1934), p. 3; A.J.M. Smith, "Old Games, New Rules," *Poetry* 47 (1935):43; quoted in Allan Seager, *The Glass House* (New York: McGraw-Hill, 1968), p. 78.

12. C. Day Lewis, "Paging Mankind," *Poetry* 49 (1937):228; T. C. Wilson, "Plenty of News," *Poetry* 52 (1938):41, 42, 40.

13. Lewis, *Poetry*, p. 228; James G. Southworth, "Wystan Hugh Auden," *Sewanee Review* 46 (1938):195–96.

14. F. Cudworth Flint, "New Leaders in English Poetry," *Virginia Quarterly Review* 14 (1938):508, 510, 512–13, 516.

15. Stephen Spender, *World within World* (New York: Harcourt Brace, 1951), p. 46; W. H. Auden, "Art and Psychology," in *The Arts Today*, ed. Geoffrey Grigson (London: John Lane, 1935), p. 18; R. G. Collingwood, *The Principles of Art* (Oxford: Oxford University Press, 1938), p. 291; Auden, "Sigmund Freud," *New Republic* 127 (1952):16–18.

16. Joseph Adelson, "Freud and America: Some Observations," cited in *Freud and the Twentieth Century*, ed. Benjamin Nelson (New York: Meridian Books, 1957), pp. 182–83; Robert Lowell, "A Talk with Robert Lowell," *Encounter* 24, no. 2 (1965):40; Ernest W. Burgess, "The Influence of Sigmund Freud upon Sociology in the United States, *American Journal of Sociology* 45 (1939–40):356–74.

17. Lionel Trilling, *Sincerity and Authenticity* (Cambridge: Harvard University Press, 1972), pp. 134–72.

18. David Daiches, "W. H. Auden: The Search for a Public," *Poetry* 54 (1939):148–56; Delmore Schwartz, "The Two Audens," *Kenyon Review* 1 (1939):23–45; Randall Jarrell, "Changes of Attitude and Rhetoric in Auden's Poetry," *Southern Review* 7 (1941):326–49; John Berryman, "On Poetry and the Age," in *Randall Jarrell: 1914–1965*, ed. Robert Lowell, Peter Taylor, and Robert Penn Warren (New York: Farrar, Straus and Giroux, 1967), p. 10.

19. Daiches, pp. 151, 152, 155; Karl Shapiro, "The Death of Randall Jarrell," in *Randall Jarrell: 1914–1965*, p. 225.

20. Delmore Schwartz, *Selected Essays*, ed. Donald A. Dike and David H. Zucker (Chicago: University of Chicago Press, 1970), pp. 147, 152; John Crowe Ransom, "Poetry: I. The Formal Analysis" and "Poetry: II. The Final Cause," *Kenyon Review* 9 (1947):436–56, 640–58.

21. Randall Jarrell, *The Third Book of Criticism* (New York: Farrar, Straus and Giroux, 1969), pp. 117, 148, 149–50, 118; Jarrell, *Poetry and the Age* (New York: Vintage Books, 1955), p. 213; *The Third Book of Criticism*, p. 119.

22. W. H. Auden, "A Note on Order," *Nation* 152 (1941):131; Auden, "Mimesis and Allegory," in *English Institute Annual 1940*, ed. Rudolf Kirk (New York: Columbia University Press, 1941), pp. 14–15, 17; Auden, "Tract for the Times," *Nation* 152 (1941):25; Auden, "Squares and Oblongs," in *Language: An Inquiry into its Meaning and Function*, ed. Ruth N. Anshen (New York: Harper and Brothers, 1957), p. 174; Auden, "A Preface to Kierkegaard," *New Republic* 110 (1944):683; Auden, "The Poet of the Encirclement," *New Republic* 109 (1943):580; Auden, "Sigmund Freud," *New Republic* 127 (1952):17; Auden, "The Greatness of Freud," *Listener* 50 (1953):593.

23. Spender, p. 46; John G. Blair, *The Poetic Art of W. H. Auden* (Princeton: Princeton University Press, 1965), pp. 37, 70–71.

24. Jarrell, *Third Book of Criticism*, p. 162; W. H. Auden, *Modern Canterbury Pilgrims* ed. James Pike (New York: Morehouse-Gorham, 1956), p. 39; *Third Book of Criticism*, pp. 154, 156, 158; Jarrell, "Verse Chronicle," *Nation* 165 (1947):424; *Third Book of Criticism*, p. 146; Auden, "The Anglo-American Difference," p. 214n.

25. Randall Jarrell, "The End of the Line," *Nation* 154 (1942):228; Jarrell, "Poetry in War and Peace," *Partisan Review* 12 (1945):125; Jarrell, *Poetry and the Age*, pp. 192, 213; Jarrell, "Recent Poetry," *Yale Review* 44 (1955):605, 604, 607, 606.

26. Schwartz, *Selected Essays*, p. 11.

27. Louise Bogan, *The Achievement in American Poetry* (Chicago: Gateway Editions, 1951), p. 102; W. H. Auden, "In Praise of the Brothers Grimm," *New York Times Book Review*, 12 November 1944, p. 28.

28. "The State of American Writing, 1948," *Partisan Review* 15 (1948):855–94.

29. Bewley, *The Complex Fate*, p. 152; James G. Southworth, *Some Modern American Poets* (Oxford: Basil Blackwell, 1950), p. 9; John Ciardi, Foreword to *Mid-Century American Poets* (New York: Twayne Publishers, 1950), p. xxix; Selden Rodman, Introduction to *A New Anthology of Modern Poetry*, rev. ed. (New York: Random House, 1946), p. xlvi; Thorp, *American Writing in the Twentieth Century*, p. 225.

30. Alvarez, *The Shaping Spirit*, p. 188; Mark Strand, Editor's Preface to *The Contemporary American Poets* (New York: World Publishing Co., 1969), p. xiii; M. L. Rosenthal, *The New Poets* (New York: Oxford University Press, 1967), pp. 13, 15.

31. Donald Hall, "The New Poetry," *American Literary Essays*, pp. 215–25; Bewley, *The Complex Fate*, pp. 155–56.

32. Stephan Stepanchev, *American Poetry since 1945* (New York: Colophon Books, 1967), pp. 4–5.

2

Between Two Worlds: Randall Jarrell

In his lifetime (1914–65) Randall Jarrell found his poetry consistently praised in reviews yet excluded from Oscar Williams's influential anthologies and, except for a National Book Award in 1961, ignored by all prize committees. As a result, his poetry never quite succeeded into popular acceptance or acclaim. The occasional recognition it did get from the *Southern* or *Sewanee Review*, the Guggenheim foundation, or *Poetry* merely reinforced the image of a poet with an intense but narrow audience. *The Complete Poems* (1969) provides a basis for discussing why this image occurred as well as for determining Jarrell's proper place among the poets of his generation. The view that Karl Shapiro expressed in 1966, shortly after Jarrell's death—that he had outpaced all of his contemporaries—seems already overgenerous. The decision that Helen Vendler offered three years later seems no more lasting. Her review of *The Complete Poems* leans heavily on Oscar Wilde's self-estimation when she asserts that Jarrell "put his genius into his criticism and his talent into his poetry." Jarrell's own sense in *A Sad Heart at the Supermarket* (1962) that all poetic audiences were falling before "the habitual readers of Instant Literature" (p. 28) indicates how he might have explained the neglect, but one has the sense, too, from essays like "The End of the Line" (1942) that with the other immediate heirs of the modernist movement, Jarrell was "wandering between two worlds, one dead, / The other powerless to be born." [1]

More accurate is the metaphor that Jarrell used about Wallace

Stevens: "In a lifetime of standing out in thunderstorms," he managed to be "struck by lightning" (PA, 124) enough times to secure
himself a notable but not paramount place among those poets who
came into their own during and after World War II. Though individually laudable, the twenty or so outstanding poems Jarrell
wrote do not allow for the "continuing," "significant, consistent,
and developing personality"[2] that Eliotic critics have made requisite to a major writer. Instead, like the period which prompted
them, the poems stand as isolated crystalizations of a mind that
may have been too various and responsive to the discrete experiences of modern life to settle them into a single overriding pattern.
It is as if in giving up the assurances of the modernists, the poet
could not impose his own views with any finality. Like those of his
predecessors, any assurances required constant reexamination and
revision until at Jarrell's death the total pattern of the vision was
either incomplete or obscure. The technological advances that
revolutionized transportation, communication, and living settled
too many questionable options to propose a final direction. Given
Jarrell's own need to excel, to go on living life to the fullest and
highest reaches and aims, this judgment of the work may seem
harsh; but it is one which he often made of the work of others and
which in his last volume he seems to have understood about his
own poetry.

More than any of his contemporaries, Jarrell took seriously
Matthew Arnold's hope that the writer should see the world
"'with a plainness as near, as flashing' as that with which Moses
and Rebekah and the Argonauts saw it" (PA, 118). To this hope
Jarrell had added Arnold's statement in "The Study of Poetry"
(1880) that "more and more mankind will . . . have to turn to poetry to interpret life."[3] Arnold contended that most of what was
considered religion and philosophy would be replaced by poetry.
Without poetry even science would seem incomplete. This attachment in poetry of emotion to the idea and the attachment's refusal
to materialize in the fact would allow poetry to realize certain
psychological and rhetorical truths. Indeed one way in which
Jarrell differs from the poets of the previous generation is a postmodernist's acceptance of Freud's view of the psyche. "The English in England" (1963) hypothesizes of Rudyard Kipling's late
stories: "If the reality principle has pruned and clipped them into

plausibility, it is the pleasure principle out of which they first rank-
ly and satisfyingly flowered" (TBC, 282). Similarly "Stories"
(1958) establishes, "the writer is, and is writing for, a doubly- or
triply-natured creature, whose needs, understandings, and ideals
—whether they are called id, ego, and superego, or body, mind,
and soul—contradict one another." In the same essay, Jarrell asserts, "Reading stories, we cannot help remembering Groddeck's
'We have to reckon with what exists, and dreams, daydreams
too are also fact; if anyone really wants to investigate realities, he
cannot do better than to start with such as these. If he neglects
them, he will learn little or nothing of the world of life'" (SH, 141,
140–41).

Mrs. Jarrell reports that by the end of his life *The Interpretation
of Dreams* (1900) and *The Psychopathology of Everyday Life*
(1904) were recommended readings for the poet's classes, friends,
and family. "The volumes of [Freud's] *Collected Papers* [were]
strewn with little bent page corners and [Ernest] Jones' *Life and
Work* . . . smeared with lemonade and tennis sweat, . . . and the
coincidence that Randall and Freud shared the same birthday was,
in his word, 'astronomical.'"[4] The familiarity with Freud and
Georg Groddeck may have begun as early as Jarrell's undergraduate days as a psychology major at Vanderbilt, but it was undoubtedly strengthened by the early poems of W. H. Auden into a literary possibility. Often the two analysts' separations of life into
stimuli colored by subjective interpretation explain the "factitious-
ness" that Jarrell's writing recurs to. Particulars dissolve into
rhetorical predicaments whose emotions then act as bridges to
those emotions Arnold would attach to the unmaterialized idea.
The psychological coloring of an event defines the reality of a situation by defining the character of the person undergoing the experience and the "reality" evolves into an ideal world by extending
these distortions into art whose essence is "the union of a wish and
a truth" or a "wish modified by a truth" (SH, 26).

The previous generation's rejection or neglect of Freud frequently left it without a means for handling the discrepancies of inner
and outer experience except through the terminologies of philosophy and religion and with no language to speak of to handle the
area of the age's tendencies toward self-consciousness. Stevens
accordingly erred for Jarrell by "thinking of particulars as primar-

ily illustrations of general truths, or else as aesthetic, abstracted objects, simply there to be contemplated"; he "often treats things or lives" so that they seemed "no more than generalizations of an unprecedented low order." Jarrell goes on to insist that "a poet *has* to treat the concrete as primary, as something far more than an instance, a hue to be sensed, a member of a laudable category" (PA, 127–28). Yet William Carlos Williams, who does treat particulars as primary in his early poetry, errs by neglecting the "organization, logic, narrative, generalization" of poetry, thinking it enough to present merely *"data brought back alive"* (PA, 222). Kipling's description of his writing suffers from a comparable failure in that he, according to Jarrell, "was a professional but a professional possessed by both the Daemon he tells you about, who writes some of the stories for him, and the demons he doesn't tell you about, who write others." "Nowadays," he continues, reverting to psychoanalytic terminology, "we've learned to call part of the unconscious *it* or *id;* Kipling had not, but he called this Personal Daemon of his *it*" (SH, 124). In "From the Kingdom of Necessity" (1946) Jarrell praised Robert Lowell's "detailed factuality" and the "contrary, persisting, and singular thinginess of every being in the world" which set themselves against the "elevation and rhetorical sweep of much earlier English poetry" (PA, 196).

For Jarrell the expression of all art involves a balance between emotion and idea or id and superego along lines similar to those which Arnold and Freud drew and carries in their mediation residues of both extremes. In "The Age of the Chimpanzee" (1957), for example, he presents the hands of a figure in Georges de La Tour's *St. Sebastian Mourned by St. Irene* as resembling "(as so much art resembles) the symptomatic gestures of psychoanalysis, half the expression of a wish and half the defence against the wish";[5] and Jarrell's few comments on music suggest a corresponding emphasis. Jarrell may even have believed that art was a kind of medium to make the forces of the id acceptable to the superego and that, in literature, language worked as wit or dream works in Freud to allow passage through an ontogenetic censor of what Jarrell consistently depicts as dark and phylogenetic feelings. Certainly wit and dream form several of his main stresses when dealing with poetic language. His review of Walter McEl-

roy's translation of Tristan Corbière (1947), for instance, makes
"puns, mocking half-dead metaphors, parodied clichés, antitheses,
and paradoxes, idioms exploited on every level . . . the seven-
league crutches on which . . . poems bound wildly forward" (PA,
147); and, as if to emphasize the connection, Jarrell entitles his
own next volume of poetry *The Seven-League Crutches* (1951)
and includes in it his own versions of Corbière's "La Poète con-
tumace" and four "Rondels pour Après."

Likewise, as early as "Poetry in War and Peace" (1945), Jarrell
is investing the previous generation's poetry with Freudian equivalents, dividing it along conscious and unconscious lines, and indicating of Williams that "the tough responsible doctor-half that
says and does" and "the violent and delicate free-Freudian half
that feels and senses" contribute to one of the "great mythological
attitudes" of the country—"the truck-driver looking shyly at the
flower."[6] In "The Situation of a Poet" (1952) he notes further of
Williams that "he speaks for the Resistance or Underground inside
each of us" (PA, 244–45), and he says of Walter de la Mare
(1946) that "from his children and ghosts one learns little about
children and nothing about ghosts, but one learns a great deal of
the reality of which both his ghosts and his children are projec-
tions, of the wishes and lacks and love that have produced their
'unreality'" (PA, 139). Much of the discussion in his "Robert
Frost's 'Home Burial'" (1962) is given over to distinguishing the
characters' rational and compulsive behavior; and, in "Changes of
Attitude and Rhetoric in Auden's Poetry" (1941), he cites the pre-
human forms which lurk always behind Auden's individuals in the
early poems and concludes: "Many of the early poems seem produced by Auden's whole being, as much unconscious as conscious,
necessarily made just as they are; the best of them have shapes (just
as driftwood or pebbles do) that seem the direct representation
of the forces that produced them." He then generalizes on poetry
that it "represents the unconscious (or whatever you want to call
it) as well as the conscious, our lives as well as our thoughts; and
. . . has its true source in the first and not the second" (TBC,
148, 149).

The unique character of the ontogenetic half-self assures Jarrell
that its presence in the language of art without any additional
mannerisms will make that art human and individual. He lauds

Frost for "a verse that uses, sometimes with absolute mastery, the rhythms of actual speech" (PA, 28). In reviews of Auden's later work, Jarrell sees increased mannerisms subverting the unconscious. In "Poetry in a Dry Season" (1940) he says of *Another Time*: "Auden at the beginning was oracular (obscure, original), bad at organization, neglectful of logic, full of astonishing or magical language, intent on his own world and his own forms; he has changed continuously toward organization, plainness, accessibility, objectivity, social responsibility. . . . Now, in too many of the poems, we see not the will, but the understanding, trying to do the work of the imagination." Jarrell dismisses the volume as "moral, rational, manufactured, written by the top of the head for the top of the head." He repeats the complaint a year later in a review of *The Double Man*. "Auden's ideas once had an arbitrary effective quality, a personality value, almost like the ideas in Lawrence or Ezra Pound. They seem today less colorful but far more correct—and they are derived from, or are conscious of elements over most of the range of contemporary thought." [7] Thus, given a situation where the "thought" of Arnold's overt moral view of art conflicts with an honest resolution of life's "realities," Jarrell chooses Freud and Groddeck; and one gets the first suggestion of the two worlds which his art would wander between.

Later, when Jarrell returns to praise Auden for *The Shield of Achilles*, he does so in the *Yale Review* (1955) with statements that indicate his impatience at Auden's having let art's morality conflict with life. In an effort to keep art moral, Jarrell proposes that "perhaps Auden had always made such impossibly exacting moral demands on himself and everybody else partly because it kept him from having to worry about more ordinary, moderate demands; perhaps he had preached so loudly, made such extraordinarily sweeping gestures, in order to hide himself from himself in the commotion. But he seems, finally, to have got tired of the whole affair, to have become willing to look at himself *without doing anything about it*, not even shutting his eyes or turning his head away." Writing of the same volume in *Harper's*, Jarrell repeats his reluctance to abandon his belief that moral and artistic senses lie very close together. He attributes their separation in Auden's writing to a lack of Arnoldian high seriousness. "A few of the poems are good, and all of them are brilliant, self-indulgent, marvelously individual: if Auden sometimes loses faith with something as frivolous as poetry, he never loses it in anything as serious as Auden." [8]

This last is an illusion to *The Age of Anxiety* (1947), which Jarrell had reviewed, complaining of Auden's statement that "all art is . . . essentially frivolous." Even later in "The Old and the New Masters" (1965) he will reply to Auden's "Musée des Beaux Arts" (1939). Auden had contended in his poem that the great artists were never wrong in placing suffering "in a corner" of their work, leaving the center for someone else "eating or opening a window or just walking dully along." Jarrell, for whom suffering is a central concern of poetry, sees the Auden position as passive and asserts that "the old masters disagree." Some like La Tour and Hugo van der Goes make suffering central to their paintings as humanity is central to their meaning. In contrast, modern painters are guilty of abstractions like those of Auden's *New Year Letter*: "How hard it is to set aside / Terror, concupiscence and pride / Learn who and where and how we are, / The children of a modest star." They, too, depict the earth as "a bright spot somewhere in the corner" of canvases devoted to cosmic perspectives. Implied in Jarrell's description is his lament in "The Age of the Chimpanzee." Modern art denies the evolutionary process by equating the art of the chimpanzee to that of man. Of course, Jarrell adds, "there is an immense distance between my poor chimpanzee's dutiful, joyful paintings and those of Jackson Pollock," yet he regrets not living "in an age when painters were still interested in the world. . . . All the poet must do, Rilke said, is praise: to look at what is, and to see that it is good, and to make out of it what is at once the same and better, is to praise." [9]

Conversely "The Age of the Chimpanzee" indicates Jarrell's opposition to a complete submergence of art into the unconscious half-self where it would have at no time the redeeming factors of individuality, Freudian reality, or Arnoldian morality. "Abstract-Expressionism," he writes, "has kept one part [the unconscious] of this process, but has rejected as completely as it could the other part and all the relations that depend on the existence of this other part; it has substituted for a heterogeneous, polyphonic process a homogeneous, homophonic process." This opposition to unconscious art is expanded to include such notions of man as his being an objective uncensoring recorder. In a review of *Paterson* (1951) Jarrell complains of Williams that he should not have left so much of book 2 "real letters from a real woman. . . . What has been done to them," he asks, "to make them part of the poem *Paterson?* I can think of no answer except: 'They have been copied out on the typewriter'" (PA, 238). Trite and unexamined language comes in for similar condemnation. In "These Are Not Psalms" (1945) he objects that the work of A. M. Klein "has none of the exact immediacy, the particular reality of the language of a successful poem; it has instead the voluntary repetition of the typical mannerisms of poetry in general—mannerisms that become a generalized, lifeless, and magical ritual without the spirit of which they were once the peculiar expression." [10]

The redemption of language by this spirit prompts Jarrell to fall back on Goethe's statements concerning technical facility and risk. In "Poetry, Unlimited" (1950) Jarrell asserts: "Goethe said that the worst thing in art is technical facility accompanied by triteness. Many an artist, like God, has never needed to think twice about anything." In "The Profession of Poetry" (1950) he attacks the timidity of Howard Nemerov: "He knows very well that the poet, as Goethe says, is someone who takes risks (and today most intellectuals take no risks at all—are, from the cradle, critics); but he thinks romantic and old-fashioned, couldn't believe, or hasn't heard of something else Goethe said: that the poet is essentially naive." This naiveté, which would allow a dark-world layer into the poem, provides the basis through which Jarrell would merge Freud and Arnold so that poetry might outlast religion and philosophy. As he explains in "Ernie Pyle" (1945), "what he cared about was the facts. But the facts are only facts as we see them, as we feel them; and he knew to what a degree experience . . . is 'seeing only faintly and not wanting to see at all.' The exactly incongruous, the crazily prosaic, the finally convincing fact—that must be true because no one could have made it up . . . was his technical obsession." [11]

Jarrell's stress on naiveté—the individually unreflective as opposed to the overly refined—may have led him, as John Berryman in "Randall Jarrell" (1967) contends, to overvalue Williams considerably. "I'm very fond of Bill Williams' poetry," Bettyman writes, "but not as fond as Jarrell was." Moreover the view would ally Jarrell with John Ruskin, who had written in *Modern Painters* (1855) of the soul's need "to *see* something and tell what it saw in a plain way" as "poetry, prophecy, and religion,—all in one." Jarrell in his preface to *The Best Short Stories of Rudyard Kipling* (1961) refers to Ruskin's stand on perfectibility in art: Kipling's stories "are not at all the perfect work of art we want—so perhaps Ruskin was right when he said that the person who wants perfection knows nothing about art" (SH, 121–22). A precise lack of naiveté in the overly refined, lifeless perfection of Richard Wilbur's poetry turns Jarrell against it. In "A View of Three Poets" (1952) he accuses Wilbur of being "too poetic," of letting life become an excuse for poetry and, as Ruskin would have it in the opening volume of *Modern Painters* (1843), of letting art "sink to a mere ornament" and "minister to morbid sensibilities, ticklers and fanners of the soul's sleep." [12]

The strongest indication of the role of language as a mediator between one's senses of art and life and the descending priorities which Jarrell attaches to the mediation as its impulses move progressively outward comes in a review of Rolfe Humphries's *Forbid Thy Ravens* (1948): "What Mr. Humphries's poems say is agreeable, feeling common sense, necessarily a little too easy and superficial, since it has neither the depth of the unconscious, nor that of profound thought, nor that of profound emotion, nor that of the last arbitrary abyss of fact." Under such conditions, poetry in its inmost and purest state would work as Groddeck's It or a Hegelian Geist so that a sequence of its manifestations provides proof of that motivating inner force adumbrated by psychoanalysis or a history of the highest and noblest thoughts of man similar to the imperfect picture of God that results from a Hegelian survey of history. Jarrell's view in "The Profession of Poetry" that "a poet in the true sense of the word [is] someone who has shown to us one of those worlds which, after we have been shown it, we call the real world" substantiates such an hypothesis. Jarrell proposes what critics typically hold for psychoanalysis. For them Freud "thought of the artist as an obdurate neurotic who, by his creative work, kept himself from a crack-up but also from any real cure." The artist fashioned his fantasies into a "new kind of reality" that men conceded "justification as valuable reflections of actual life." [13]

The contexts of Jarrell's view which in its desirability embraces Hegelian "highest and noblest thoughts" is the German poet Rainer Maria Rilke. "Rilke, in his wonderful 'Archaic Statue of Apollo,' ends his description of the statue, the poem itself, by saying without transition or explanation: *You must change your life.* He needs no explanation. We know from many experiences . . . we have shared the alien existences both of this world and of that different world to which the work of art alone give us access—unwillingly accuses our lives." The view also coincides with the starting point of existential philosophy, that existence precedes essence and that man knows his essence by reflection. As early as "The Dramatic Lyricism of Randall Jarrell" (1952) Parker Tyler hinted at a connection when he framed Jarrell's view of existence and knowledge to echo Jean-Paul Sartre's famous pronunciamento. Tyler wrote: "*Existence* comes before *knowledge* because it retains, even after knowledge has arrived, the unknowable that is often the unpredictable." [14]

The Sartrean position which moves beyond Groddeck's It has led to the development of an existential psychoanalysis. One difference of this psychoanalysis and Freud's is, as Rollo May in *Existence* (1960) maintains, the belief that "what an individual seeks *to become* determines what he remembers of his *has been*. In this sense, the future determines the past"; but the future makes the determination in order to change the *present*. The pattern of potentiality that the individual perceives becomes his instrument for handling the domains of past and present. As Hendrik M. Ruitenbeek writes in his introduction to *Psychoanalysis and Existential Philosophy* (1962), "unlike Freudian analysis, which deals with the *Umwelt* and the *Mitwelt*, the biological and social worlds, but almost ignores the *Eigenwelt*, existential analysis stresses the self and the mode of the patient's relationship to that self." [15] Existential psychoanalysis offers to the patient the future directedness and the choice that the Rilke poem suggests, but its Dasein—unlike Hegel's Geist or Groddeck's It—shows a conscious and willful shaping force which, like his reliance on naiveté rather than consciousness, a need for metaphysical mystery will not let Jarrell wholeheartedly accept. As he formulates the present's relation to the future in "A Sad Heart at the Supermarket" (1960), Hegel and Arnold seem most influential: "An artist's work and life presuppose continuing standards, values extended over centuries and millennia, a future that is the continuation and modification of the past, not its contradiction or irrelevant replacement. He is working for the time that wants the best that he can do: the present, he hopes—but if not that, the future" (SH, 73).

Upon the sequence of the changes brought about by one's re-actions to art, the present world shapes its future along with an evolving new poetry, conceived of for such purposes and, as Arnold believes, in terms "worthily and more highly than it has been the custom to conceive of it" and "capable of higher uses, and called to higher destinies, than those which in general men have assigned to it hitherto."[16] Thus a second, more practical disjunction between future and present arises from Jarrell's efforts to fuse psychoanalysis and Arnold, and his refusal to accept the consciousness of existential psychoanalysis prevents its resolution. Throughout his criticism Jarrell can complain, on the one hand, of living in a time that is worse than Arnold's or Goethe's and, on the other, admit that he is "old-fashioned enough to believe, like Goethe, in Progress—the progress I see and the progress I wish for and do not see" (PA, 20). The blindness and optimism of this progress—since for Jarrell only the future can judge the best of the past and that by what it has knowingly incorporated—raises certain questions about the purposefulness of the present which repeatedly, as Arnold before him, Jarrell tries to solve but which, unlike Auden, he is not willing to dismiss by disowning the seriousness of art.

The failure to collapse these visions into one suggests a schematicization of the world—an inner lens—through which one is to see darkly the darkling plain with the "plainness near and flashing" that Arnold called for. Moreover the failure seems to be built into the vision, for as Moses and Rebekah and the Argonauts had cosmic views against which to measure their daily experiences and which never dissolved into an atmosphere of complete immediacy, so, too, in Arnold and Jarrell forces outside their work dictate the choice of words. Goethe's view that the poet must be naive is at least to that extent negated; the "ignorant armies," for instance, which end Arnold's "Dover Beach" are ignorant not because of anything in the poem but because of the world view out of which the poem springs. The same may be said of the emotive language of many Jarrell poems. Delmore Schwartz registers such a complaint in "The Dream from Which No One Wakes" (1945): "In his first two books many of the poems were weakened by a thinness and abstractness of texture and reference; it was as if the poet saw his subjects through opera glasses. . . . For all the genuineness of the poems, the net result resembled the dim and ghastly negative which has to be held up to the light, and not the developed photograph full of daylight and defined objects."[17]

Jarrell's various positions on Auden demonstrate, in addition, an unwillingness to resolve the matter of these disjunctions by focusing necessarily on one persona or about the writings of a single man. This suggests another kind of disjunction hinted at by Shapiro: a yearning for and an opposition to Authority. Shapiro writes of Jarrell's opposition: "It became necessary for everyone my age to attack Auden, as sculptors must attack Mount Rushmore. Nevertheless Auden and Mount Rushmore still stand and probably always will."[18] Nor was Williams a more suitable subject. Jarrell notes of him: "He is a *very* good but *very* limited poet, particularly in vertical range" (PA, 240). Jarrell adds: "He keeps too much to that tenth of the iceberg that is above water, perhaps" (PA, 245). Jarrell is more generous toward Frost: "Frost is that rare thing, a complete or representative poet, and not one of the brilliant partial poets who do justice, far more than justice, to a portion of reality, and leave the rest of things forlorn" (PA, 61). And Jarrell says of Whitman: "Of all modern poets he has, quantitatively speaking, 'the most comprehensive soul'—and, qualitatively, a most comprehensive and comprehending one, with charities and concessions and qualifications that are rare in any time" (PA, 115). But he reduces his praise of Frost by adding: "If we compare this wisdom with, say, that of the last of the Old Ones, Goethe, we are saddened and frightened at how much the poet's scope has narrowed, at how difficult and partial and idiosyncratic the application of his intelligence has become, at what terrible sacrifices he has had to make in order to avoid making others still more terrible" (PA, 62).

As an alternative to shaping his views into a single voice, Jarrell seems at times to suggest multiple personae. He champions, for example, anthologies as an ideal critical expression and exposition of an age's taste and laments the fact that Arnold's touchstones "never evolved into an anthology" (PA, 155). He also praises individual poets like Williams, Whitman, and Frost for their abilities to get out of themselves, to suggest other voices than their own in their poetry; and he complains of Robert Lowell in "A View of Three Poets" that "you can't tell David from Bathsheba without a program: they both (like the majority of Mr. Lowell's characters) talk just like Mr. Lowell" (PA, 231). A decade earlier, "Poets: Old, New, and Aging" (1940) had noted the same of Pound: "Everything is seen as through a glass darkly, the glass being Mr. Pound: 1766 B.C. talks exactly like 1735 A.D., and both exactly like Ezra Pound. To the old complaint, 'All Chinamen look alike,' Mr. Pound makes one add, 'And talk alike, and act alike—and always did.'"[19] Jarrell repeatedly insists on dramatic monologue as the poetic vehicle, though, at times, as in the case of Elizabeth Bishop, he is willing to grant morality to description and landscape as had Ruskin.

All three suggestions—anthologies, flexible voices, and the dramatic monologue technique—seem part of a philosophical relativism which Jarrell betrays in statements like "Williams had a real and unusual dislike of, distrust in, Authority; and the Father-surrogate of the average work of art has been banished from his Eden. His ability to rest (or at least to thrash happily about) in contradictions, doubts, and general guesswork, without ever climbing aboard any of the monumental certainties that go perpetually by, perpetually on time—this ability may seem the opposite of Whitman's gift for boarding every certainty and riding off into every infinite, but the spirit behind them is the same" (PA, 220). His enlisting of readers to join him on such journeys recalls Oswald Spengler's position in *The Decline of the West* (1918). Spengler branded this philosophical relativism the modern counterpart to classical skepticism which was ahistorical and denied outright. The new skepticism which "is obliged to be historical through and through" gets its solutions "by treating everything as relative, as a historical phenomenon, and its procedure is psychological."[20] It leads to a voice in Jarrell's poetry that is consciously nonauthoritative or whose authoritative tone is undermined by the poem's context in the volume or by other tones within it. Only in his criticism was Jarrell willing to become authoritative, and this may have prompted Helen Vendler's remark that his poetry had talent but that his real genius lay in criticism.

Jarrell's treatment of the childhoods of Auden and Kipling and his poems like "A Story" (1939) indicate that there may be other personal reasons behind his dislike of Authority. The accounts in these works strangely blend into each other and, one suspects, Jarrell's own boyhood. In "Freud to Paul: The Stages of Auden's Ideology" (1945) he says of Auden's childhood and its part in the creation of "the wicked Uncle": "It is no surprise to learn, in *Letters from Iceland* and other places, that Auden's parents were unusually good ones, very much venerated by the child: Auden moralizes interminably, cannot question or reject Authority except under the aegis of this pathetically invented opposing authority, because the superego (or whatever term we wish to use for the mechanism of conscience and authority) is exceptionally strong in him." Jarrell then cites a statement by Abram Kardiner that "the superego is based on affection, not hatred" (TBC, 164). Of Kipling's boyhood Jarrell notes, "For the first six years of his life the child lived in Paradise, the inordinately loved and reasonably spoiled son of the best of parents; after that he lived in the Hell in which the best of parents put him, and paid to have him kept" (SH, 129). After six years they rescued the boy "and for the rest of their lives they continued to be the best and most loving of parents, blamed by Kipling for nothing, adored by Kipling for everything" (SH, 130). Jarrell goes on to conclude: "It is *this* that made Kipling what he was: if they had been the worst of parents, even fairly bad parents, even ordinary parents, it would have all made sense, Kipling himself could have made sense out of it. As it was, his world had been torn in two and he himself torn in two: for under the part of him that extenuated everything, blamed for nothing, there was certainly a part that extenuated nothing, blamed for everything—a part whose existence he never admitted, most especially not to himself" (SH, 130).

Jarrell's "A Story" details the same emotions in the son of "the best of parents." The lad eventually extenuates everything and blames his parents for nothing while at the same time he extenuates nothing and blames them for everything. He arrives at the "Hell" of a boarding school whose emptiness is juxtaposed to the "good" mother's concern—even to the point of using the "right"

language: "Remember to change your stockings every day— /
Socks, I mean." Recollection of the concern changes to resentment
as the boy's "mail-box is still empty, / Because they've all forgotten
me, they love their / New friends better." The boy plots to punish
his parents by disappearing. The same "concern" and "indictment" fill late poems like "Windows" (1954), in which the parents
who have been accused by their son of being "indifferent" show
their concern in noting "you have not slept." For Jarrell, whose
parents were divorced, these "parents" are often his paternal
grandparents with whom he lived for a while in Hollywood. Significantly the movement in these later poems runs ever away from
indictment to forgiveness. "In Those Days" (1953) he recalls:
"How poor and miserable we were. / How seldom together! / And
yet after so long one thinks: / In those days everything was better."
The sentiment extends to both "The Lost World" and "Thinking
of the Lost World" (1963), which concludes that, having spent
most of his life learning to forgive his parents for having damaged
him, he is left with "nothing" as his reward. The mechanisms by
which one's self has been defined, once withered away by forgiveness, leave one nothing by which to define self—a fear implicit in
any real skepticism and here expressed "in happiness."

Jarrell had come to a similar conclusion twenty-three years before in "For an Emigrant" (1940), and the despair of nothingness,
so much complained of by reviewers, runs through the early
books. In one of his last poems, "A Man Meets a Woman in the
Street" (1967), the narrator gives up identity and the human drive
of imagination and contents himself with the wish of the birds that
"this day / Be the same day, the day of my life." Faced with these
various disjunctions, his advice in "The Obscurity of the Poet"
(1951) is that "there is nothing to do different from what we already do: if poets write poems and readers read them, each as best
they can—if they try to live not as soldiers or voters or intellectuals
or economic men, but as human beings—they are doing all that
can be done" (PA, 20). Here he falls back on the thesis of Groddeck's *The Book of the It* (1923) that at man's inception he incurs
a force that shapes his destiny, and things like breathing which
have much to do with the It have little to do with the will. Man
may, as Jarrell indicates in "To Fill a Wilderness" (1951), find that

the world imaged by poetry is "our nation's life as Yeats saw his own—as a preparation for something that never happened."[21]

"A Girl in a Library" (1951), the opening selection of *The Complete Poems*, depicts the conditions of such a perverse preparation. Centering on a girl, a "student of Home Economics and Physical Education, who has fallen asleep in the library of a Southern College," it evolves into a colloquy between the poem's speaker (the present) and Tatyana Larina (the past), who materializes out of Aleksandr Pushkin's *Eugene Onegin* (1833). Tatyana wonders at the value of a life of sleep where "the soul has no assignments, neither cooks / Nor referees; it wastes its time." Without ideas against which to shape the present, a person is no more than a "machine-part"; dream and reality are one and homogeneous like the homogeneous abstract expressionism attacked in "The Age of the Chimpanzee." Indulgent with this "machine-part," as often Jarrell's speakers are not, the narrator responds that since "the ways we miss our lives are life," it is better at death "to squawk like a chicken" and meet Death's challenge "with a last firm strange / Uncomprehending smile" and, then, to see the "blind date that you stood up; your life," than to be aware of the failure beforehand. Incorporated in this response is Jarrell's inconsistent view that, whatever the innate or obscure and expanding reaches of excellence, like Rebekah and the Argonauts, people should strive after them. As with Groddeck's patients, this striving may take the form of a self-examination to make one adjust himself to the It, but no amount of will can shape an It that is not there.

Knowledge by way of Tatyana emphasizes literature as an important source of reform. Jarrell repeats this stress in "The Intellectual in America" (1955) where he speaks of the writer again as "the man who will make us see what we haven't seen, feel what we haven't felt, understand what we haven't understood—he *is* our best friend" (SH, 15). The student's failure, like the failures of the children of "Lady Bates" (1948) and "The Black Swan" (1951) and of the pilot of "The Dead Wingman" (1945), relegates her to an unearned oblivion of "everlasting sleep." In contrast the "saved"—those whose visions help shape the future—become part of a hovering Spirit which "Burning the Letters" (1945) shows inspiring the present. But even there it must be finally abandoned in order to let new life evolve. In time, as "The Memoirs of Glückel of Hameln" (1942) asserts, "We take your place as our place will be taken." In both instances "The Knight, Death, and the Devil" (1951) maintains, man achieves his judgment not by any human design but by doing what he must. Under such non-traditional terms "The Night before the Night before Christmas" (1949) indicates that "to use God's name" (that is, to imagine him) is "to misuse His name," for what can be imagined, as "In the Ward: The Sacred Wood" (1946) makes clear, can also be un-made. "A Sick Child" (1949) depicts God as "all that I never thought of," and "Eighth Air Force" (1947) shows Christ not as divine but as a "just man" without fault, whom the speaker has tried to imitate. This imitation causes "suffering" and a final self-image as Pontius Pilate, and in "Seele im Raum" (1950), it pro-duces the "eland," that imaginary creature of the mind which gives life to the soul and humanity to the "machine" and which in German translates as "wretched" (*elend*).

The human designs which result from this wretchedness—often dictated in terms of daydream, wish, fairy tale, make-believe, dream, myth, miracle, and masterwork—are the products, Jarrell insists, only of children and men, and men only insofar as they are childish. In no case are they as idiosyncratic as Heideggerian Daseins. Girls have them until they marry and become women. Then, as "Woman" (1964) states, they become "realists; or as a realist might say, / Naturalists," for it is "woman's nature / To want the best, and to be careless how it comes." "Cinderella" (1954) records a coy but significant conversation between a day-dreaming girl and her daydream godmother (the Virgin Mary) in the absence of Prince Charming and Christ, who are out childish-ly imagining. It ends with God's mother inviting the girl to await inside the return of their men, which might be soon or never. "Mary" herself has taken on the aspects of the Devil's grandmoth-er in Grimm's "The Devil with the Three Golden Hairs." In the light of man's inability to imagine correctly the Divine Will, the "wisdom" of their position is obvious, for what they do realize by becoming mothers is a role in Jarrell's almost Darwinian evolution and divinely willed preservation of the species. Here, however the individual may be disregarded, the form or species will be cher-ished. Yet, as Jarrell seems to say in variations of the "Cinderella" situation such as "The End of the Rainbow" (1954), "Seele im Raum" (1950), and "The Woman at the Washington Zoo" (1959), becoming a woman is not very easy. The women of these poems are looked on by their worlds as machine-parts. Only in their imaginations do they preserve their humanity, often by dreaming of fairy-tale and animal creatures in whom to invest their love.

As in Arnold the cherishing of this species takes the form of the perfection of the state—"the nation in its collective and corporate character"—rather than of the individual. Many of the essays in *A Sad Heart at the Supermarket* are directed toward this end, which critics of Jarrell's early poetry mistook for Marxism. In such essays as "The Taste of the Age" (1958) Jarrell presents himself as a latter-day Arnold or as Arnold's favorite, Goethe. The essay opens with a negative reaction to the age: "When we look at the age in which we live—no matter what age it happens to be —it is hard for us not to be depressed by it." Jarrell then goes on to note: "We can see that Goethe's and Arnold's ages weren't as bad as Goethe and Arnold thought them: after all, they produced Goethe and Arnold" (SH, 16, 17). The rest of the essay unfolds as an attack on popular culture and an appeal for continuing to upgrade culture, as Arnold had thought to do, through education. Similarly, in recommending the second book of William Wordsworth's "The Excursion" in the *New York Times*'s "Speaking of Books" column (1955), Jarrell writes: "I feel Matthew Arnold's approving breath at my shoulder, and see out before me, smiling bewitchingly, the nations of the not-yet-born." [22] The state thus conceived becomes organic, and war in "The Range in the Desert" (1947) is looked upon as the pitting of one state against another in a struggle for survival much as the lizard of the poem survives by devouring "the shattered membranes of the fly."

Caught in a movement from greater to lesser imperfection similar to man's, the state at no time is perfect and incapable of change. Yet, as "The Night before the Night before Christmas" indicates, only a just state may triumph, for the triumph of an unjust state is an indication of an unjust God. The view of this relationship between the state and God is declared in "Kafka's Tragi-Comedy" (1941): "God is the trust, the state, all over again at the next higher level. God's justice and the world's contradict each other; and yet what is God's justice but the world's, raised to the next power, but retaining all the qualities of its original." [23] Rather than legally centered upon the protection of the many, the justice of this state is built upon "poetic justice"—the good receiving rewards and the bad, punishments. This central wellspring of art adds a vein of aestheticism which is not obvious in Arnold but which is consistent with nineteenth-century philosophy. It frequently held that the act of poetic creation was closest to the nature of God.

Such pieces as "A Sad Heart at the Supermarket" are willing to admit the aestheticism: "To say that Nature imitates Art . . . is literally true. . . . Which of us hasn't found a similar refuge in the 'real,' created world of Cézanne or Goethe or Verdi?" (SH, 78–79). But the aestheticism which existential psychoanalysis relegates to the past and present by creation of the Dasein is negated in part by Jarrell's drive toward the future. While granting, as had Wilde, "that the self-conscious aim of Life is to find expression, and that Art offers it certain beautiful forms through which it may realize that energy," [24] Jarrell in locating the real force of art in the realm of the spirit—the phylogenetic or Groddeck's It—gives it a timelessness which transcends, as he supposed Freudian analysis might, the otherwise past-directedness of recollected childhood. In "The State" (1945) the poet tries to make acceptable through wit a state's having killed a child's mother and drafted his sister and cat. Although the acts lead finally to the child's wish to die, they may in the realm of the spirit be ultimately right. The deranged nature of the speaker prevents any clear assurance, but Jarrell's concluding remarks in "Auden's Ideology," published in the same year, indicates a willingness to put up with some inconveniences to direct his efforts toward a larger enemy. One senses this "larger enemy" is fears like those expressed in Arthur Miller's *Situation Normal* (1944). Miller defined World War II as a struggle to maintain "the right of each individual to determine his freedom" against "the tyrannic corporate control of the minds and wills of men." [25]

"A Lullaby" (1944) had approached these fears directly. Its soldier's life is submerged to the service of the state. He "is lied to like a child, cursed like a beast," and generally so nonhumanly treated that his life "is smothered like a grave, with dirt," forgotten or "recalled in dreams or letters." "A Field Hospital" (1947) describes an injured soldier being so sedated by the state that he "neither knows" nor "remembers" but "sleeps, comforted." The volumes in which these poems appeared express the hope that the personal sacrifices and losses of the war may be offset by a willingness to create a better world afterward, based on the cost to the individual to let the past continue or to allow its recurrence. A later poem, "A Well-to-do Invalid" (1965), tells of a self-interested nurse (the individual?) who tends a self-indulgent invalid (the state?), taking to herself his care so that she feels her justification and her hope of his inheritance in his not being able to get along without her. She dies, and the poem's speaker sees the invalid "well with grief," realizing in the act how easily her vacancy will be filled. The premise of the poem echoes Jarrell's comments on Alex Comfort (1945). Recognizing "that the states themselves are at present the main danger their citizens face," Jarrell adds reluctantly: "It is we who wither away, not the state" (PA, 142–43). In the "radically-pastoral, romantically nostalgic, bittersweet idylls" that followed these war poems and caused him to begin to lose him his audience, Jarrell began to see even more conclusively that the resolve he hoped might come from the war was not forthcoming. Veterans preferred to forget their sacrifices and accept the sleep that the postwar culture offered. Meaninglessness set in.

Jarrell comes to these views slowly, and even more slowly is a reader able to put them together. Some are already formed by *The Rage for the Lost Penny* (1940), but their presence is obscured in a more conspicuous admixture of Audenesque phrases. These include "efficiently as a new virus," "the star's distention," and "the actuaries end." They later disappear, but their presence here affirms Jarrell's statement in the preface that "Auden is the only poet who has been influential very recently; and this is because, very partially and uncertainly, and often very mechanically, he represents new tendencies, a departure from modernist romanticism." One tendency was the dream poem and its mediation of subconscious and conscious levels, typified by the second poem in Auden's first collection. The poem, which was dropped in subsequent reprintings, forms one reason why Jarrell always cited the 1930 edition of *Poems*, though for convenience he tended to quote from the 1934 edition. A second tendency was Auden's millennialism rooted in "Darwin, Marx, Freud and Co., . . . all characteristically 'scientific' or 'modern' thinkers" about whom the previous generation had "concluded, regretfully: 'If they had not existed, it would not have been necessary to ignore them' (or deplore them)."[26] A third was the power of women to motivate history, as typified by the mothers of Auden's *Paid on Both Sides*. These women keep the feud between their families alive and bloody; and their power, which occurs often in the backgrounds of these early poems, becomes more apparent as women move into the foreground of Jarrell's poetry with *Losses* (1948).

In *The Rage for the Lost Penny* are located a number of poems which belong to the child's sing-song world and whose half-lines and themes occasionally foreshadow lines and themes in Theodore Roethke's *The Lost Son* (1948). The narrator of "A Little Poem" (1940) speaks to his yet-to-be-conceived younger brother in the womb with such Roethkean expressions as "My brother was a fish" and references to the world as "this sink of time." The opening lines of "The Ways and the Peoples" (1939) add: "What does the storm say? What the trees wish" and "I am the king of the dead." This last assertion finds itself repeated in Berryman's *The Dispossessed* (1948), at the end of the second and psychologically based "Nervous Songs" ("The Song of the Demented Priest"). Jarrell's introduction to *The Golden Bird and Other Fairy Tales* (1962) makes the connection between these poems and Freud apparent: "Reading *Grimm's Tales* tells someone what we're like, inside, just as reading Freud tells him. *The Fisherman and His Wife*—which is one of the best stories anyone ever told, it seems to me—is as truthful and troubling as any newspaper headlines about the new larger-sized H–bomb and the new antimissile missile: a country is never satisfied either, but wants to be like the good Lord." Earlier Jarrell in his essay on Kafka had described *Amerika* as "a charming and often extremely funny story, a sort of Candide *à la* Hans Christian Andersen, with extraordinary overtones": "This world is hardly *judged* at all; its cruelties and barbarities elicit only the blankly anthropological interest we extend to the vagaries of savages or children. The conscientious naïveté, the more-than-scientific suspension or tentativeness of judgment of the later books, are already surprisingly well developed in *Amerika*. In its capacity for generating ambiguity and irony (reinforced in the later books by the similar possibilities of allegory), the attitude resembles that of Socrates, that of the scientist making minimal assumptions, or that of the 'humble observer': child, fairy-tale simpleton or third son, fool." [27]

In addition Jarrell knows enough about the Arnoldian future of his poetry to begin *The Rage for the Lost Penny* with "On the Railway Platform" (1939). Like the later "A Girl in a Library" it has as its theme the ideas that man travels "by the world's one way" and that his "journeys end in / No destination we meant." What man leaves, he leaves forever. "When You and I Were All" (1939) continues the Arnoldian cast with the lines: "What kiss could wake / whose world and sleep were one embrace?" The influence reappears as well in the telling question of "The Refugees" (1940): "What else are their lives but a journey to the vacant / Satisfaction of death?" "For the Madrid Road" (1940) adds the prospect of people who die to preserve their ideals and who ask continually, "But when were lives men's own? . . . Men die / . . . that men may miss / The unessential ills." Malcolm Cowley's review of *Blood for a Stranger* (1942) lists the further echoes of Wilfred Owen's "The Snow" in "The Automaton" (1937) and of Allen Tate's "Ode to the Confederate Dead" in "A Description of Some Confederate Soldiers" (1936). But the reader's task has been formed; he must reject the surface and work backward from the language of Jarrell's writing not to influences but to the conscious and unconscious impulses which fashioned the work.

Moreover the views translate into an over-all sense of a poetry which, in striving after the noblest thoughts of men and a style which might serve the higher destinies to which poetry has been called, consistently appears unreal and valueless. Often the unreality is necessary, for, by believing that imagination must precede change, Jarrell must stress moments of imagination—daydream, fairy tale, and wish—and minimize the fact. In this he faces a problem similar to that faced by Dante and Gerard Manley Hopkins: weighing the sensuous beauty of the world which attracts the artist against the idealism which leads him to reject that world for the idea. In reviewing, Jarrell faced the problem by beginning his reviews with his most adverse statements, reversing the usual order of reviewers and prompting Berryman's comment: "Jarrell's reviews did go beyond the limit; they were unbelievably cruel." But their cruelty was often the way Jarrell had for forcing readers out of their complacency into realms where the imagination might function. Since the highest and noblest thoughts of men exclude the ugly, Jarrell tended to exclude it from his poetry or redeem it by means of sentimentalism and romanticism. In a war situation like that opening "Transient Barracks" (1949), the ugly may intrude and allow a sense of life to emerge, but this is rare, and one suspects the additional influence of Pyle. Miller's analysis of Pyle here proves relevant: "Ernie Pyle's thought *was* in his columns. His thought is people. His thought is details about people. War is about people, not ideas. You cannot see ideas bleeding."[28]

More common are the moments in Jarrell's last volume where man is located amid a gross commercialism that hawks its panaceas of Cheer and Joy and All and where things are stripped plain. At those moments, as ever where the fact and idea clash, Jarrell's wit intrudes to work, as Freud indicates all wit works, to overcome the valuelessness by letting an unaltered or nonsensical ambiguity of words and multiplicity of thought-relations appear to the consciousness at the same time senseful and admissible as jest. In "A Man Meets a Woman in the Street" Jarrell is willing to forego such ambiguity by accepting the factuality of the world, but the willingness is itself indication that the fact has not occurred. These instants when idea and fact clash are most often the occasions where the purposelessness of the present fades into the brilliance of Jarrell's lines as the concerted direction of his life lay always obscured by the veneer of an incessant instinct of expansion and a refined sensibility. This sensibility, for all its stress on modernism, relished sports cars, bucolic atmospheres, traditional art, good music, poetry, technological advances, and Russian ballet. Lowell in "Randall Jarrell" (1967) recalls: "His mind, unearthly in its quickness, was a little boyish, disembodied, and brittle. His body was a little ghostly in its immunity to soil, entanglements, and rebellion. As one sat with him in oblivious absorption at the campus bar, sucking a fifteen-cent chocolate milk shake and talking eternal things, one felt, beside him, too corrupt and companionable. He had the harsh luminosity of Shelley—like Shelley, every inch a poet, and like Shelley, imperiled perhaps by an arid, abstracting precocity."[29]

Only the imaginary portrait of the poet—akin to the Imaginary Portraits of fin-de-siècle writers—shifting among Goethe, Arnold, and Auden and formed early by Jarrell—offered him something worldly and static and positive against which to shape his life. That portrait is sketched in the allusions to these writers, the self-comparisons with them, and the appropriations of their tastes that run through all of Jarrell's work. These appropriations go hand in hand with an attack on idiosyncratic individualism which he associated in "The End of the Line" with modernism. This sense led early to a growing drift from the personal that was not reversed until *The Woman at the Washington Zoo* (1960) and *The Lost World* (1965). Here, as M. L. Rosenthal in *The New Poets* (1967) observes, "a change had begun to take place, heralded by three poems in the former book: 'In Those Days,' 'The Elementary Scene,' and 'Windows.' These are poems of private memory—of a time in the past that seemed, often was, 'poor and miserable' (and yet 'everything was better'); of the sadness of what appears, in 'The Elementary Scene,' to have been an unsatisfactory childhood, with a last ironic allusion to the speaker's adult condition ('I, I, the future that mends everything'); and of the impossibility of recovering the dead, simple past of parents who 'have known nothing of today.'" This reversal which brings Jarrell into the confessional school, so much a part of the age, was roundly applauded by reviewers who, like Philip Booth, tended to refer to *The Lost World* as a "great new book."[30]

In fact one might chart the progress of *The Complete Poems* as a succession of efforts by Jarrell to rid himself of the "aloneness" which he felt—without resorting to the condemnations of parents which he associated with both Kipling and Auden. Repeatedly one senses what in *The Divided Self* (1960) R. D. Laing calls "ontological insecurity": "The individual in the ordinary circumstances of living may feel more unreal than real; in a literal sense, more dead than alive; precariously differentiated from the rest of the world, so that his identity and autonomy are always in question." Jarrell's personae are always involved with efforts to escape engulfment, implosion, and petrification, by demanding that they somehow be miraculously changed by life and art into people whose ontologies are psychically secure. The changes may allow them then to drop the mechanism by which in their relations they preserve themselves and to feel gratification in relatedness. Laing, who indirectly cites Kafka as a prime example of a writer of ontological insecurity, strikes close to Jarrell's own sensibility. Something there along with Rilke's Apollo or Norman O. Brown's *Love's Body* (1966) announces: "Meaning is not in things but in between; in the iridescence, the interplay; in the interconnections; at the intersections, at the crossroads." [31]

For a person with less skill, such purposelessness and such militating against the fact might be enough to make his life and poetry unwelcome. Without Williams's rhythms of descent or a comparable instrument of sacramentalization to bridge inner and outer existences, Jarrell's world remains disparate; and he must rely on language as his major means for keeping it together. This reliance runs explicitly through much of his criticism and is implicit in his poetry; yet, as he perceived in "The Taste of the Age," even language was failing him: "The more words there are, the simpler the words get. The professional users of words process their product as if it were baby food and we babies: all we have to do is open our mouths and swallow" (SH, 28). Without a complex language, a language capable of multiplicity, of the ambiguity necessary to wed conscious and unconscious realms, successful poetry would become impossible. Nevertheless a thingy liveliness might be preserved and, because the future always holds something better, hope as well. Like Arnold, who never realized his dream of some day supplanting Tennyson and Browning as the poet of the mid-nineteenth century because of the self-defeating nature of his momentary stays against the confusion of the world, Jarrell seems destined because of his overwhelming reliance on the translucency of language for a secondary role. Here the excellence and abundance of wisdom, hope, humanity, and despair that the in-betweens of Jarrell's poetry contain, affirm his role in bringing psychological techniques to American themes. If, as Shapiro senses, he failed in that role, all the same by his efforts he made others aware of the course poetry must take. His nostalgic laments for the passing may be perhaps not so centrally important as the celebrations of renewal by other poets of his generation, but Jarrell remains by virtue of the laments imposingly significant.

Notes

1. Karl Shapiro in *Randall Jarrell: 1914–1965*, ed. Robert Lowell, Peter Taylor, and Robert Penn Warren (New York: Farrar, Straus and Giroux, 1967), p. 201; Helen Vendler, "The Complete Poems," *New York Times Book Review*, 2 February 1969, p. 5. The following abbreviations of Jarrell's books have been adopted for internal citation: PA—*Poetry and the Age* (New York: Vintage Books, 1955); SH—*A Sad Heart at the Supermarket* (New York: Atheneum, 1962); TBC—*The Third Book of Criticism* (New York: Farrar, Straus and Giroux, 1969). The abbreviations are accompanied by page citations.

2. T. S. Eliot, *Selected Essays*, rev. ed. (London: Faber and Faber, 1951), p. 203. For Jarrell's subscription to this view, see his remarks on Theodore Roethke in *The Third Book of Criticism*, pp. 326–27.

3. Matthew Arnold, "The Study of Poetry," in *Essays in Criticism: Second Series* (London: Macmillan and Co., 1888), p. 2.

4. Mary von Schrader Jarrell, "Reflections on Jerome," *Jerome: The Biography of a Poem* (New York: Grossman, 1971), p. 13.

5. Randall Jarrell, "The Age of the Chimpanzee," *Art News* 56 (summer 1957), 34.

6. Randall Jarrell, "Poetry in War and Peace," *Partisan Review* 12 (1945): 123.

7. Randall Jarrell, "Poetry in a Dry Season," *Partisan Review* 7 (1940): 166; Jarrell, "New Year Letter," *Nation* 152 (1941): 440.

8. Randall Jarrell, "Recent Poetry," *Yale Review* 44 (1955): 607; Jarrell, "The Year in Poetry," *Harper's* 211 (October 1955): 100.

9. Randall Jarrell, "Verse Chronicle," *Nation* 165 (1947): 424; "The Age of the Chimpanzee," p. 35.

10. Randall Jarrell, "These Are Not Psalms," *Commentary* 1 (November 1955): 88.

11. Randall Jarrell, "Poetry, Unlimited," *Partisan Review* 17 (1950): 191; Jarrell, "The Profession of Poetry," *Partisan Review* 17 (1950): 726; Jarrell, "Ernie Pyle," *Nation* 160 (1945): 573.

12. John Berryman in *Randall Jarrell: 1914–1965*, p. 16; John Ruskin, *Modern Painters*. Illustrated Library Edition. 3 vols. (Boston: Aldine Book Publishing Co., 1900): 3:330–31, 1:108.

13. Randall Jarrell, "Verse Chronicle," *Nation* 166 (1948): 360; "The Profession of Poetry," p. 731; René Welleck and Austin Warren, *Theory of Literature*, 3rd ed. (New York: Harvest Books, 1962), p. 82.

14. "The Profession of Poetry," p. 728; Parker Tyler, "The Dramatic Lyricism of Randall Jarrell," *Poetry* 129 (1952): 344.

15. Rollo May, "Contributions of Existential Psychotherapy," in *Existence*, ed. Rollo May, Ernest Angel, and Henri F. Ellenberger (New York: Clarion Books, 1958), p. 69; Henrik M. Ruitenbeek, Introduction to *Psychoanalysis and Existential Philosophy* (New York: E. P. Dutton, 1962), p. xx.

16. "The Study of Poetry," p. 2.

17. Delmore Schwartz, "The Dream from Which No One Wakes," *Nation* 161 (1945): 590.

18. Shapiro, p. 225.

19. Randall Jarrell, "Poets: Old, New, and Aging," *New Republic* 103 (1940): 800.

20. Oswald Spengler, *The Decline of the West*, trans. Charles Frances Atkinson (New York: Modern Library, 1965), p. 35.

21. Randall Jarrell, "To Fill a Wilderness," *Nation* 173 (1951): 570.

22. Randall Jarrell, "Speaking of Books," *New York Times Book Review*, 24 July 1955, p. 2.

23. Randall Jarrell, "Kafka's Tragi-Comedy," *Kenyon Review* 3 (1941): 118.

24. Oscar Wilde, *The Artist as Critic*, ed. Richard Ellmann (New York: Random House, 1969), p. 320.

25. Benjamin Nelson, *Arthur Miller: Portrait of a Playwright* (New York: David McKay, 1970), p. 55.

26. Randall Jarrell, "A Note on Poetry," in *Five Young American Poets* (Norfolk, Conn.: New Directions, 1940), p. 89; "New Year Letter," p. 440.

27. Randall Jarrell, "Grimm's Tales," *The Golden Bird and Other Fairy Tales* (New York: Crowell Collier, 1962), p. v; "Kafka's Tragi-Comedy," pp. 116–17.

28. Berryman, p. 16; Arthur Miller, *Situation Normal* (New York: Reynal & Hitchcock, 1944), p. 166.

29. Robert Lowell in *Randall Jarrell: 1914–1965*, p. 102.

30. M. L. Rosenthal, *The New Poets* (New York: Oxford University Press, 1967), p. 330; Philip Booth in *Randall Jarrell: 1914–1965*, p. 22.

31. R. D. Laing, *The Divided Self* (Baltimore: Penguin Books, 1965), p. 42; Norman O. Brown, *Love's Body* (New York: Random House, 1966), p. 247.

3

The Failure of Language: Theodore Roethke

A reader of Theodore Roethke's *Open House* (1941) soon comes upon a problem that bothered the writer throughout most of his career—the problem of voice. Even as late as 1959, he felt the need (in "How to Write Like Somebody Else") to respond to charges by critics that after *Praise to the End!* (1951) his poetry became too imitative of others and himself. *Open House* had appropriated tones from Elinor Wylie, theories from W. H. Auden, and cadences from Léonie Adams in what he describes as a metaphoric Adams-Roethke literary "affair": "I loved her so much, her poetry, that I just *had* to become, for a brief moment, a part of her world. . . . I *had* to create something that would honor her in her own terms." He adds in his defense, "I didn't cabbage those effects in cold blood" (PC, 66).[1] He opposes this affectionate theft to his later "conscious imitation" of established writers. Here, he asserts, the very fact that the poet "has the support of a tradition, of an older writer, will enable him to be more himself—or more than himself" (PC, 69). In between, when he was reordering in verse memories of Saginaw and the greenhouse world of his childhood, he confessed in an "Open Letter" to John Ciardi (1950) that he served as an "instrument" for the poems much as W. B. Yeats claimed his wife had in the writing of *A Vision* (1917). Jim Jackson, who taught with Roethke at Bennington when Roethke began the poems, supports such a view: "*Lost Son* was written in huge swatches. With run-on chants, dirges coming forth pell-mell. Sense of continuity uppermost at all times—even though particular poems in *Lost Son* were later detached and presented as individual poems" (GH, 146).

This role of poet-as-instrument coincides with the notion of style Goethe proposes in "Simple Imitation of Nature, Manner, Style" (1789). For Goethe, style "rests on the deepest fundamental ground of knowledge, on the essence of things, insofar as it is granted us to know this in visible and tangible forms." Roethke derives the role from Rainer Maria Rilke, who in *The Notebooks of Malte Laurids Brigge* (1910) mentions the writer's need to be able to think back with more than memories. This thinking back resembles Wordsworth's "emotions recollected in tranquility" in that "one must be able to forget [past experiences] and have vast patience until . . . they become blood within us, and glances and gestures. . . . Then first it can happen that in a rare hour the first word of a verse may arise and come forth."[2] In 1935 Louise Bogan was sending translations and analyses of the German poet to the young Roethke, and in "On 'Identity'" (1963) he uses Rilke as a model for heightening one's awareness of the universe: "To look at a thing so long that you are a part of it and it is a part of you—Rilke gazing at his tiger ["Der Panther"?] for eight hours, for instance" (PC, 25).

Reversing an early aversion to tradition, Roethke extends this heightening to the dead as well as to the living. "If the dead can come to our aid in a quest for identity, so can the living—and I mean *all* living things, including the sub-human." He claims to be influenced in his view by St. Thomas, who said: "God is above all things by the excellence of His nature; nevertheless, He is in all things as causing the being of all things" (PC, 24–25). The process, Seager reports Judith Bailey as telling him, was extended also to inanimate objects. "She says she believes that Ted actually abused his mind by concentrating on single objects for so long at a time, and she says he would also take deliberate flights of free association—she saw him stand and stare at a refrigerator handle one night and begin, 'Refrigerator handle—Frigidaire—air-hose—snake. . . .' It went on for half an hour with incredible quickness. Any object, a refrigerator, a tree, a house, seemed to be to him not only itself but the sum of the associations he could wreathe around it, a microcosm, in fact, and out of these exercises came his symbols and many new word combinations" (GH, 189).

Auden in "Rilke in English" (1939) likewise singled out the German poet as the figure "to whom writers are becoming increasingly drawn," and as early as 1934 Rolfe Humphries had begun recommending Auden to Roethke as a writer from whom he might learn. In *Theodore Roethke* (1966) Karl Malkoff describes the particular influence of Auden on the use of landscape to evoke psychological states and of melodramatic settings to image the change from adolescence to maturity. Malkoff assigns the Freudian intuition and "crippling effects of one's immediate family" especially in "the devouring mother" of "Feud" to such works as *Paid on Both Sides*. "Lull (November, 1939)" is even considered "not sufficiently detached from Auden's 'September 1, 1939' to stand on its own." Entire lines and sentiments in the Roethke poem cannot be understood without reference to the Auden work. Roethke's contribution to *Conversations on the Craft of Poetry* (1961) affirms that the influence extends beyond *Open House* into the writing of *The Lost Son* (1948). He acknowledges Auden as having made him aware of the "memorable speech" that is Mother Goose and as writing poetry which employs "the rhythms of children, of folk material" with shifting "like the tail of a fish" or "the sound of the sea or the arbor bees" to accommodate the subject. It is Auden, too, who in his review (1941) of *Open House* points the postmodern direction Roethke will take by indicating that "one grows up in the degree to which . . . unconscious order becomes conscious and its potentialities developed." Auden praises Roethke particularly for transforming "the physically soiled and humiliated" into something beautiful, and he encourages the young writer to go beyond English poetry to "the poetry of other cultures" and "books that are neither poetry nor about poetry."[3]

Anyone familiar with Arthur Rimbaud's "deliberate derangement of all the senses," Hart Crane's poetry, Yeats's "Magic" (1901), and T. S. Eliot's view of the metaphysicals (1921) can see the widespread acceptance among modernist poets of the theory of heightened awareness. Georges Lemaitre summarizes Rimbaud's techniques in *From Cubism to Surrealism in French Literature* (1947): "A visionary state cannot be achieved by one who is in a condition of complete mental equilibrium; the spirit must be wrenched from the grip of rational conceptions. The senses, which are the great means of communication with the ordinary world, must be put systematically out of their proper working order: 'Le poète se fait voyant par un long, immense, raisonné dérèglement de tous les sens.'" Lemaitre cautions that this visionary state "is not to be effected by means of artificial devices but simply by forcing the senses into a paroxysm of action exceeding the limits of their normal working power. When the fiery intensity of 'toutes les formes d'amour, de souffrance, de folie,' has caused a breakdown of our conventional receptive and interpretative mechanism, when the very excess of strain has filled our material nature with numbing 'poisons,' then only is the mind liberated from all its shackles. Then, even though he may have become a physical wreck, a criminal in the eyes of the world, a being accursed, man at last enters into supreme knowledge; he attains the unknown."[4]

According to Brom Weber in *Hart Crane* (1948), Crane, who was also an early influence on Roethke, had been directed to Rimbaud's techniques by Ezra Pound's "A Study of French Modern Poets" (1918): "Pound's observation that the key to Rimbaud's accomplishment was the utilization of intense emotional feeling, with direct entrance by the poet into the subject as the method, undoubtedly was significant to Crane."[5] In "Magic" Yeats associates the style with concepts of a Great Mind and a Great Memory, and Roethke, in phrases reminiscent of Eliot, extends it in "On 'Identity'" to John Donne and the metaphysicals. For Roethke the poet "thinks with his body: an idea for him can be as real as the smell of a flower or a blow on the head" (PC, 27). Yet, rather than think of the process in terms of a return to origins, as a modernist poet might, Roethke denies "that the soul, my soul, was absorbed in God." God remains for him, as he does for most postmodernists, "someone to be confronted, to be dueled with" (PC, 26). Desired instead is "a primitive attitude: animistic perhaps" (PC, 24) that relates to childhood recollection and innocence and establishes the poet's own identity. It is in Heideggerian terms the reintegration of *physis* (physics and nature) and *logos* (idea or reason).[6]

The role of poet-as-instrument and the Goethean notion of style as basic to this reunion coincide, too, with Carl Jung's belief in an "original undivided harmony of plant, animal, man and God," whose restoration might be accomplished through a process of psychological self-realization—an opening of conscious forces to the unconscious so as to avoid a onesidedness that may contribute to neurosis. This phylogenetic undivided harmony whose loss is symbolized in the Fall is repeated ontogenetically in the lost individual harmonies of childhood. Echoing Yeats's idea of a Great Memory, Jung notes in "Psychology and Poetry" (1930) that the great artist touches "that salubrious and redeeming psychic depth . . . where all still feel the same vibration, and where, therefore, the sentiment and action of the individual reach out to all humanity." In the particular case of Roethke, whose return to redeeming self-realization involves a return to childhood, Jung's statement in *The Theory of Psychoanalysis* (1913) is especially apt: "The little world of childhood with its familiar surroundings is a model of the greater world. The more intensively the family has stamped its character upon the child, the more it will tend to feel and see its earlier miniature world again in the bigger world of adult life." But "what youth found and must find outside," Roethke now "in middle life must find within him." [7]

Thus, although Roethke's search for harmony must be an inner search, as Jung indicates in "Concerning Birth" (1940), an outer increase of experience must carry with it the sense of inner expanding spatiality: "Everything which comes from without becomes our own only when we are capable of an inner spaciousness which corresponds to the size of the outer increase. The actual increase in personality is the becoming conscious of a widening, which flows from inner sources." [8] But what Roethke becomes conscious of in *Open House* is not a spaciousness but a widening separation of inner and outer worlds blocking his development through a failure of language to act properly as a mediator of deeds and rage. Relatives, scenes, limits come crashing in with the epigrammatic forms and tight rhymes. Most of the space is negative. Few of the landscapes and journeys of the later poems are present. "Doors" may be "widely swung," but "corruption" erodes "blood" and "cell." "Cages" appear in poems like "Silence" and "Prayer before Study," and Roethke's final attempt to leave everything behind in "Night Journey" occurs while he is in a pullman berth as an imaginative loop as crazy as that of "The Bat." One gathers that whatever increase of experience occurs in the volume is either fantastic or perverse or vicarious.

Part of the failure of language is caused by linguistic differences between the internalized, primal, familial world of the greenhouse, Saginaw, and the tradition which Roethke sought to escape in *Open House* and that of Roethke's literary adult life. He focuses on one root of this difference in *Twentieth Century Authors, First Supplement* (1955): "I had no interest in verse after an intense period of pleasure in nursery rhymes in English and German and songs my mother and nurse sang me" (PC, 15). The same mixture of English and German sounded in the greenhouse, and Seager notes that the John Moore School (which Roethke attended for eight years) out of deference to the district's large German population required students to spend an hour a day learning German. Yet, though from five to fourteen years of age he had taken German, the poet resisted learning it. Seager reports: "He never spoke it except for a few idiomatic phrases he may have picked up in the greenhouse from the workmen; he could barely read it or write it. This may have been, with his parents' unspoken consent, some dim, attenuated hangover of the immigrant's rejection of the Old Country" (GH, 20–21).

Roethke says for *Twentieth Century Authors* that "I really wanted at fifteen and sixteen, to write a beautiful, a 'chiseled' prose as it was called in those days" and cites, as possibly the source for Seager's position, models in "Stevenson, Pater, Newman, Tomlinson, and those maundering English charm boys known as familiar essayists" (PC, 15). In the light of the poet's defenses of the German character in letters to Dorothy Gordon (1934) and Katherine Stokes (1939) and of his later admiration for Rilke, one might as accurately ascribe his rejection of German to simple adolescent rebellion. In either case the German-American world and basis of what became his educated Anglo-American language would lead to the kind of separation between emotions and their expression that Roethke complains of in his first volume. The situation is not quite that of the devoted parents who are to be "extenuated everything, blamed for nothing" so much as a disadvantaged culture that must be extenuated nothing and blamed for everything. Nonetheless it involves the same displacement of a real emotional center for an imaginary one that Randall Jarrell describes occurring for Rudyard Kipling and W. H. Auden and that Jarrell himself seems to have suffered from.

A second kind of linguistic separation entering *Open House* and contributing more generally to the failure of language is that suggested in Paul Verlaine's dictum that poets strangle rhetoric. The "nakedness" or "plainness" which Yeats embarks upon in such poems as "A Coat" (1914) and the "Martian generalities" and abuses of language which Pound complains of in *Homage to Sextus Propertius* (1917) and "How to Read" (1928) have their correspondence in Roethke's "plainness" and calls for precision. Somehow words had to be brought out of their embroidered mythologies to reestablish relations with experience much as language's "lateral sliding" and divorcement from experience had to be overcome for William Carlos Williams. But, in *Open House*, the poet seeks to overcome the separation more in the management of adjectives and the manner of past poets' depiction of experience than by what, in "Marianne Moore" (1925), Williams designates as her practice of "wiping soiled words or cutting them clean out, removing the aureoles that have been pasted about them or taking them bodily from greasy contexts" so that the word stands "crystal clear with no attachments; not even an aroma."[9] "No Bird," for example, with its strong structural and linguistic ties to Emily Dickinson appears in Roethke's *Selected Letters* (1968) after a statement that he had "been reading Emily Dickinson considerably"; and, even without such admissions, one senses about many poems in the volume that their attempts through imitation at precision are but another move away from primal language.

Moreover, if the practice of poets like Yeats, Pound, Wylie, Auden, Adams, and Dickinson was not enough to warn Roethke of a discrepancy between rhetoric and poetry, his dual capacity as a publicity man and creative writer at Lafayette College from 1931 to 1935 would bring him experientially into the realm both of language's abuses and its clarifications. His letters during these years make this apparent. Their continual preoccupation with exaggeration and self-promotion on the one hand, or, on the other, with cliché, influence, didacticism, dryness, grunt and fart rhythms, precision, concreteness, and syntax illustrates the dichotomy Pound detects in twentieth-century discourse. This dichotomy will be resolved eventually in Roethke's acceptance of the "aggregate self," which "can grow gracefully and beautifully like a tendril, like a flower" (PC, 21); but, for the present, as he explains in "On 'Identity'" and as the *Selected Letters* makes very clear, it leads, out of ignorance and a "desire for the essential," into a series of necessary and willful psychic betrayals.

The particular complaints about language that the poet registers in *Open House* are severally connected with his overriding effort in the volume to appropriate Yeats's "enterprise in walking naked" and to keep the "spirit spare." In the title poem, having established "no need for tongue," Roethke opposes the "strict and pure" language of deed to "the lying mouth" and ends by asserting: "Rage warps my clearest cry / To witless agony." He repeats this discrepancy between rage and language in "Silence," where "The spirit crying in a cage / To build a complement to rage" remains undistorted by language, "terribly within the mind." But even when language exists, as in "Orders for the Day" and "The Signals," it may not lead to communication. The first shows "decision's smoking fuse" being smothered by the carelessness of clumsy fingers whose lack of contact with spirit prompts them to "bruise / The spirit's tender cover." The second asserts: "Sometimes the blood is privileged to guess / The things the eye or hand cannot possess." In "Death Piece" death becomes by extension invention's being completely cut off from the world; and in "Idyll" a world evolves where all objects are caught up in an other-excluding "self-talk." In "Prognosis" the poet allies excessive language with spiritual cowardice, and in "Academic" he makes the growing limpness of style a sign of spiritual degeneration. At the same time in "Feud" he insists on the need to reject primal language, for "the spirit starves / Until the dead have been subdued." Yet, however close these mutually excluding inner and outer worlds of *Open House* are to a Cartesian subject-object dichotomy or to what, in *Poets of Reality* (1965), J. Hillis Miller calls the dualistic dispute of romanticism, Roethke's resolution of them in this and in his next volume shows his conception of them to be not philosophical but clearly linguistic and psychological.

The techniques in *Open House* which embody the resolution of Roethke's familial and educated worlds are deliberate attempts to submerge the ontogenetic and particular into larger, more universalizing classes. The volume's language, rhythms, and metaphors evince a general avoidance of the idiosyncratic, the specific, the particular, or whatever might be termed the individual. Out of his primal German-American "gut" responses, Roethke chooses what can be blurred and warped into an educated, imitative Brahmin diction. As Imlac advises the reader in *Rasselas* (1759), the artist "does not number the streaks of the tulip, or describe the different shades in the verdure of the forest," but "remarks general properties and large appearances." [10] In the title poem, for instance, adverbs and adjectives which usually capture the individual and which might reveal the poet's backwoodsy non-English origins appear vague, normative, and impersonal. Roethke's secrets cry "aloud." Had they cried "murder," one might have had a different, less controlled condition for the heart's keeping "open house." Here truths are "all foreknown," anguish is "self-revealed," and language "strict and pure." Only at the poem's end with "lying mouth," "clearest cry," and "witless agony" does a wave of modifiers collect, and, although descriptive, none is particular enough to alter the poem's generalizing tone.

In poems such as "Epidermal Macabre" and "Prayer" this submergence of individualizing particulars extends to Roethke's willingness to "dispense / With false accoutrements of sense" and to value sight above all other senses because it is least tied to the individualizing properties of the body. This hierarchy may itself derive from John Donne's remark in a 1628 sermon that "the sight is so much the Noblest of all the senses, as that it is all the senses." Still Roethke's entry for *Twentieth Century Authors* reveals in his encounter with Robert Hillyer some of the feeling of cultural inferiority that contributes as well to the normative language. He goes to meet the poet "complete with fur coat and a fancy suit" and adds, in a telling aside, "those Harvards weren't going to have it over me" (PC, 16). The same sense of inferiority appears in a letter to Rolfe Humphries (1934) when he describes a meeting with Louise Bogan: "I was like a country boy at his first party,— such an oaf, such a boob, such a blockhead. I don't think I was ever much worse" (SL, 25). His recurrent hatred of his "epidermal dress," his wanting to be with the fish, the bears, the slugs, conveys a complementary, more personal embarrassment with his physique that might also have contributed to his tendency away from self.

Literary justification for this tendency to blur individual responses into normative language is offered in Genevieve Taggard's anthology of metaphysical poetry, *Circumference* (1929). In "A Greenhouse Eden" (1965) Louis L. Martz mentions its importance to *Open House*, although as early as 1934 Roethke was discrediting it. The book presents Dickinson and Donne as the twin beacons to guide any would-be metaphysical poet safely to port. In delineating their attractiveness, Taggard notes: "Ideas being for this temperament as real as grass blades or locomotives, the poet's imagination is always riding the two horses in the circus, Idea and Fact; they gallop neck and neck in his work, he has a genius for both the concrete word and the dazzling concept." But more importantly, in a skeleton metaphor foreshadowing Roethke's in "Open House," she stresses impersonality: "To give an idea no form but itself, to show it as organic by an inner music, as if the bones of the skeleton were singing in their own rhythm—that is the technical obsession of the metaphysical poet." Tied to the impersonality is compression: "The wit, the power to make an epigram which Donne's age so loved, is all in Emily Dickinson." This compression, this seeing (like William Blake) the world in a grain of sand, is an element that remains constant in Roethke's writing. Later, detailing for Ann Winslow's *Trial Balances* (1935) the qualities she most prized in Roethke's verse, Bogan chose for special emphasis the same, impersonal epigram-making power reduced now to epithet. "His feeling for epithet is also marked. The gift of poetic epithet, in a high degree, is comparatively rare. Such a gift presupposes sensibilities beyond the average in the poet, since the good epithet is the result of a true and hard impact between the thing felt or seen and the poet's natural power of emotion and perception." [11] But the change to epithet in no way decreases the objectivity of the style.

The rhythms and metaphors of *Open House* are normalized to the point of prompting William Meredith to state in "A Steady Storm of Correspondences" (1965) that "the issues of the poems were resolved by poetic formulas." Roethke did not yet understand Donne's practice of counterpointing speech rhythms against the normal stresses of iambic verse; nor had he moved to what, in *The Forgotten Language* (1951), Erich Fromm, another Bennington colleague, calls "symbolic language." Although influenced by Taggard's view of the two horses of Idea and Fact, the poetry manifests no widespread expression of "inner experience as if it were a sensory experience, as if it were something we were doing or something that was done to us in the world of things." The world outside is not yet sufficiently a symbol of the world inside, "a symbol for our souls and our mind." Nor has there occurred, as Jung indicates in self-realization there should, any sense of increasing inner spatiality to accompany the outer increase of experience. The blurring of the individual into the universal on this deliberate public level precludes the kind of inner self-discovery that allows for the formation of such symbolic language. This language, which Fromm roots in an Eliot-like "affinity between an emotion or thought, on the one hand, and a sensory experience, on the other" has a transcultural commonality which permits, when Roethke moves to it, the discovery of the universal from within, from the particular or local.[12] "Mid-Country Blow," which, with its regression into the womb, looks forward to later poems like "Big Wind" and "The Storm," or "The Premonition," which prefigures Roethke's treatment of his father in "The Lost Son" and "Otto," or "On the Road to Woodlawn" and "The Heron," which increase significantly the number of concretely descriptive adjectives and adverbs, indicate the direction of Roethke's next volume; but in *Open House*, he engages wit as the exclusive device to mediate metaphoric tenor and vehicle, inner and outer worlds, and primal and educated languages.

In such poems as "Dolor" Roethke carries this preoccupation with the failure of language into *The Lost Son*. Here his awareness of the failure's source in the giving way of primal to educated language is translated into the deadly "inexorable sadness of pencils" and "dust from the walls." This dust is "more dangerous than silica" in shaping the world's "duplicate grey standard faces." Auden's influence is apparent in the language of the poem's closing line, but the awareness of the evil of "the trivia of the institution" enables Roethke to abandon the universalizing detail and to move to symbolic language and the psychic corrections which he attempts in the volume. Part of the move to symbolic language is tied to an acceptance of Rilke's belief in a useful, unified life-death existence which permits Roethke to abandon the rejection of his familial world evident in poems like "Feud." In "On 'Identity'" Roethke associates the acceptance of "the great dead" with a remark that John Peale Bishop made during a writers conference at Olivet College in 1940, but that took Roethke "some years to learn": "You're impassioned, but wrong. The dead can help us" (PC, 23). Part is tied to writing techniques derived from D. H. Lawrence and W. C. Williams, and part to the personal encouragement of Kenneth Burke. In the long poems which comprise the volume's final section and which, for Roethke and critics alike, constitute its major accomplishment, additional influences of nursery rhyme, Elizabethan rant, Gerard Manley Hopkins, James Joyce, and E. E. Cummings are present.

Seager dates the poet's active involvement with Rilke's poetry to the arrival of Philip Shelley at Penn State in 1939 and a course that Shelley and Roethke jointly taught in Rilke, Yeats, and Auden. As Rilke explained his view of existence in a letter to his Polish translator, Witold von Hulewicz (1925): "Death is the *side of life* that is turned away from us: we must try to achieve the fullest consciousness of our existence, which is at home in *the two unseparated realms, inexhaustibly nourished by both*. . . . The true figure of life extends through *both* domains, the blood of the mightiest circulation drives through *both: there is neither a here nor a beyond, but the great unity*, in which those creatures that surpass us, the 'angels,' are at home."[13] In translating this belief into images of subsurface, surface, and oversurface, Roethke adds a psychological vitality indebted in part to Lawrence, whose work he had encountered at the University of Michigan in 1930 and who then was being championed by Auden. Like Rilke, Lawrence believed in a unified life-death existence. In *Etruscan Places* (1928) he had written: "Death, to the Etruscan, was a pleasant continuance of life, with jewels and wine and flutes playing for the dance."[14] This continuance past death and "non-existence to far oblivion" is a preoccupation of Lawrence's *Last Poems* (1932).

What Roethke publicly acknowledges in "Some Remarks on Rhythm" (1960) as his debt to Lawrence is more technical than ideological. The devices of enumeration and of varying line-length which these poems use, he deems "the favorite devices of the more irregular poem" and allies them to Whitman and Lawrence: "It was Lawrence, a master of this kind of poem (I think I quote him more or less exactly) who said, 'It all depends on the pause, the natural pause.' In other words, the breath unit, the language that is natural to the immediate thing, the particular emotion" (PC, 83). Yet Lawrence's introduction to the American edition of *New Poems* (1918), wherein he writes of his indebtedness to Whitman and which, along with Williams, furnishes the Roethkean terminology, also makes clear that poetry is self-expression and that free verse, as "the soul and the mind and body surging at once," cannot leave ideology out. Bogan, whose favor Roethke had courted since the thirties, in reviewing Lawrence's *Selected Poems* (1948), tellingly attributes to the English poet a revival of nature poetry in a nonsentimental and an unembarrassed way; and one does sense that Roethke's handling of nature is closer to the Lawrence of *Birds, Beasts and Flowers* (1928) than to any other modern poet. The sense is even strengthened when one reads Roethke's letter to Burke detailing his project for a Houghton Mifflin fellowship (1945). In it Roethke describes the greenhouse poems which comprise the opening section of *The Lost Son*. He employs the mixture of nature, eroticism, and mysticism common to Lawrence: "The poems done so far are not sufficiently related and do not show the full erotic and even religious significance that I sense in a big greenhouse: a kind of man-made Avalon, Eden or paradise" (SL, 113).

What Roethke wished publicly to have acknowledged about the Williams influence upon him is similarly misleading. In objecting to a comment in *100 American Poems* (1948) that he "derived his undressed and deceptively simple style from the cross-grained imagist, William Carlos Williams," the poet told Selden Rodman: "I do owe him a debt for jibing me in conversation and by letter to get out of small forms; but his own work I don't know as well as I should. . . . His (Wms.) rhythms are more staccato, more broken, seems to me" (SL, 146). Yet, in a letter to Williams (1944), he had acknowledged some affinity: "Anything with images equals Imagism equals Old Hat. Oh well, you know all that better than I; have seen it, have been fighting it" (SL, 111). And in a letter to Burke (1946), he admitted to a Williams-like literalness: "Do I betray myself as too literal? But I try to be true to the actual (be exact) and also to get the widest yet most honest symbolical richness too" (SL, 119). Moreover Jackson wrote Seager in this connection: "In rough-draft the long poems appeared to be in free verse (or rather, a line closer to what William

Carlos Williams calls *versos sueltos*, loose-limber verse with enough exactness and repetition in measure to avoid free-verse monotony)" (GH, 146).

Williams had hit upon the technique of *versos sueltos* after 1923 in an effort to capture in his writing not the mere copy of life but art's inner life. As he notes in his *Autobiography* (1951), "it is to make, out of the imagination, something not at all a copy of nature, but something quite different, a new thing, unlike any thing else in nature, a thing advanced and apart from it." But for Roethke who is given to mysticism, this imitation is involved with a metaphysical introspection not common to Williams. In fact Williams in the introduction to *The Wedge* (1944) insists: "Let the metaphysical take care of itself, the arts have nothing to do with it." [15] Seager offers a second personality difference in Roethke's summary of a first meeting with Williams in 1942: "We had a powerful lack of interest in each other's poetry" (GH, 118), and one suspects, as Roethke suggests in a letter to Williams enclosing "The Lost Son" (1946), that the connection between the two poets lies in Williams's lifelong courtship of a natural American language and a metrical breath-unit. Roethke was fond of quoting Lewis Jones's statement that Roethke was "a grass roots American with classic tastes" (SL, 109); and, in the Williams letter, he writes: "Here's a long one which I think is the best I've done so far. It's written, as you'll see right away, for the ear and not the eye. It's written to be heard. And if you don't think it's got the accent of native American speech, your name ain't W. C. Williams, I say belligerently" (SL, 122). Yet even here there were differences. Williams's view of language as "bricklaying" in which words are solidified against translucency and connotation much in the way pigment was solidified by the cubists is different from Roethke's Yeatsian view of words as a means for the evocation of memory.

Nor can one minimize the enthusiasm of Kenneth Burke in the writing of these poems. Roethke was bothered by various personal, cultural, and professional insecurities throughout most of his life, and the enthusiasm of an eminent hard-nosed critic like Burke for poems which began to open the childhood German-American world Roethke intended in his first volume to shun out of embarrassment would permit the poet to chance the self-expression of Lawrence and risk even greater entry into this world. Though perhaps not as directly seminal, since the new style of the greenhouse poems had begun to evolve in such works as "City Limits" (1941), "Germinal" (1943), and "The Minimals" before Roethke's arrival at Bennington, it was nevertheless important. Seager reports that Burke came into Roethke's room one day in 1945 and, hearing two greenhouse poems, reacted by saying: "Boy, you've hit it." His demands for more produced a series of poems which Roethke published in 1946 and led to Roethke's admission in the Williams letter (1946) that the two were greatly responsible for the new style. In a separate letter to Burke (1946) Roethke confesses: "But my real point is: Your belief and interest in the piece has set me up very much" (SL, 116). Yet Roethke's objection in a 1949 letter to Burke about his trying to make out of the long poems "a kind of *collage*" and Roethke's insistence to Rodman and others on the poems' seeming "to come from a tapping of an older memory— something that dribbled out of the unconscious, as it were, the racial memory or whatever it's called" (SL, 162, 130) suggest a degree of initial misreading even on Burke's part toward surface and an implied Williams-like poetics.

In "Open Letter" Roethke cites as additional "ancestors" of these poems: "German and English folk literature, particularly Mother Goose; Elizabethan and Jacobean drama, especially the songs and rants; the Bible; Blake and Traherne; Dürer. . . . Rhythmically, it's the spring and rush of the child I'm after—and Gammar Gurton's concision: *mütterkin*'s wisdom" (PC, 41). He was doubtlessly put on to these "ancestors" and rhythms by Hopkins's famous preface to his *Poems* (1918). Noting the nature and history of sprung rhythm, Hopkins writes: "Sprung Rhythm is the most natural of things. For (1) it is the rhythm of common speech and of written prose, when rhythm is perceived in them. (2) It is the rhythm of all but the most monotonously regular music, so that in the words of choruses and refrains and in songs written closely to music it arises. (3) It is found in nursery rhymes, weather saws, and so on; because, however these may have been once made in running rhythm, the terminations having dropped off by the change of language, the stresses come together and so the rhythm is sprung. (4) It arises in common verse when reversed or counter-pointed, for the same reason." [16] Joyce's *Finnegans Wake*, Bogan would have it, is also important. Seager reports that "it is her opinion that it was Joyce, not Yeats, the verbal exuberance of the Joyce of *Ulysses* and *Finnegans Wake* that influenced Ted in *The Lost Son*" (GH, 149).

Certainly Bogan's review of *Praise to the End!* (1952) contains (in words like "nonsense" and "gibberish") echoes of her review of *Finnegans Wake* (1939). Of Roethke she writes: "It is witty nonsense and effective gibberish, since the poet's control over this difficult material is always formal; he knows exactly when to increase and when to decrease pressure, and he comes to a stop just before the point of monotony is reached. Behind Roethke's method exists the example of Joyce, but Roethke has invented a symbolism, in his searching out these terrors, marginal to our conciousness, that is quite his own." Of Joyce, she notes: "It is not gibberish unless it wants to be. It has rules and conventions. . . . [It] is related to what Panurge called the "puzlatory," and it is cousin to the language of E. Lear, L. Carroll, and writers of nonsense verse in general." [17] Yet the device of "paranomasia," which she mentions as Joyce's peculiar contribution and which involves a great deal of translingual punning, is not used by Roethke; and one feels more the nursery rhyme opening of *A Portrait of the Artist as a Young Man* (1916) than the dream language of *Finnegans Wake*. Roethke seems to have sensed this difference, too, in a letter to Burke (1949) in which he disowned a connection between his evocations of the wholeness of childhood and Joyce's dreamlife evocations of a racial past: "Offhand, I don't know anyone who's tried this before, with any success. Joyce is something else. . . . Also Faulkner in *As I Lay Dying*" (SL, 149).

The kind of verbal displacement which occurs in the volume's final section happens in the manner that Northrop Frye describes in "Emily Dickinson" (1962): "In popular poetry there is a clearly marked rhythm and the words chosen to fill it up give approximately the intended meaning, but there is no sense of any *mot juste* or uniquely appropriate word. . . . For a great many of her poems she has provided alternative words, phrases, even whole lines, as though the rhythm, like a figured bass in music, allowed the editor or reader to establish his own text." [18] In "The Long Alley" "Tricksy comes and tricksy goes" owes more to the rhythms of the saw "Handsome is as handsome does" than to any sophisticated paranomasia. The same is true of "For the waltz of

To, / The pinch of Where" in "The Shape of the Fire," which owe their being more to the Cummings of "anyone lived in a pretty how town" (1940) than to Joyce. The child swing-rhythms of the Cummings poem are later modified into the jumping-rope rhythms of Roethke's "I Need, I Need," and, contrary to Seager's contention that Cummings had no literary influence on Roethke despite his being the only poet of Roethke's contemporaries he always praised in the privacy of his notebooks, in this matter of verbal displacement along a figured bass Cummings proves to be an influence. He is able most "to blow up the language," and, as Roethke repeatedly insists, the key to the structure of the volume's long poems lies not in the narrative sense but in the rhythms.

These alterations in technique which seemingly bring Roethke closer to the modernists prompt reactions from postmodernist readers such as Jarrell's response in "Fifty Years of American Poetry" (1962). In going to rhythms, the "childish," and the "unconscious," Roethke neglects "hydrogen bombs, world wars, Christianity, money, ordinary social observations, . . . everyday moral doubts." His pursuit of ontogenetic identity results in a slighting of the socially defined self. Yet the very separation of this ontogenetic identity from the godhead makes it essentially social and moral in the manner that Auden and Freud describe. The separation makes possible the historical development of one's personality where each significant experience builds on the next so that the final outcome of one's life is an integration of these experiences. The effect of each pursuit of the unconscious becomes an interpretation of self rather than a return to an essential *nul* and so can assume the "impressive 'positive' endings" that Jarrell considers "rhetorically insincere" because the process does not have as its end a destruction of language.[19] Instead it has something closer to the idea of one's changing and perpetual self-definition as the continuity of life, much as consciousness is seen by Descartes as the basis of being. The changes of identity that the various pursuits discover are presumably the results of choice; yet the act of choosing is not Roethke's focus. Like Rilke he prefers to celebrate the ongoing renewal.

The poems of the opening section of The Lost Son define the elements of this kind of existence. Thoughts rise as images from the unconscious mind where, having been accorded cognition, they return. Submerged there, they collect about them other experiences and sensations and, with new accretions, on occasion erupt again into consciousness. This psychological approximation of the Rilkean life-death cycle fosters a new language of image rather than of word in which slime represents subsurface and air, consciousness. The Rilkean "angel" who inhabits the fulness of both worlds is replaced, as in Yeats's poetry, by the "Roethkean" symbol. In the symbols of the new poems, "Cuttings" establishes that birth is life coming through the slime. With strong phallic imagery the reproduction of "Cuttings Later" pulls the worlds of plant and man together. "Root Cellar" posits a cemeterial slime in which things refuse to die and go on living a perverse subsurface life. "Forcing House" enlarges the unity of "Cuttings Later" to machines by imaging the steam pipes that keep flowers alive as a pulse. "Weed Puller" betrays perhaps most patently the cycle's Rilkean influence. The speaker tugging all day under the concrete benches feels the intrusion of perverse subsurface life rather than the joys of blossom. As in Rilke death becomes an aspect of life, but Rilke's death, which seems more attractive than life, differs from this poem's less attractive world. The swamp of "Moss-Gathering" becomes a sanctuary for perverse life which thrives to become eventually coal and opposes the greenhouse of "Big Wind," which heaves the evils of the world like a ship bearing souls to heaven. The poem leads to the image of the florist in "Old Florist" as a magician, as a redeemer, like Jung's poet, pulling blossoms into being, and of the three ancient ladies of "Frau Bauman, Frau Schmidt, and Frau Schwartze" as three fates.

The cyclical nature of this existence creates a flow which opposes the arresting confrontations of *Open House*. There is little attempt in these poems to put on form *ab exteriore* and, by imposing form, encounter "the dullness, confusion or remplissage or the 'falling between two stools'" that Pound indicates can occur.[20] The natural breath unit is used; the fusion of tenor and vehicle exists on a preconscious level. In accepting the descriptive language in positing the objects, the reader accepts the poems' implicit metaphors. There is, as a consequence, a clarity that marks the group as a whole and which manages, by keeping to basic emotions and experiences of birth, death, and physical and spiritual transfigurations, a commonality through particulars which

Fromm assigns to symbolic language and Yeats to symbol. But the kind of Lawrentian one-ing, which now occurs in the conscious or subconscious before a poem's start rather than at its close, requires a new kind of nakedness if the artist is to remain precise. Stephen Spender writes of this need in "The Objective Ego" (1965): "'Separateness' like 'swaying' is a word that bears much weight of meaning in his poems. It is not the separateness of things from one another which concerns him so deeply, but to see their separateness from himself" (TR, 3). The mystic who has oned himself and the world lacks the aesthetic distance with which to describe the world. Without it there can be no adequate outlet for communication; and, as Spender indicates, Roethke, at such times, "becomes the egotist who burdens the reader with his problems" (TR, 10). Jackson reports that during the years when Roethke developed his symbolic language, rather than stripping descriptive adjectives he was "popping out of his clothes, wandering around the cottage naked for a while, then dressing slowly, four or five times a day." Seager remarks: "There are some complex 'birthday-suit' meanings here, the ritual of starting clean like a baby, casting one's skin like a snake, and then donning the skin again. It was not exhibitionism. No one saw. It was all a kind of magic" (GH, 144). These magic rituals which actualize Yeats's metaphor of walking naked serve also the symbolic purpose of separating Roethke from the skin of his world so that he can with literalness reproduce that world.

As *Praise to the End*'s opening section establishes this cycle of perverse and blooming life, the long poems establish the cycle's dimension of inner time. In so doing, they allow a spatiality absent from *Open House*, wherein adult worlds can be shaped to the images of a child. This shaping, which permits Roethke to merge his German-American childhood and his Anglo-American adult world, lessens the sense of mutually excluding inner and outer worlds unmediated by language. There are no two circus horses galloping neck and neck and no complaints of emotions' being warped or trapped within the mind. In fact the flow of language suggests that the poet is an instrument of what Rilke called the glances and gestures that become blood within the writer and which now will out. The ease at which images arise and mediate between cultures opposes the earlier anguish at blurring the individual into the species, the ontogenetic into the phylogenetic. A sense of joy appears similar to that which in *Psychological Types* (1921) Jung assigns generally to metaphors of "childlikeness": "The feeling of bliss accompanies all those moments which have the character of flowing life, . . . 'when it goes of itself,' where there is no longer any need to manufacture all sorts of wearisome conditions by which joy or pleasure might be stimulated. The age of childhood is the unforgettable token of this joy, which, undismayed by things without, streams all-embracing from within." Thus Roethke's placement of easeful self-expression into the "'as if' of the child's world," nursery rhyme, and fairy tale is taking precedence. In the same way his insistence in letters and essays that the world of these long poems is sexual in no way negates its childlikeness, for, as Jung indicates in "Experiences Concerning the Psychic Life of the Child" (1910), "fairy-stories seem to be the myths of childhood, and therefore, among other things, they contain the mythology which the child has woven around the sexual processes. The fascination which the poetic charm of the fairy-story has for adults is also perhaps due not least to the fact that some of these old theories are still alive in the unconscious."[21]

Roethke's refusal in "Open Letter" to be "some kind of oversize aeolian harp upon which strange winds play uncouth tunes" (PC, 37) forces him to admit to some degree of having consciously written the poems. But even if he had not, one has only to follow his use of "sleep song" through the pages of "Where Knock Is Open Wide" and note the precise way "away" (hell) is distinguished from "somewhere else" (heaven) to believe the careful outlines that Jackson reports the poet constructed before beginning the poems. Still, in reading them, one realizes that even with these outlines and Roethke's explanations as guide the poems are unintelligible. Part of the unintelligibility comes from the nature of their "symbolic language." Symbols of the unconscious have always bipolar potential, at times meaning a thing and its opposite coevally. Often explications that appeal to a reader's cognitive faculties do not account for this bipolar tendency or for the rhythms and evocative situations which insinuate themselves deeply into any response. Meredith allows that "the obscurity is that of a lucid dream, where only the causes and connections, not the facts or events, are in doubt" (TR, 42), and in "The Anguish of Concreteness" (1965) W. D. Snodgrass, adding his admiration for the originality of the poems, is compelled to admit as well that "even now, more than twelve years since those poems appeared, I do not feel that I really understand them, or feel certain how ultimately successful they are" (TR, 81). Similarly, in "The Power of Sympathy" (1965), Roy Harvey Pearce ventures: "In a sense, they are not poems but rather pre-poems; so that the reader, working through them, must bring his own capacities as protopoet most actively to bear on them. In effect, the reader *completes* them. One can hardly talk about these poems, or in terms of them. One can only try to talk through them—which perhaps is a way, a way we too much neglect, of learning, all over again, to talk" (TR, 180).

The attempts of these critics to come to grips with the unintelligibility of the poems together with other tendencies to misread them provide insight into how the poems may affect readers generally. Their constructed self-expressions of the wholeness of the poet through ongoing recoveries of childhood become evocations for the reader's own tendency toward a different wholeness. Though related, the two processes remain completely independent of each other. In *The Craft of Fiction* (1921) Percy Lubbock describes the phenomenon as it affects the reader's creation, in his reading, of a novel different from the author's. By allowing something akin to the "self-talk" of "Idyll," the poems undergo comparable transformations. To the degree that the poems succeed, words function much as they do in Yeats's "Magic"—not to communicate directly between self and other but to evoke images out of the Great Mind and Great Memory which the reader can feel. What one has in the long poems, then, is intersubjectivity used for communication. What of childhood overlaps in a reader and poet gets mediated; what does not is lost. Intersubjectivity is possible in this instance because at the root of the Goethean notion of style is a connaturality of subjectivity and the reality which poetic knowledge has caused the poet to see. This subjectivity and reality are alike in nature and essence. Thus, when poems reveal the inner sides of things, they reveal the inner depths of self, and the self arrives by the revelation at a spiritual communion with being. In such a poetics, which tends to slight the reader, the failure of language as communication becomes subordinated to the reader's sensitivity in translating accurately the emotions set off by the word. For complete interaction his sensitivity to symbolic language must equal the poet's.

The ten poems which Roethke adds to complete the sequence, extending its range backward and forward, begin to show the strain of invention which set in after *The Lost Son*. Louis Martz complains that the poems of the next volume "too often destroy themselves by violent experiments in a Tom o' Bedlam style" (TR, 29), and Meredith wishes to dismiss *Praise to the End!* as Roethke's least successful collection, commanding admiration only "as a feat of exploration" (TR, 44). Rather than rhythms and a precision to capture the movements of the mind in form, one senses, in its mechanical arrangements and repetition, design as an overriding principle. Simple transpositions increase as rescuing devices for cliché. "Once upon a tree / I came upon a time," for example, is saved by such a device. Likewise there is a growing literariness in the number of lines and half-lines echoing past poets, Dr. Seuss, and nursery rhyme. Evidently a new blockage has occurred. Either, as Snodgrass conjectures, the ventures into the incredible inner landscapes of self-expression produced a fear and a "need to step back and regather his forces" (TR, 81) or the consternation at the poems' inability to communicate forced Roethke into more traditional forms as a remedy. Yet not until "The Dance" (1952) do the extremes of such a remedy occur, and one gets for Roethke's educated Anglo-American language the same kind of interiorization and ease that one encountered in the greenhouse poems. The poem came after "a longish dry period" in which the poet felt he was through. Roethke reports in "On 'Identity'": "Suddenly, in the early evening, the poem, 'The Dance,' started and finished itself in a very short time—say thirty minutes, maybe in the greater part of an hour, it was all done. I felt, I *knew*, I had hit it. . . . But at the same time I had, as God is my witness, the actual sense of a Presence—as if Yeats himself were *in* that room" (PC, 24).

The poem begins with the poet's learning to dance alone, moving in what became the other parts of "Four for Sir John Davies" to a living partner, then to embrace the dead, and finally into an all-embracing Dantean light. That Roethke should feel the need to sense a Presence is explained by Jung in "The Phenomenology of the Spirit in Fairytales" (1948) in the endopsychic automatisms that appear in hopeless and desperate situations from which only profound reflection or a lucky idea, compensating the deficiency, can extricate the self. These endopsychic automatisms or personified thoughts come often in the shapes of sagacious and helpful old men. Williams's poetry is filled with them, either as his grandmother or as representations of himself at various points of his life; and, like Williams, Roethke seems fated in his work to go on discovering and to evince an inability at filling in those territories he discovers. In *The Theory of Psychoanalysis* Jung writes about this need to make peace with an educated language as well as a childhood language. He details the dangers of one's remaining perpetually a child, for without such an integration that would be, in effect, what artistically Roethke would be doing. Jung states: "We know that the first impressions of childhood cannot be lost, but cling to the individual accompanying him throughout his whole life, and that certain educative influences which are equally indestructible are capable of restricting the individual within certain bounds for life. Under these conditions it is no wonder and in fact even a frequent experience that conflicts break out between that personality which was shaped by education and other influences of the childhood's milieu and the true individual line of life." Jung singles out for this specific conflict people especially "who are ordained to lead an independent, creative life."[22]

That this educated language should be so indebted to Yeats has become an embarrassment to Roethke critics. In an interview (1971) Robert Creeley laments: "One of the incredibly nostalgic and poignant situations of Roethke's writing . . . is that I don't ever feel he came to a person. He looked with deep insistence and longing to find that person, himself, but that person never emerged. I mean it's as if you need to say, will the real Theodore Roethke please stand up? It's intriguing, he's not realized." Earlier, in the *Black Mountain Review* (1954), Creeley had attacked the forces that may have prompted the impersonation. "Certainly it is not Roethke's fault that those very characteristics in his work which are most lamentable, e.g., diffusion, generality, and a completely adolescent address to the world in which he finds himself, should be the ones on which his reputation is maintained. But it is to the point to attack such a maintenance." [23] Critics have also been bothered by Roethke's notion of "aggregate voice." Described in "On 'Identity,'" the device challenges the unified voice of romanticism and modern criticism. Roethke quotes his poem "A Light Breather" to show how voice takes and embraces its surroundings, "never wishing itself away." Identity becomes both the self perceived in *Open House* and the operative perceiving "I."

By the kind of playing-at-roles which George Herbert Mead encourages in *Mind, Self, and Society* (1934) Roethke seems to have discovered the existence of this perceiving and changing "I." Being quite distinguishable from the body and not at all a blossoming flower, the "I" resists being found in any one shape or poem but is the regenerative spirit which infuses the whole. The flower metaphor simply makes the concept comprehensible and brings symbolic language into Roethke's criticism. Snodgrass, who in his essay accepts the literalness of a form, would have readers see Roethke's poem "The Kitty-Cat Bird" as the history of his voice's being swallowed into Yeats's. The acceptance forces Snodgrass to distort the poem's moral. Consistent with Roethke's "aggregate voice," the poem encourages the bird's cat mews, jay grates, and mouse squeaks as preferable to an assignment of self to a single role, be it in or out of a real cat. Such assignment is to "up and die." It is the duel with God and not the absorption in his godhead that constitutes one's purpose and produces the "four or five . . . best poems," each "in a decidedly different style" that Jarrell cites. [24]

The concept of a unified voice that readers would make requisite to a major writer and that is at odds with the flexible listening of Goethean style demands an authoritative language which Roethke never possessed. Always the country boy, the oaf, the boob, the pot poet, he could do no better linguistically than to become a ventriloquist of those voices approved by his contemporaries. Even here, as John Crowe Ransom in "On Theodore Roethke's 'In a Dark Time'" (1961) argues, Roethke manages despite a "reference to Yeats, who has influenced him" to remain "original" and to assert quickly "his own voice in paying tribute to the other poet." [25] Yet the very act of ventriloquism supplies a voice for his adult emotions and enables the poet to tap and channel an energy that depth psychologists claim is American. Emanating from the discrepancy between the high level of the country's conscious culture and an unmediated unconscious primitive landscape, the energy provides inhabitants with a spirit of enterprise and enthusiasm lacking in Europeans who are still possessed by their ancestors' spirits. In the case of Roethke, as in the cases of the immigrants whom H. L. Mencken celebrates in "The Anglo-Saxon" (1923), the energy, translated into the cultural distance between the language of an Anglo-American conscious culture and an unmediated European earthiness, provides avenues of cultural, technological, and scientific growth. On occasion, particularly in *The Lost Son*, Roethke is able with this energy to achieve a voice, a rhyme, a line, a poem that redirects and enlivens contemporary letters. Regardless of whether or not the voice is his, the effect, like that voice of the prudent kitty-cat bird, is to exact from the failure of language something that leads not to obliteration but to psychic and artistic growth.

Notes

1. The following abbreviations have been adopted for internal citations: PC—Theodore Roethke, *On the Poet and His Craft*, ed. Ralph Mills, Jr. (Seattle: University of Washington Press, 1965); GH—Allan Seager, *The Glass House* (New York: McGraw-Hill, 1968); SL—*Selected Letters of Theodore Roethke*, ed. Ralph Mills, Jr. (Seattle: University of Washington Press, 1968); TR—*Theodore Roethke: Essays on the Poetry*, ed. Arnold Stein (Seattle: University of Washington Press, 1965). The abbreviations are accompanied by page citations.

2. Quoted in Alfred Hofstadter, *Truth and Art* (New York: Columbia University Press, 1965), p. 25; quoted in C. F. MacIntyre, *Rilke Selected Poems* (Berkeley: University of California Press, 1964), p. 5.

3. W. H. Auden, "Rilke in English," *New Republic* 100 (1939):135–36; Karl Malkoff, *Theodore Roethke* (New York: Columbia University Press, 1966), pp. 24, 31; Theodore Roethke in *Conversations on the Craft of Poetry*, ed. Cleanth Brooks and Robert Penn Warren (New York: Holt, Rinehart and Co., 1961), pp. 48, 50, 57; Auden, "Verse and the Times," *Saturday Review* 23 (5 April 1941):30–31.

4. Georges Lemaitre, *From Cubism to Surrealism in French Literature* (Cambridge: Harvard University Press, 1947), pp. 34–35.

5. Brom Weber, *Hart Crane* (New York: Bodley Press, 1948), p. 145.

6. For an excellent analysis of the relationship between the ideas of Heidegger and antimodernist poetics, see Joseph N. Riddel's *The Inverted Bell* (Baton Rouge: Louisiana State University Press, 1974).

7. C. G. Jung, *Psychological Reflections*, ed. Jolande Jacobi (New York: Harper Torchbooks, 1961), pp. 175, 183–84, 125.

8. Ibid., p. 276.

9. William Carlos Williams, *Selected Essays* (New York: Random House, 1954), p. 128.

10. Samuel Johnson, *Rasselas*, ed. G. B. Hill (Oxford: Oxford University Press, 1887), p. 62.

11. John Donne, *The Sermons*, ed. Evelyn M. Simpson and George R. Potter, 10 vols. (Berkeley: University of California Press, 1953–62), 8:221; Genevieve Taggard, *Circumference* (New York: Covici Friede Publishers, 1929), pp. 6, 10, 11; Louise Bogan in *Trial Balances*, ed. Ann Winslow (New York: Macmillan, 1935), p. 139.

12. Eric Fromm, *The Forgotten Language* (New York: Evergreen Books, 1957), p. 12.

13. Quoted in the notes to Rainer Maria Rilke's *Sonnets to Orpheus*, trans. M. D. Herder Norton (New York: Norton, 1942), p. 132.

14. Quoted by Christopher Hassall, "Black Flowers: A New Light on the Poetics of D. H. Lawrence," in *A D. H. Lawrence Miscellany*, ed. Harry T. Moore (Carbondale: Southern Illinois University Press, 1959), p. 373.

15. William Carlos Williams, *Autobiography* (New York: New Directions, 1951), p. 241; Williams, *Selected Essays*, p. 256.

16. Gerard Manley Hopkins, *The Poems and Prose*, ed. W. H. Gardner (Baltimore: Penguin Books, 1953), p. 11.

17. Louise Bogan, *Selected Criticism* (New York: Noonday, 1955), pp. 384, 143.

18. Northrop Frye, "Emily Dickinson," in *Modern American Poetry: Essays in Criticism*, ed. Jerome Mazzaro (New York: David McKay, 1970), p. 24.

19. Randall Jarrell, *The Third Book of Criticism* (New York: Farrar, Straus and Giroux, 1969), pp. 326–27.

20. Ezra Pound, "Dr. Williams' Position," in *William Carlos Williams*, ed. J. Hillis Miller (Englewood Cliffs: Prentice-Hall, 1966), p. 35.

21. Jung, pp. 278, 114–15.

22. Ibid., p. 273.

23. Robert Creeley, "Interview," *Unmuzzled Ox* 1, no. 1 (December 1971):34; Creeley, "Comment," *Black Mountain Review*, no. 3 (Fall 1954):64.

24. Jarrell, pp. 326–27.

25. John Crowe Ransom in *The Contemporary Poet as Artist and Critic*, ed. Anthony Ostroff (Boston: Atlantic–Little, Brown, 1964), p. 29.

4

Circumscriptions: David Ignatow

David Ignatow began his poetic career by announcing that he was "a man with a small song," and the years since *Poems* (1948) have seen him extend the range of his poetry but never the magnitude of any single work. His individual poems are all "small songs," and it is as a totality that they amount to something approaching a major voice. Randall Jarrell's remark in a review of *The Gentle Weight Lifter* (1955) that "one reads the poems with a mild blurred feeling of seeing them and not seeing them, a clear daze like water or late evening air" is especially apt. One is never sure whether one is reading a new poem or rereading an old one, and it does not make a difference. The impression of *Tread the Dark* (1978), though at times conveying a greater sense of alienation, is not markedly different from that of *Poems*. Ignatow is a poet of and about habit, and daily recurrence rather than the intensity of what he chooses to celebrate is important. In this focus on common recurrence he resembles William Carlos Williams, who achieved a reputation and wide recognition only after he had published a large quantity of work and his audience had undergone a change in sensibility. Jarrell's main objection to Ignatow's poetry does not substantially vary from the objection R. P. Blackmur raised in "John Wheelright and Dr. Williams" (1939). Resorting to a view that personality is best revealed under crisis, Jarrell complains of *The Gentle Weight Lifter* that it lacks "some last heat or pressure, concentration and individualization, that would have turned a photograph into a painting, a just observation into a poem." [1]

To argue the merits of whether personality is better revealed in exceptional situations or by blurring habitual behavior or to consider whether progress is individual or collective seems absurd. All four positions appear eminently true and, carried to their extremes, very limited. What good, for instance, are the perceptions of an extraordinary personality if there is no interaction with an audience? One will simply carve out a solipsistic and masturbatory world and frame the "imperial self" that Quentin Anderson finds typical of a number of American artists, and while it may be consoling to write for the future, it also seems a bit foolish to ignore the present. This seems to be Ignatow's position in regard to T. S. Eliot and the New Critics: "By their own acknowledgement, they have taught a studied withdrawal from society, in which is implicit a condemnation of the present state of our culture" (CR, 154). The view also lies behind the distinction between Wallace Stevens and Walt Whitman he makes in an interview (1971): "Stevens wrote to affirm himself, as did Whitman, but without the illusion that he was affirming others" (CH, 28). It prompts, in addition, Ignatow's reservations (in 1964) about Barbara Guest's *Poems*: "Deeply attracted to life with all that it involves, she seeks to escape it in the mistaken idea that life can be abstracted from its sources and be enjoyed purely" (CR, 123). He would insist a writer remain in contact with life and the masses: "The world will always fail us, but by the grace of life we dare not fail the world, we dare not accuse it or denounce it without love for it in what we have to say—or death strikes us and the poem" (CR, 128).

Jarrell's stresses on extraordinary character and on singular expression and experience are emphases which Ignatow repeatedly regards as negative, isolating, and elitist: "The folk theme," his *Notebooks* states, "is of suffering together and joy together. Orestes suffers alone exiled from his inheritance. Iphigenia alone, Oedipus alone. The aristocrats of Greek society. Their theme has become the national theme of America, for in this country each man counts himself free and alone" (L, 88–89). "An ordinary man is a message to the world," *Poems* affirms, not the individual "looking for fame and glory." What Ignatow is seeking, *Note-books* makes clear, is "the abandonment of the principle of individual life in order to give ourselves a larger, stronger basis in community" (APR, 6). His desire is "to bring the world together in one song fest, in one eternal spring by singing the song that would start the fete" (NYQ, 92). In this desire his precursors are Russian writers like Anton Chekhov, whom he read as a child, and Whitman: "I guess the Russians finally had the biggest say in my work, the sense of compassion they convey about others, particularly Chekhov—his gentle irony, his sympathy for the worst characters, about whom he was truthful all the same. I guess that led me to a like sympathy and truth-telling but Whitman enlarged the scene for me and gave me some kind of hope about people in general, about change and about failures in human relationships" (CH, 27). Yet, in defense of Jarrell, who nowhere proposes an extreme position of individualization, one might counter by saying that all changes begin with the individual and as a minority movement.

Realizing that poetry of and about habit must be rewritten as habits originate, alter, and cease, Jarrell proposes what is at root a utilitarian stance. He believes that changes in habit are too ephemeral a condition for a critic to ground his energies in; it is instead to a cultural historian, a sociologist, or a psychologist that he would have such changes relegated so that they might be charted as trends. He would take art up at the moment that it fuses into permanence. The intensity that he would have as a prior condition of this fusion and which removes art immediately from the normal pace of life approaches the fire which in "Diaphaneité" (1864) Walter Pater made a precondition of art. The intensity can itself become monotonous and blurred as every now and then, by being less intense and eschewing the monumental and individual, a poet like Ignatow proves. By not proposing those mirages of unlimited ceilings that seem foisted upon Americans almost at birth and whose collapses for all but a few result in the nostalgias and guilts of later life, such poets remind their audiences of important small moments of life that otherwise go ignored and forgotten. As early as *The Seven Lamps of Architecture* (1849) John Ruskin had seen that by the accumulation of these small "moments" artisans of the Middle Ages were able to achieve intensity and amass monumental artistic structures that in every way proved as uplifting and satisfying as those structures overseen by individual geniuses.

It was not Ruskin's discovery but Roy Harvey Pearce's *The Continuity of American Poetry* (1961) that provided Ignatow with a theoretical articulation of his own prior and implicit opposing utilitarian practice, although a number of traditionally intense lyrics indebted to Emily Dickinson and resembling those of Theodore Roethke's *Open House* (1941) appear in *Poems*. Pearce's book encouraged Ignatow to continue a rejection of older, larger, consciously monumental forms along with what A. Alvarez in *The Savage God* (1972) would eventually call "extremist poetry" for a view of the epic as "the life of the poet in the ordinary rounds of existence from birth, growth, maturity, and death." Readers would be drawn to the poetry by "a likeness of themselves, their aspirations, failures, and successes" (CH, 30), not by any vicarious eccentricity of subject or by a prolonged flirtation with suicide. Part of this likeness is the poet's careful manipulation of natural idiom so that it both suggests normal conversation and exceeds it. By means of such near-mirroring the audience may gain not only entrance but also, by the distortion, perhaps some understanding, for just as few Americans ever grow up to be president of the United States, few ever experience, even imaginatively, those extreme heights and depths which Jarrell or Alvarez's "extremist" pose would have all poetry restricted to. In "Consolation" Ignatow describes the impulse to set oneself above others as a fever preventing a revelation of love, and in "The Poet Is a Hospital Clerk" he attributes to the impulse man's sadistic as well as his masochistic tendencies.

Still, within Jarrell's criteria of intensity and extraordinary personality and in opposition to Ignatow's own statements, one might argue that in the depiction of daily recurrence the very smallness of the early poems constitutes a kind of concentration. "All small things," as Gaston Bachelard proposes in *The Poetics of Space* (1958), "must evolve slowly, and certainly a long period of leisure, in a quiet room, was needed to miniaturize the world. Also one must love space to describe it as minutely as though there were world molecules, to enclose an entire spectacle in a molecule of drawing." Bachelard sees the inclination to miniature

as the opposite of intuitional perception which takes everything
in at one glance, for "in looking at a miniature, unflagging attention is required to integrate all the detail." This "unflagging attention" forces the detachment of the artist from the normal world so
that he resists his dissolving into surrounding atmosphere. In the
case of Ignatow's miniatures, one critic is willing to posit their
origin in a corollary to the love of space—the love of time—and
in a proverbial motto of business that "time is money." Victor
Contoski in "Time and Money" (1968) shows how Ignatow's
awareness of time forms the subject of a number of poems and
characterizes the style of the pieces as "short and to the point, like
business letters." Contoski also indicates the presence in the work
of an element approximating Anderson's "imperial self," resulting
perhaps from the detachment that must be part of an "unflagging
attention." Contoski envisions Ignatow as wanting to play God:
"He sees everything from the point of view of eternity, a myste-
rious eternity that offers him no consolation for his suffering."[2]

Reviewers like Robert Bly and Louis Simpson, on the other
hand, have noted the need for unusual concentration on the part
of the reader if he is to respond to Ignatow's early work, and
Hayden Carruth in reviewing *Figures of the Human* (1964) and
Rescue the Dead (1968) has called for an understanding of the
dynamics of the small poem as a prerequisite to an appreciation
of Ignatow's skills. Bly's sense of the situation is part of a larger
complaint that readers generally do not know how to read poetry
unless the ideas of the poem have been denuded and presented
"under stark enough light" so that they can be grasped. While
admitting an element of snobbery may have prompted a resistance
to Ignatow's work, Simpson describes the effect of the poems as an
uncomfortable but necessary "drilling through asphalt." The
reader is required to look at the collections of detail not as part
of a superficial or sentimental cataloguing of ephemera that may
include designs of Coca Cola bottles as well as histories of motion-
picture actors, but as something that shows these phenomena as
effecting deeply the psyche of Americans, often as something that
may substitute for or obscure the perception of real danger. Thus
Carruth's suggestion that for a proper appreciation of the poetry
a reader begin with an understanding of the dynamics of small
poems seems especially wise. In many ways Ignatow's reinterpre-

tation of the small flat poem of Williams ideally illustrates both his singular world view and a pivotal change in the shift in sensibility from the postmodernism represented by Jarrell to that typified by the next generation.[3]

By redirecting the emphasis of Williams's small poem away from marriage and into matters of succession and by reinterpreting its scope to include urban and political matters, Ignatow touches on the principal concerns of both generations: how to succeed poets like Ezra Pound, T. S. Eliot, and William Carlos Williams; and how to achieve identity without undergoing dehumanization in a society that has gotten progressively urban, conformist, and impersonal. Bly in "Slipping Toward the Instincts" (1968) deceptively suggests that although Ignatow is of the generation of John Berryman, Robert Lowell, and Karl Shapiro, none of these poets have defended his work. That is true, but Jarrell and William Meredith have both praised Ignatow's poetry, and Winfield Townley Scott was among the first to see the positive effects of concentration in the poems. William Carlos Williams even proposed that "the best of them . . . be printed on pulp and offered at Woolworth's, a dime a copy." Thus, when Bly contends that "it is men younger than Ignatow who have insisted that his poetry be reviewed and published,"[4] he ignores for polemical considerations what is common to Ignatow and his generation: the acceptance, as Jarrell calls it, of "Darwin, Marx, Freud and Co.," the importance of history, and the restatement of philosophical problems as psychological states. Bly misses thereby what may be the real attraction of readers to the structure of the small poem in addition to those stresses on daily recurrence and continuity that Ruskin, Pearce, and Ignatow have each maintained.

Critics have often asserted that smallness is part of the appeal of Emily Dickinson's poetry, and in beginning his discussion of miniatures, Bachelard discourages a view that the tendency to smallness be thought of as geometric, "*exactly the same thing* in two similar figures, drawn to different scale." Such a "simple relativism of large and small," he maintains, belies the unequal conviction with which the imagination approaches the objects. Thus a reader should not think of small poems as shrunken large poems or (as Ignatow's publisher did once) of their necessarily being parts in the creation of "a grand and tragic vision." Thom Gunn in reviewing *Say Pardon* (1961) rightly affirms: "The point is, surely, that [the] poetry does not even *set out* to be grand or tragic." Still, in regard to Ignatow's work, one would be as wrong to accept without qualification Bachelard's dismissal of the view that "the tiny things we imagine simply take us back to childhood, to familiarity with toys and *the reality of toys*."[5] In his miniatures Ignatow, as does Emily Dickinson, tends to oppose authority, to equate it and largeness—those "aristocrats of Greek society" that one accepts in childhood—but not quite to enter those encapsulations from ordinary life that one associates with toys and sometimes feels with miniatures.

In Ignatow's case there is instead an open-endedness that Carruth describes as producing a "certain abruptness" when the poem ends just as "the reader is beginning to get interested." Carruth wisely asks whether "going back over the poem again, even a dozen times, will make up for this foreshortening"; but he does not suggest that the abruptness may be similar to that gnomic quality one gets from Miss Dickinson's poetry in which, when the reader must resort to interpretation, the particulars of the poem are rendered universal and yet personal. Nor does he suggest that sense Ruskin writes of in regard to gothic architecture when, at the moment the eye leaves one part of the structure, it lights upon another as interesting and where abruptness works to liberate the viewer into his next observation. Instead, despite a plea for understanding the dynamics of small poems, Carruth's own manner of dealing with the situation is a "geometric" scaling down: "When I examine them closely to see what part is missing—beginning, middle, or end—I find that I cannot make up my mind." He goes on to imagine the poems not as parts of some ongoing vision but as "complete in embryo; or, as Ignatow would no doubt prefer to say, in essence."[6] The approach presupposes with no apparent explanation that the deliberately limited techniques and subject of an Ignatow poem may be extended at will with no appreciable loss of interest.

It might be better, then, not to begin with these views but with the effects of miniature that Claude Lévi-Strauss in *The Savage Mind* (1962) would have readers accept. The discussion does much to bring these otherwise divergent positions into coincidence with one another and with Eliot's sense that the oeuvre of a major writer assumes the unity of a single developing personality. Lévi-Strauss distinguishes as the principal characteristics of miniatures their senses of being humanly produced and of reflecting a real experiment with the nature of an object. Miniatures tend as well to compensate "for the renunciation of sensible dimensions by the acquisition of intelligible dimensions." [7] Thus the dynamics of small poems should work ideally to stress the poet's humanity and should diminish the reader's tendency to lose himself in art. In Ignatow's poetry this emphasis on humanity is conveyed through a complex strategy of intimacy: his subject is often domestic and personal; his diction, direct and informal; his manner of speaking, given to partial statement; and, finally, the whole is given to silences rather than conclusions. Poems like "Physical Love" deal openly with sex; "The Rightful One," "I Was Angry," and "I Can Be Seen" with the breakdown and hospitalization of his son; "Droll Husband," "Consolation," "Marriage," "Brooding," and "The Debate" with the close and sometimes absurd moments in every marriage; and any of these concerns may be taken up again at some later point. There is, in addition, the corresponding reduction in sensible detail that Lévi-Strauss mentions. Adjectives are most likely not to occur or, if they do appear (as in "Prologue") they will be conceptual or fade (as in "In Absentia") into stereotype or symbol. Only the bawdy poems contain real sensual detail, and one might argue the detail is conceived of as part of the obscenity.

Hence readers of Ignatow's work are led to conclude that the essential meaning and value lie, as Gunn would have it, in personality rather than, as Carruth wishes it, in the formal "dynamic inner relationships" that the New Critics believe are necessary for art—or even, as Jarrell wants to believe, in a reinterpretation of these formal inner relationships as psychic characteristics. Here the observations of critics like Bly begin to assume a proper significance, for they often point more to the experiment with perception that the short poem attempts than to the nature of miniatures. Bly, in particular, likes to stress "leaping" in these reconstructions, restricting the term to include only jumps "from the conscious to the unconscious." Norman O. Brown, on the other hand, prefers "meaning," relegating it not to leaps but to the gaps, the iridescences and interplays that a reader must bridge, for as poets have known since the time of Sappho, leaps can be made among levels of conscious perception as well. Ignatow's poetry does both. Indeed the most interesting aspect of an Ignatow poem inclines to be its use of gaps. It will leap on one level from one conscious perception to the next or from the conscious to the unconscious, setting up for readers at least these distinct patterns of inner relationships. "A Recounting" (from *Tread the Dark*) beautifully illustrates both patterns at work. The poem begins with sounds of innards rotting and crickets whirring and leaps consciously to dance "to silence" their sound "by listening / to the rhythm of [his dance] steps." The leap from sound to dance is reinforced by a gap of stanzas, and the decision prompts in the poem's next stanza a realization that dancing, walking, and dying are all "states of things." At the same time the impression of isolation on which the poem begins drifts unconsciously into a countering, closing, conscious, communal image of "an angry, clamorous cry."

Facing the Tree (1975) shows Ignatow's efforts to deal with the same gaps in prose poems. By his own account he had begun to feel "uneasy about the direct lyrical method" that he was using and continues to use: "I had begun to feel it repetitious for me, keeping me in a kind of groove." The prose poem allowed him instead "to disregard end lines and to concentrate on the total poem itself which, after all, was the original purpose of the rebellion against the formalism of the traditional poem patterns" (B, 475). The prose poem allowed, too, more control over emotion and, because it minimized the intensity and gaps of the lyric form, a message closer to the everyday life. Fewer things remain unsaid, and the form itself offers—as does the prose of Williams—a new "gap" testing the lyric form. All the same, as in "The Diner," readers have "small poem" leaps between conscious perceptions in the shifts among sentences and paragraphs. In the speaker's perception that he himself may be the owner of the diner who, in a "breakdown of communications," has given himself "an order of ham and eggs instead of a sandwich" and now wonders "when in hell did I buy this diner and who needs it," readers have also experienced shifts from the unconscious to conscious. In either form the resolution of gaps into meaning requires interpretation, and like the gnomic poems of Dickinson, Ignatow's poetry works best when the interpretation involves person-to-person transference.

For these transferences, basic understandings of the poet's views on art, the conscious and unconscious levels on which the views function, and the various possible psychodynamics of expectation and fulfillment are all necessary.

Whatever their differences over what may be the best manner in which to depict personality or convey understanding, both Jarrell and Ignatow begin with an awareness that art is an instrument for moral change. Both believe, in addition, that art is the expression of man's noblest and highest aspirations and that the state is "the collective and corporate character" of a people whose development toward perfection as reflected by art represents an important evolving picture of Deity. Ignatow in his *Notebooks* acknowledges a deep respect for "ideas, especially as they reflect moral integrity" (L, 80). The book is also a confession of the poet's being haunted by goodness, of measuring "every act, every idea . . . by abstract standards of goodness" (L, 79), even to writing in part "to influence myself toward good" (L, 87). This "good" involves a kind of cohesiveness that accepts community as its ultimate end and man as basically social. Yet, while committed to the moral integrity of ideas, Ignatow is never committed to a view that one should falsify in order to make art uplifting. He prefers the truthtelling of Chekhov or Allen Ginsberg to such falsification or to the continuation of beliefs no longer workable, however uplifting they may have been once or now seem: "Dante's answer of individual salvation does not apply to us today" (APR, 6). To indicate that the answer may apply to us is to jeopardize the credibility of the near-mirroring on which Ignatow's poetry relies.

Implicit in Ignatow's various gaps is the rejection of the role of poet as *alter deus* that has existed since the Renaissance. Entailed instead is the acceptance of Williams's belief that what a poem describes must be measured against the nature it depicts as well as James Joyce's view that the lyrical form is "the simplest verbal vesture of an instant of emotion" and that it arises out of a response to nature. Thus what Ignatow chooses to portray exists first as a duality of imagination and nature and, once depicted, must then be bridged by a mediation of art and life. The duality is not to be resolved at the expense of nature, as Jarrell sometimes accomplishes his resolutions; nor is it to dissolve into those imaginative visions that poets use to separate themselves from their

societies; nor does it accept, as did W. H. Auden, the defeatist
view that "poetry makes nothing happen." Instead the gaps in and
among the lyrics and prose poems work to keep the poet and reader from any "last heat or pressure" that might create these visions.
Similarly the poet avoids overt detached didacticism, for abstract
moralizing may become as divorced from nature as that "false"
world of closed art. The superiority of the poet—as it exists—results from a superior moral character. In an ongoing "cooperative
effort to raise each person to his greatest height and all of us then
standing together to celebrate each other's life" (APR, 7), his work
"will be spent pointing out the bad from the standpoint of forgiveness and peace rather than improvement" (NYQ, 86).

While finding that daily life makes it increasingly difficult to
make crucial moral decisions, Ignatow rejects for his poetry a view
that man can acquire moral character without enlightenment from
God. The acceptance of this "enlightenment" does not mean the
acceptance of orthodoxy as it had for Auden. In "The Past Reordered" (1967) he may state that "God, Zion, and preordination
are either abolished or, having vanished in the daily struggle for
existence, are now forgotten without regret or afterthought"; but
"The Permanent Hell" (1966) indicates that the result is not freedom or an advantage but "a permanent hell from which no *mea
culpa* can save."[8] The abolition or distancing of God does not
eliminate guilt, and here, differing from Jarrell's view of Deity as
"all that I never thought of," Ignatow rejects any effort to abolish
such guilt in a view of an evolving comprehensive self spurred on
by suffering. The "good" that Ignatow's poetry will strive for is
modeled on a perfect Creator rather than on a series of imaginatively spun natural adaptations. *Say Pardon* ends with a long, Old
Testament wrangle with this Creator to understand and accept
setback, for, as *Notebooks* asserts, to avoid the wrangle in favor
of a natural progress like that of Jarrell can lead to perversion:
"My theory of homosexuality is that it is man worshipping himself
instead of God, worshipping his own possibilities and making of
these his illimitable goal of perfection, attributes that belong to
God. Homosexuality is a rebellion against God, against man's limitations" (L, 82). The very presupposition of gaps, then, constitutes a vital means for understanding guilt and man's limited nature; and the continuous bridging of these gaps through glimpses

of a traditional Deity earns for the poet and reader alike an expanding awareness of truth.

Various personal and ideological reasons make the city ideal for both Ignatow's requisite of moral improvement and his reworking the small poem away from that form used by Williams. Ignatow was born and raised in Brooklyn and consequently feels most at ease with urban situations, but his social view of man makes the city equally apt for realizing cohesion. In the strangeness of its life man meets fleetingly those challenges to identity that give rise to self-definition and the very diversity of urban experience provides a model for leveling variety that Ignatow in particular seeks. For him the city "is the world in small—especially New York" (TPJ, 30). It is, in addition, "the nature of reality today. . . . The concentration of population where everything is happening—the whole political crux, the crucible in American life" (TPJ, 37). An action like that in Vietnam is even interpreted as "an extension of American life, of city life, of city living, and of our conception of life as it flows from this" (TPJ, 37). Yet, as Ignatow told Scott Chisholm in 1970, in order to get these experiences into his writing and "emerge with all the facts," he had to learn "to meet the city on its own terms." This meant being "overwhelmed" on the occasion of each new poem: "I was not going to write in the iambic pentameter when the very tone and pace of the city denied such a regular, predictable, and comfortable style." He wanted "the spirit of the city" in his work while, as a city man, he was able to manipulate that spirit "in terms of its language" (TPJ, 23). The pragmatic tentativeness that results from such an aim prompts Ignatow's disavowal of the role of "social poet" with its attendant, abstract, preconceived positions. He claims instead to be a poet of "individuality," and by individuality he means "interacting with others" (TPJ, 27). This individuality (expectation) and interaction (fulfillment) form the personal and social bases of his poetry and invite confusions with more widely appealing existential concepts of "being," "bad faith," and "intersubjectivity."

The personal center of the poetry as well as of the city lies in a classic Freudian family situation that Ignatow describes in the 1971 interview. During his formative years he was close to his father; but as Ignatow reached maturity, they quarreled. The father wanted the poet to join the family trade, a bindery; and only through the mediation of his mother was he permitted to try writing. She provided him with a plan that got him on the WPA payroll so that he could join the Writers' Project. The action came despite her feeling that he was a "lost" son inclined to waste his energies, intellect, and strength "on a futile course" (CH, 26). Ignatow had by this time already published a story in *New Talent*, and the story had gained him mention in Edward O'Brien's *Best Short Stories* (1934) together with an invitation from Orrick Johns to join the writing group. The incident seems to have contributed greatly to shaping the poet's moral vision and to creating the pattern of expectation and fulfillment that his work would take. As he remarks in his *Notebooks*, the closeness to his father during his boyhood kept him from the "sublimated homosexuality" that marred Whitman's view of Deity. In addition the rebellion, like that disobedience of Adam and Eve, produced a guilt and a standing alone which, seen as a pressure to keep on writing, becomes an equivalent of Jarrell's "suffering." At one point, in the absence of a sense of God, he refers to this guilt as his "one attachment to reality"; but more important, at moments of despair bordering on suicide, it forces the poet to prove himself anew as a writer. It reminds him that "in killing myself I leave behind me those I consider so much beneath me, little as I myself have achieved: my father, mother, M. . . . Why, I ask myself, should I give them the satisfaction of feeling confirmed in their judgment of me! . . . What could be more perfect confirmation of their suspicion of me than my suicide?" (L, 81).

Elsewhere in his *Notebooks* Ignatow seems to lend support to Contoski's sense of a key relationship between business and poetry by noting of the despair on a less theological level: "I wouldn't knock myself off and give M the satisfaction of saying to his wife, my sister, 'See, he couldn't take it. The shop was too much for him. He liked easy work. Now who was right about him? I told you so'" (NYQ, 91). The gaps in his poetry may well be due to a pressure that he feels has shaped his "thinking into a form derived from impatience, skepticism, mingling with despair . . . like a businessman under pressure to produce for a profit with time working against him" (L, 78). He has certainly worked hard to create a life where the failures of art and business are not at odds: "Neither business nor art can afford to be sentimental given the facts and the objective. In business we cut off an account without a moment's hesitation. . . . In art, we cannot expect the reader to carry us along simply from good nature" (NYQ, 84). At one point he admits that Whitman sent him originally into business: "From him I got the idea that business could do no harm to a man whose sights are set on transcendent values. But the kind of business I do and the petty thievery I practise are not in agreement with my original idea" (NYQ, 87). Poems such as "Origins" and "The Orange Picker" build upon the relationship between business and poetry by equating the work of the poet to that of other laborers. The first depicts a poet presenting poems to a friend, only to have her so question the sufficiency of the efforts that he turns "the vehicle of his wealth" in her direction. The second compares the efforts of orange pickers to those of writers.

Faced with similar pressures of a life divided between medicine and art, Williams in his short poems hit upon a basically biological myth to unify his occupations: imagination strives to be reborn through a wedding with place. Ignatow's solution is framed in more mechanical terms, as a balance against one's having to undergo self-destruction or "bad faith": "We write when we think we are wrong or the world or an individual is wrong" (L, 87–88). He also adds that however much such situations make of art "an instrument of retaliation or revenge which it is not," the feelings "are with what art must involve itself for its own vitality" (NYQ, 80). He would prefer the retaliation to be a challenging love like that of "Origins," but he is willing, as in "Aesthetics II," to make it a response to boredom. There poetry is forced on him "like doodling," while he is waiting for an interview that will decide his job and after he has exhausted a supply of "dated periodicals and books." In fact poem after poem begins with an incident that throws the poet or life itself off stride; the rest of the work seeks to reestablish verbally and emotionally the violated "necessary balance for good living" (L, 87). "News Report," for example, begins with a Dionysian urge "jumping out of a manhole" to "run down the street, / emitting wild shrieks and merriment and lust" and ends with the victims restoring themselves to habit by turning their experiences into unreal adventures and trying to drown the telltale signs in perfumes and baths. "The Bagel" shows the poet's annoyance at himself for dropping a bagel and turns to absurdity as his own doubling over "head over heels, one complete somersault after another like a bagel," restores him to peace.

By an enlargement of these personal concerns, Ignatow develops the corresponding social center of his work. Here the conflicts of identity and "bad faith" are collective. Often their beginnings are defined in psychohistorical terms that echo Williams's view of the Puritan in *In the American Grain* (1925), and like Williams, Ignatow uses the conflicts to explain both the violence and the apathy of modern culture. Williams had theorized that, by a failure of sensibility, the Puritan had "come to impersonate, and to marry, the very primitive itself" so that America in the twenties had "become 'the most lawless country in the civilized world,' a panorama of murders, perversions, a terrific ungoverned strength, excusable only because of the horrid beauty of its great machines." [9] In the 1970 interview Ignatow notes similarly of American society that it is "laboring under a sense of predestined guilt. We're Puritan. No matter how you turn it or how you phrase it, we're guilty for cultural reasons—or lack of reasons which the culture withholds from us" (TPJ, 24). Again this residue of guilt leaves the individual no recourse except through a reform that will—like Auden's in *The Orators* (1932)—embrace the community; and this reform, as Ignatow points out in *Notebooks*, will have to consider that people "do not have the leisure or freedom to choose their own way. . . . People feel themselves forced into patterns from which as it seems to them to rebel is to invite death" (NYQ, 82). Ignatow goes on pessimistically to conclude that "for man to assert himself, he will have to destroy this world and begin all over again. That is the fantastic truth of our times and we are propelled toward it with the speed of a jet plane carrying its bomb load to the front" (NYQ, 83).

In the light of these situations of personal and collective bounds, Ignatow will pronounce an indebtedness to Charles Baudelaire and a difference from Whitman and Williams. "Sometimes," he told Chisholm, "I think my own work is an attempt to reconcile the very profound skepticism of Baudelaire with Walt Whitman's sanguine hopes. But I feel that it's these three—Whitman, Williams, and Baudelaire—who are most important to me" (TPJ, 14–15). Baudelaire confirmed doubts that the poet had earlier found in the Russians concerning man's innate goodness. Unlike

Whitman, who accepted Jean Jacques Rousseau's belief in man's natural goodness and predicted an eventual evolution of man and society into a perfect democracy, Baudelaire subscribed to what Jean-Paul Sartre calls a "dream of anti-nature." This dream would replace the environment of Rousseau's "noble savage" with a human order that "would be directly opposed to the errors, injustices and blind mechanical forces of the natural world." This "higher" order would be achieved through a revaluation of work. By placing an emphasis on collective rather than individual man, the order would check the individualism that both Whitman and Williams celebrate. The existence of this cohesive order would, moreover, reaffirm an honored, theologically based purpose in community as an expiation of Cain's crime. These beneficial aims are already implicit in Ignatow's love of the city, his emphasis on collective rather than individual goals, and his view of man's innate need for "interaction," and they complement in both Baudelaire and Ignatow a general view of man's susceptibility to social conditioning. Like the voyagers of Baudelaire's "Le Voyage," man is forever bringing with him his past and finds shedding any of its social preconceptions difficult.

The use of Baudelaire to temper the optimism of Whitman and Williams provides an additional glimpse into the way literary influence will be handled as part of Ignatow's social structure. Artistic lineage will follow a pattern of conflict and resolution much in the way Williams in "America, Whitman, and the Art of Poetry" (1917) proposes: "The only way to be like Whitman is to write *unlike* Whitman." [10] Just as Dante's answers earlier had to be superseded, and Ignatow's father's insistence that he go into business was met by a quarrel, would-be oppressive literary influences will be reshaped in order that Ignatow may achieve his own authenticity. Ignatow told Chisholm that, although he felt Whitman was still exerting an influence in American letters and that he remained "the important factor to whom we must address ourselves . . . as sons to a father," he was a father "who finds his sons no longer believing in what he has to say." These "sons" were now "taking, point for point, everything he had to say and showing how it is the opposite of what he thought or hoped for" (TPJ, 25). In the specific case of Williams, Ignatow in "Williams' Influence: Some Social Aspects" (1964) registers the same reservation to an outmoded emphasis on individuality while in *Notebooks* he openly admits: "Today I received a letter (note) from WCW which made me feel my status (Dickinson-Chase) has been reaffirmed in his eyes. Nothing makes me so jittery as to think I may have sunk low in his estimate, having been 'reevaluated' by him through the influence of others. I say jealously, since I know I would be jealous and am jealous of his esteem for others. . . . It is only myself I see in direct, full-powered descent from his line and this I say is damned egotistical of me" (L, 79). Amateur analysts would not be hard pressed to see a Freudian relationship in the recurrent gun-and-knife imagery of Ignatow's work and these statements, and some critics like Richard Howard are even brought to the verge of embarrassment by the insistent "tough-guy approach."

From any absolutist point of view, the philosophical and theoretical bases that give support to these social positions emerge as confused and perhaps irreparably defeating. Their mythos is that either of Prometheus and Zeus as realized by the romantics or of the Saviour and God as seen by biblical interpreters. They make man a creature, by origin or imitation, directly of a Demiurge and indirectly of an all powerful Deity. This time-bound shaper of man is sometimes called Necessity. In Ignatow's poetry, as in Marx, History becomes this Demiurge that has created man, often by means of the social conditioning which is part of Baudelaire's attraction and which prompts the pleas for social reform. At some further remove is that perfect Force which the poet and reader are permitted to glimpse amid gaps in the poems and, on occasion, amid wrangles like that which closes *Say Pardon*. Generally what rules man is the Demiurge and what evil exists exists in his domain. Thus Ignatow revives for readers problems associated with Gnosticism and Manichaeanism. Either there is a God who is omnipotent and sees evil and refuses to correct it and hence Himself becomes evil (Gnosticism), or there is a dualism in which a continual battle between good and evil occurs (Manichaeanism). Ignatow's own inclination—like Jarrell and Arnold, and Hegel before them—is to dissipate these problems by seeing History in an almost deistic way: what man knows as good and evil is a partial vision beyond which lies ultimate good. Like Shelley, but one step closer, Ignatow will propose that, as a secondary demiurge to the History (Zeus) which shapes him, man should rebel against this tyranny and establish a new order. Here the translation of Hegel's disembodied Zeitgeist into something akin to Freud's view in *Totem and Taboo* (1913) of community as ritualistic murder of father figures by sons who then engage in totemic feasts seems to be occurring, but the transformation gives rise as well to complaints like those in Howard's "Poetry Chronicle" (1965).

History is either a fiction created by collective man and for which collective man must be culpable or it is a force beyond man that is imposed by Deity. If the former situation obtains, as Howard points out, Ignatow "is not really concerned . . . with the events of human history, . . . for he does not regard events as part of a history," since the nature of the events can be changed by man's altering the nature of the Demiurge. If the latter obtains, then the "dreadful unitary devices" that Howard finds, "meaningless and mostly vicious, rising from the chaos within the self, exhibiting no design and allowing none to be imposed on them" work to make delusionary any expectation of real reform that the poet projects.[11] However much he believes that apparently contrary philosophical positions may be resolved by successfully turning them into psychological states, Ignatow cannot avoid his readers' being confused. Two distinct orders are being delineated—one which is not changeable and one which is changeable—and the very bridging of them returns a reader to the Gnostic-or-Manichaean dilemma. Either, as man in the Middle Ages believed, the world has no reality, or there are two orders in real conflict. In the first instance the reader will have to confront Ignatow's belief that poets "dare not fail the world" and dismiss as silly the objection to withdrawal from what would then be "unreal" society. In the second instance the terms of the conflict exclude man permanently from Deity. This position has increasingly become that of modern poets, but it leads for Ignatow to an equally unacceptable perversity and to an "imperial self." Here again, gaps—much as grace and mystery in religion—allow the poet whatever escape from contradiction he achieves.

More practically the confusion accounts for a modulating indirectness in Ignatow's poetry. The stance he adopts, as Sartre in his *Baudelaire* (1951) would explain, is not that of the revolutionary but of the rebel: "The revolutionary wants to change the world; he transcends it and moves toward the future, towards an order of values which he himself invents. The rebel is careful to preserve the abuses from which he suffers so that he can go on rebelling against them. He always shows signs of a bad conscience and of something resembling a feeling of guilt. He does not want to destroy or transcend the existing order; he simply wants to rise up against it." [12] Rebels preserve censors or what Freud would call superegos, commonly identified by them with their fathers. Early in Ignatow's poetry when he was overtly opposing his father's will and believed in man's ability to change History, this censor took the shape of business, the stock exchange, and banks. Later, as he began to make peace with his father's ghost in "Prologue" and "The Boss," the censor became something beyond the father and man's control, something closer to a Zeitgeist, forcing the father's hoarding of lewd photographs and prompting the violences of everyday life. This modulation of man's aggressive nature by first understanding and then resignation has led to statements in *Notebooks* where Ignatow questions the energy that is wasted in rebellion. He eventually laments: "I cannot say things definitively any longer and a sense of decline has come with it, but peace too. It could be the start of death, the road down, the sense of futility and defeat that surrounds every endeavor" (NYQ, 83).

Compassion has been the means most used by religious and nonreligious writers to soften contradiction and explain capitulations like those that Ignatow's contrary philosophical positions seem to demand. In Ignatow's case the compassion arises from the perception of one's self in others. In "The Poet Is a Hospital Clerk" he advises: "In memory of yourself, in sorrow be good to others"; but no corollary means for compassion in the perception of God's likeness in others is offered, nor is the possibility suggested that men may achieve a disinterested love by responding to this Eternal likeness. Deity remains Old Testament, a God of justice rather than of mercy, except as His judgments have mercy implicit in them, and man's very need to have his identity proved by another keeps him from such Perfection. As "The Complex" has God state: "Of love you are a man. / You are yourself, apart from me." One has consequently compassion defined in terms similar to those that Irving Singer uses in *The Nature of Love* (1966) to characterize "bestowal"; one responds creatively to an object of love, making her more worthy by investing her with greater value, although not necessarily making her a better person. In the process the lover transforms himself "by subordinating his purposive attitudes . . . into a being who enjoys the act of bestowing." The creativity involved is primarily that of self-creation in which each lover "enhances the other's importance through an imaginative play with valuation itself." [13] "Pardon Keeps the Sun" indicates that one loves mainly for what a woman has to give, thinking that something in her may need what one has as well. The success of this mutually self-interested, self-completing love is celebrated in "Marriage," and in a later untitled poem Ignatow extends the self-interest to the emotions surrounding the birth of a daughter. These emotions become subordinate to the speaker's own sense of being reborn. Behind this compassion lies a view expressed in "The Gentle Weight Lifter"—that each individual has his own special dazzling grace to bestow.

The social character of the compassion is made explicit in Ignatow's remarks to Chisholm regarding Bly's misunderstanding of the poem "Rescue the Dead." There the line "Not to love is to live"—which is intended as an ironic attack on Sartrean "freedom"—becomes in the context of its associations with nature something akin to racial instincts. Bly exaggerates the "noble savage" image, perhaps because he did not then have available two early poems, "Money and Grass" and "Come!". In these works Ignatow uses nature as a vantage point for a reexamination of city life much in the way that Shakespeare in *As You Like It* makes Arden a place where courtiers come to reform themselves before their eventual return. In no instance is natural existence shown as superior to proper civilized life. Ignatow tells Chisholm that man cannot really live without love: "In the last analysis, you love yourself, which is manifested in the fact that you continue to live. . . . Having gone through the poem stage by stage showing what it is to live without love and then to return to those who are living through love and in love, I turn back to those who think they are living without love and ask them to save us who are under the influence of love. But it would be quite obvious from what I have said about living without love, that they who would help us, must first help themselves." He adds later: "People make an effort to live with one another, to understand, and to help and support

one another" (TPJ, 32–33). If this effort is thwarted, one gets
the derelicts of "Emergency Clinic" or the criminal of "The
Murderer."

Ignatow's capitulation to an unalterable History has as significantly brought about an increase in his attempts to bypass this
Demiurge by unconscious means. Since *Poems* his poetry has
enmeshed its calls for reform almost exclusively in gallows humor,
irony, and incongruity; and the poetry is embodied in a poetic
structure that moves by rhythm, rising to crisis and resolution
more like dream or the separate frames of a movie montage than
by the exigencies of uninterrupted narrative. Freud in *Wit and Its
Relation to the Unconscious* (1916) speaks of wit as a device for
bypassing censors as well as the relation of wit to expectation.
Laughter forms a release from overpreparation and results from
a saving of psychic energy. In the case of gallows humor, the
energy that is saved derives from what would otherwise go into
feelings of sympathy. In Ignatow's case the conditions which
would form the sentence for the condemned man ensue from the
bleak outlook that Ignatow projects for mankind and that he perceives in man's helplessness at either altering the existing order or
destroying the censor. The suicide of "Beautiful and Kind,"
prompted by the same social pressures that force the murders of
"Ritual Three" and the suicide of "A Dialogue," is stated in such
romantic terms that the reader forgets for a moment that when the
speaker prepares "to step out the window" to meet his dream girl
he also lives "on the top floor." The intense pity one might normally have extended to the death—like that of Freud's example—
is "inhibited" because the individual who is most concerned is
quite indifferent to the conditions which are producing his suicide,
and the expenditure for pity which was being built up subcon-
sciously becomes inapplicable in the light of the poem's apparent
"happy ending."

Less comic and pessimistic in outlook, the ironic poems offer
an often slim possibility that what is being attacked may be
changed. At times, as in "Rescue the Dead," this possibility is
illusory; for, as Ignatow has said, those to whom the speaker
appeals must help themselves before they can help others. "All
Quiet" attacks the government for beginning a bombing pause
without telling its citizens, and the charge that "you can't take my

fate in your hands, / without informing me" is rendered similarly comic by its being precisely what the government has done all along, both in starting and in stopping the aerial maneuvers. His only protest—suicide—which indeed will remove him from government manipulation—will also remove him from existence and seems far more extreme a remedy than the situation calls for. More hopeful, however, are poems like "Love Poem for the Forty-Second Street Library," in which the irony works to suggest that one's absurd behavior can alter multitudes. Here incongruity serves, as it generally does in Ignatow's poetry, to return the reader to personal situations and to optimism. As Freud's example of the woman who prepares to lift a heavy basket only to find it light, Ignatow's readers prepare themselves for individual disasters that finally do not occur. "How Come?", for example, begins with one's being "in New York covered by a layer of soap foam," but the poem's emphasis proves to be the people who survive not "the many / who will die of soap foam." A comparable saving of energy is effected by "The Bagel," in which whatever sympathy one might express at the loss of the bagel is saved by the speaker's turning into the lost object. That these disasters do not occur prevents Ignatow from believing in sacrifices that alter character and hence protects him from the disappointments that Jarrell feels in a world that learns nothing from having survived two world wars.

In *The Interpretation of Dreams* (1900) Freud assigns a similar function of bypassing the censor to dream work, and, whereas generally one might argue from "The Relation of the Poet to Day-Dreaming" (1908) that all art is dream, the ways in which artists approach the rhythm of dream differ. By condensation, displacement, and transformation of the optative ("would it were") into the indicative ("it is"), dream attempts to effect its rebellions and define its flow. A similar process goes on in motion-picture structure. Like the dream it creates "a natural present, an order of direct apparition"; and, in the way the spectator's mind works to assemble the frames of film, its flow involves "condensation." Moreover both dream and film force the viewer through a succession of predominantly visual images which define him centrally as a participant and an observer. In dreams the dreamer is the actual center; in film the camera is, but the camera works as a catalyst to the viewer's imagining himself in control. In both the rhythm is anticipatory—a continuous state of becoming—and it differs greatly from the usual rhythm of poetry which so fuses anticipation with recollection that one tends to listen to what is to come in relation to what has been. In Ignatow's poetry this reflexive tendency is lessened by the reduced number of devices that might create static rhythms. Since the sixteenth century, rhetoricians have known that stasis can be produced by such "dynamic inner relationships" as ambiguity, paradox, and those techniques that the New Critics refer to collectively as "texture." As early as A. M. Sullivan's "Seven of Merit" (1948) critics have been able to see this anticipatory quality as an Ignatow trait, referring to its linear flow in terms like "a graphic report of ghetto life . . . to be said aloud, and not too pleasantly, while looking at Mark Hellinger's 'The Naked City.'" [14]

Equally, as Sergei Eisenstein notes in "Montage in 1938" (1939), the role of the spectator in putting together the parts of a montage is similar to that of the reader bridging the gaps of small poems: "The spectator is compelled to proceed along that selfsame creative road that the author traveled in creating the image. The spectator not only sees the represented elements of the finished work, but also experiences the dynamic process of the emergence and assembly of the image just as it was experienced by the author." Eisenstein goes on to state: "The strength of the method resides also in the circumstance that the spectator is drawn into a creative act in which his individuality is not subordinated to the author's individuality, but is opened up throughout the process of fusion with the author's intention, just as the individuality of a great actor is fused with the individuality of a great playwright in the creation of a classic scenic image." [15] Many of the late illustrations that Eisenstein uses to demonstrate how montages are created are taken from poems, including a piece by Vladimir Mayakovsky. A poet as adept as Ignatow at managing shifts in perception and the levels of perception as well as committed to leveling collective experience can expect, in turn, to have the open structures of his short poems eventually compared to that most leveling of popular media in his day—the motion picture—especially in the manner in which the personalism of his poetry enlists a comparable participation and personalism from his readers. This personalism, which has been the active goal of the generation of poets after Jarrell and which Ignatow's work allows to an unusual degree, may provide the most intelligent explanation why these younger writers, as Bly has asserted, have insisted strongly that Ignatow's "poetry be reviewed and published."

In the past, various bridges have been found to fill the gaps of short poems. Rhyme, melody, common religious and social out-looks, and, in the individualism of the Renaissance, the person of the poet. Therefore, to bridge the gaps in the disparate images of a metaphysical poem, a reader must evoke the figure who would join the elements; and this has remained generally true until the advent of Imagism in the twentieth century. All these methods have in common that they bridge with *something*, and by using *something*, each method has defined to a degree its limits. In Imagism the reader, rather than having to bridge an imagery of statement, was asked to bridge silence. This permitted his own definition of what the limits would be. Hugh Kenner in *The Pound Era* (1972) is willing to credit part of the invention of this method to the uncovering of fragments of Sappho among the papyri. More recently in *Escape from the Self* (1977) Karl Malkoff attributes it to the writings of T. E. Hulme. But the method is also implicit in the oriental sympathies of Imagism. Marshall McLuhan points this out in the introduction to the paperback edition of *Understanding Media* (1964): "The art and poetry of Zen create involvement by means of the *interval*, not by the *connection* used in the visually organized Western world. Spectator becomes artist in oriental art because he must supply all the connections." One thinks of the legendary Chinese painter mentioned by Siegfried Kracauer in *Theory of Film* (1965) as his example of the ideal film-viewer (and poetry reader?), "who, longing for the peace of the landscape he created, moved into it, walked toward the faraway mountains suggested by his brush strokes, and disappeared in them never to be seen again." [16] Readers will have to concede that the personal-ism to which they are attracted in Ignatow's poetry is predomi-nantly the result of silence and that this silence perhaps even more than the personal elements, the compassion, and the various in-directnesses accounts for the work's imaginative appeal.

Ironically most critics who have written favorably of Ignatow's work have concentrated on an opposite quality—the writer's diction—as if greatness in poetry did lie, as Yeats's "Adam's

Curse" (1902) indicates it should, in one's articulating "sweet sounds together." This criticism would emphasize not the gaps but the words being used; and, for the same purpose of Yeats's magic, it would create a false world for the real one to be summoned to. This purpose would tend to disregard the social messages that Ignatow claims underlie his very skills at mixing language levels and reduce not only his but the whole of poetry to surfaces similar to those of minimal art. In short these critics would see poetry not as a moral force so much as a cosmetic force, the value of which is authentication through a fantasy retransformation of existence rather than by the illuminations of near-mirroring. They would reverse the pattern of life's being an imitation of art by altering art's purpose in giving ideas an artistic form, endowed with higher life and detached from the artist's own personality. Like Rousseau's Pygmalion they would have art dragged by a very unreality down to the spectator's own earthly level. Hayden Carruth is willing even to pronounce Ignatow a "poet of sensibility," as if some personal outrage of taste or feeling took priority over the poet's larger and more philosophical concerns or propriety and truth-telling might be equated.

Not unless one is willing to accept a middle ground between Jarrell's intensity and unreformed normal life and admit, as Paul Goodman does in *Speaking and Language* (1971), to silence and its effects as an integral part of diction, will one be able to comprehend that Ignatow's near-mirroring by its very stylization and compression is different from both life and the self-congratulatory tone of the criticism that it has received. Silence often counts for more than its verbalization, and Ignatow is one of the last poets about whom it may be said that he is not simply a poet of sensibility. His silences are not purely explicable as reactions to situations that challenge man's ability to contain his emotions or to moments of resentment. Nor are they necessarily indications of complete familiarity or complete accord. They are interested. Ignatow derives from a culture which has traditionally regarded silence with special awe, particularly as it approaches and reveals Deity; but equally, as his review of *Buckdancer's Choice* makes clear, Ignatow himself has thought long on the problems of silence and its impact: "I have read and reread [The Firebombing], fascinated by what it omits to say. I have been seeking to make out the meaning of this gap and have come to believe it is the poem itself, as the holes in [Henry] Moore's sculpture determine its form."[17] Overcoming metaphysical silence is the subject likewise of *Tread the Dark*. An audience that would recognize what Ignatow has to say will have to seek meaning, too, in silence, gaps, and their manipulations.

Notes

1. David Ignatow, *Poems* (Prairie City, Ill.: Becker Press, 1948), p. 30; Randall Jarrell, "Recent Poetry," *Yale Review* 45 (1955–56):124. The following abbreviations for work by David Ignatow have been used in this chapter: CR—"Williams' Influence: Some Social Aspects," *Chelsea Review* 14 (1964):154–61; "Hurting Inside," *Chelsea Review* 15 (1964):122–28; CH—"An Interview with David Ignatow," *Crazy Horse* 9 (December 1971):26–32; APR—"Notebooks (1971)," *American Poetry Review* 1, no. 1 (1972):4–7; NYQ—"A Poet's Notebook," *New York Quarterly* 5 (winter 1971):79–94; L—"From the Journals," *Lillabulero* 10–11 (1971):78–94; TPJ—"On Writing" and "An Interview with David Ignatow," *Tennessee Poetry Journal* 3, no. 2 (winter 1970):14–16, 22–40; B—"A Dialogue with William Spanos," *boundary 2*, no. 2/3 (1974):443–81. The abbreviations are accompanied by page citations.
2. Gaston Bachelard, *The Poetics of Space*, trans. Maria Jolas (New York: Orion Press, 1964), p. 159; Victor Contoski, "Time and Money," *University Review* 34 (1968):212.
3. Robert Bly, "Slipping Toward the Instincts," *New Leader* 51 (20 May 1968), 31–33; Louis Simpson, "New Books of Poems," *Harper's* 237 (August 1968):76; Hayden Carruth, "First Books and Others," *Hudson Review* 18 (1965–66):134–35; Carruth, "Making It New," *Hudson Review* 21 (1968):405–6.
4. William Carlos Williams, "Poetry with an Impressive, Human Speech," *New York Times Book Review*, 21 November 1948, p. 50; Bly, pp. 31–32.
5. Bachelard, pp. 148, 163; Thom Gunn, "Outside Faction," *Yale Review* 50 (1960–61):594–95; Bachelard, p. 149.
6. Carruth, "First Books and Others," pp. 134–35.
7. Claude Lévi-Strauss, *The Savage Mind* (Chicago: University of Chicago Press, 1966), p. 24.
8. David Ignatow, "The Past Reordered," *Nation* 204 (1967):531; Ignatow, "The Permanent Hell," *Nation* 202 (1966):753.
9. William Carlos Williams, *In the American Grain* (New York: New Directions, 1956), p. 68.
10. William Carlos Williams, "America, Whitman, and the Art of Poetry," *The Poetry Journal* 8 (November 1917):31.
11. Richard Howard, "Poetry Chronicle," *Poetry* 106 (1965):299.
12. Jean-Paul Sartre, *Baudelaire*, trans. Martin Turnell (New York: New Directions, 1950), pp. 51–52.
13. Irving Singer, *The Nature of Love* (New York: Random House, 1966), p. 16.
14. See Suzanne Langer, "A Note on the Film," in *Film: A Montage of The-*

ories, ed. Richard Dyer MacCann (New York: Dutton Paperbacks, 1966), p. 201; A. M. Sullivan, "Seven of Merit," *Saturday Review* 31 (28 November 1948):26.

15. Sergei Eisenstein, *The Film Sense*, ed. and trans. Jay Leyda (New York: Harvest Books, 1947), pp. 32–33.

16. Hugh Kenner, *The Pound Era* (Berkeley: University of California Press, 1972), pp. 54–75; Karl Malkoff, *Escape from the Self* (New York: Columbia University Press, 1977), p. 36; Marshall McLuhan, *Understanding Media* (New York: Signet Books, 1964), pp. vii–viii; Siegfried Kracauer, *Theory of Film* (New York: Galaxy Books, 1965), p. 165.

17. Ignatow, "The Permanent Hell," p. 752.

5

The Yeatsian Mask: John Berryman

The Dream Songs (1963–69) opens with John Berryman's hero having to say "a long / wonder the world can bear & be," and he continues this "long wonder," warning readers in song 308 not to "seek the strange soul, in rain & mist," but to "recall the pretty cousins they kissed, / and stick with the sweet switch of the body." The advice to seek verification of the songs in the ordinary events of life proposes a mimetic process with which readers might empathize, and it echoes statements like William Carlos Williams's in *Kora in Hell* (1920): "The trick of the dance [the poem] is in following now the words, *allegro*, now the contrary beat of the glossy leg." Williams, moreover, is among the poets whose deaths move Henry in the course of the poem. Yet, as John Bayley in "John Berryman: A Question of Imperial Sway" (1973) persuasively argues, Berryman constructs his hero by a process opposite to Williams's mirroring or the mirroring that novelists do to create character. Rather than allow entrance into the poem by permitting an identification with his speaker, Berryman assembles a voice "so single that [one] cannot share with or be a part of him." In short he creates out of his speaker a new object in nature which is not him but which is not nature either. He repeats—despite his expressed reservations about Williams—Williams's eventual modernist equivalent of the enlargement of nature by imitation. As Williams had phrased it in his *Autobiography* (1951), "It is NOT to hold the mirror up to nature that the artist performs his work. It is to make, out of the imagination, something not at all a copy of nature, a thing advanced and apart from it." [1] It is to make, in terms closer to those Berryman might accept, an approximation of W. B. Yeats's mask or antithetical self and to set the result in a world colored, like that of his contemporaries, by W. H. Auden and the views of Darwin, Marx, and Freud.

In this regard Berryman advises his readers in a note to the volume against mistaking Henry House alias Henry Pussy-cat, Henry Hankovitch, and Mr. Bones for the poet. Henry is "an imaginary character (not the poet, not me) . . . a white American in early middle age sometimes in blackface, who has suffered an irreversible loss and talks about himself sometimes in the first person, sometimes in the third, sometimes even in the second." The separation of Henry and Berryman may not be easy for readers predisposed to a close coincidence between life and art, for much as one may grant that Henry is the composite of the age and that the intention of the rhetoric is to divorce him from his creator, one notices that Henry shares with his author degrees from both Columbia and Cambridge, intervals at Harvard, Princeton, and the University of Minnesota, travels in both Asia and Ireland, friendships, illnesses, loves, prejudices, prizes, reputations, and a sentimental attachment to what, in "The Death of Randall Jarrell" (1966), Karl Shapiro calls "Who's First," that game of deciding who holds first place among living American poets. Henry is obviously intended as a double figure for Berryman, and he functions psychologically in that way as Mr. Bones (Henry's death urge) and the blackface interlocutor of Henry form a still further breakdown. Mr. Bones, as Berryman told Richard Kostelanetz (in 1970), is the voice of a Job's comforter telling Henry always that "you suffer, therefore you are guilty." [2] The interlocutor, however, is never named.

Yet, just as the rhetoric of Henry is divorced from the normal language of Berryman or the eschatological view that Henry shares with many poets of the period may not, in fact, be Berryman's own, the relationship between the two figures extends beyond similarity to contrast and contiguity. As Berryman admits of Henry, "he doesn't enjoy my advantages of supervision; he just has vision. He's also simple-minded. He thinks that if something happens to him, it's forever; but I know better" (K, 341). Nor does Henry pay income taxes. Instead he represents "the individual soul under stress," opened to far more opportunities for experience than any of the poet's other personae; and he owes this openness as much to the "I" of Walt Whitman's "Song of Myself" (1855) as to any changes that might have occurred in the poet's life. If pressed, Berryman will confess that "we touch at certain points,"[3] but Henry's problems result from systems of chance and causality that are within literature's power to change, whereas those systems of chance and causality to which his creator is subject cannot be altered: they must be lived through. Moreover Henry has for his forebears the whole of western literature, its traditions and ranges, while Berryman has a precise limited ancestry and tradition and a mobility that, by comparison to Henry's, seems restricted. Yet, as the poet told Kostelanetz, he can speak of "Heisenberg's theory of indeterminacy" and "scholarly questions" and "modern painting" while, owing to the range of diction in *The Dream Songs*, Henry cannot (K, 346).

Berryman's interests in the achievement of such a discrete voice date from the thirties and his admiration for Yeats. Yeats's "mask" had been the method of his ascertaining his opposite "true" self in a philosophical system in which opposites call each other into account. Auden's Darwinism and Marxism had reinterpreted these masks along the lines of biological and social roles. Therefore a concept of aesthetic distancing like Keats's "negative capability" would lead not, as T. S. Eliot in "Tradition and the Individual Talent" (1917) supposes, to a loss of personality but—for both Yeats and Auden—to an antipersonality. In 1936 the young Berryman, full of such notions, had taken high tea with the Irish poet, whom he reports to have said: "I never revise now . . . but in the interests of a more passionate syntax" (PR, 188). As early as "A Note on Poetry" (1940) the young poet had converted these "interests" into technical matters, "a delight in craftsmanship . . . versification, rime, stanza-form, trope . . . by which the writer can shape from an experience in itself usually vague, a mere feeling or phrase, something that is coherent, directed, intelligible." This delight in craft, he adds, is "rarely for its own sake, mainly as it seizes and makes visible its subject."[4] Twenty-five years later he would still be attacking Eliot's belief in "impersonality," but "passionate syntax" was now something to shield rather than make visible the subject—a strategy of skills which, "like any craftsman," a poet "who deserves to know them deserves to find them out for himself." He would now boast of knowing "more about the administration of pronouns than any other living poet writing in English or American," of being "less impressed than [he] used to be by the universal notion of a continuity of individual personality," and add that he thought art technical: "I feel myself to be addressing primarily professional writers or will be writers and teachers."[5]

The note which prefaces his own selection for *Five Young American Poets* (1940) is devoted mainly not to these matters of syntax and personality but to an explanation of a poem, "On the London Train" (1939), clearly indebted to Auden in its flat, contemporary, class trappings and to Sir Thomas Wyatt through either Yeats or Berryman's teacher, Mark Van Doren, in its yearning for high style. The subject is a solitary man in a train compartment, whose social protective armor still does not prevent women from looking at him and fancying in their loneliness some idyllic tryst. He, in turn, imagines some virgin whom he would approach in the manner of the lovers in Wyatt's "They Flee from Me," and who subsequently, in the manner of Auden's women, will see that his wounds get proper medical attention. The narrator then intrudes to suggest that if one "could summon a lover from a former time, or summon John Donne from his grave,"[6] one would proclaim as had Wyatt that the pursuit of love is unpleasant and that the anguish persists beyond the marriage bed. In a final moralizing stanza Berryman, again in the manner of Auden, aligns the poem's various paradoxes into "shell" and "life." The "sea-shell" puzzling Destiny is also the train and the protective armor of the passenger, while the lives it contains become the train's passengers and the passengers' fantasies. The discrepancy between fixity and motion which results from obstinately remaining out of life's stream becomes in the narrator's words "too little recompense" for those like the passenger "who suffer on the shore."

The syntax of the poem is spare, "elliptical and indistinctly allusive: casual in tone and form, frightening in import,"[7] reflecting the Auden climate that Berryman claims set in by 1935. This climate, as Berryman says in "Waiting for the End, Boys" (1948), is indebted to Yeats's later poetry, although Berryman admits that safeguards prevented Auden from being overwhelmed. Jarrell in

"Changes of Attitude and Rhetoric in Auden's Poetry" (1941) views the "eccentric syntax" of early Auden as a similar "creative extension" of language; and assuredly the syntax in the early works of both Auden and Berryman does not of itself preclude novelistic ways of creating character. Both remain tied to a traditional use of predicaments—those concrete situations of personality and circumstance that allow readers to identify themselves with what is being depicted: how a man of virtue, for example, might react to a specific attempt at seduction. Over an extended number of circumstances and a variety of personal characteristics, these predicaments set up so closed a system of logic that the reader can swear the character is "real," that, in short, the reader can predict its behavior in circumstances that are not contained in the work. In briefer pieces, one makes the same logical assumptions, but one bases them on premises that are more generalized: all lonely men act this way, or one has known this to happen before. For Auden the individual qualities of personality take on the color of class values which are apparent in the Berryman poem. The ironic moralizing on which he ends the poem assumes some system of normative behavior inspired by Destiny. One's amusement at the passenger's self-satisfaction at "remaining on shore" comes from the sense that man is a social being and, painful as love may be, man cannot remain removed from it. As the poet will later tell Jane Howard (1967), "it's terrible to give half your life over to someone else, . . . but it's worse not to." [8]

Much as "On the London Train" explores one extreme of Berryman's experiments with character and passionate syntax, "At Chinese Checkers" (1939) explores the other. Its flat Audenesque game of chinese checkers is so presented as to warrant response by means not of Auden's ironic detachment but of Yeats's ceremonial involvement. Cast in eight-line stanzas that are a variation of those used by Yeats's "In Memory of Major Robert Gregory" (1918), the work navigates through a reef of echoes. One reads of "passionate activity," "dreadful leniency," the "mountainous dead world" as well as of "a voice that even undisciplined can stir / The country blood." Yet neither the stanza form nor the phrases so redeem the importance of the initial revery and the speaker's inability to concentrate on the game before him that a subsequent comparison of these activities to Delmore Schwartz's inability to bring his mind to bear on the day's needs gains the significance Berryman wants. The comparison works instead to trivialize Schwartz's efforts, much as failed Yeatsian lines like "Venus on the half-shell was found a dish / To madden a fanatic" and "Marbles are not the marbles that they were" work to trivialize the Yeatsian elegance that elsewhere appears. In an ironic structure such as "On the London Train" the poet might have succeeded with such definition; but here, remaining serious as he does in the final stanza, he is guilty of what Jarrell in reviewing *The Dispossessed* (1948) labels as a slavish adherence to "Yeatsian grandiloquence" that results at times in "monumental bathos."[9]

Thus, at the beginning at least, Berryman could be grouped with other poets of his generation as one who, though he had moved toward passionate syntax, had not yet achieved an individual voice. Like Theodore Roethke and Jarrell before him, Berryman seems more concerned in his first volume with bringing his talent into line with a tradition than in establishing himself as an independent voice albeit, as Daniel Hughes suggests in "The Dream Songs" (1966), the echoes may have resulted from a desire by the poet "to take Eliot and Yeats and Auden on their own grounds, and do it better." Although Dudley Fitts was already finding the grammar of these early poems a "fanfare of ship-wrecked syntax, textbook inversions and alliterations" and "somehow without the excitement that attends the transformation of a craft into a completely realized art," Jarrell was citing the volume's most extreme dislocations of syntax—"The Nervous Songs"—as the direction that the poet should be moving in.[10] His citation of these works and the enigmatic parts of Berryman's other pieces is part of a view Jarrell derived from Auden—namely that poetry represented the Freudian ego, embodying in its realization both id and superego. This psychological part of Auden, which had been pointed out by Schwartz and others, is precisely what Berryman is rejecting in favor of a Yeatsian view of masks.

Yeats's masks are predicated not upon an individual memory of Freud but upon a racial memory akin to Carl Jung's racial unconscious and along with that a psychological typology that goes back to the Greek Stoics. By the end of Yeats's life, these masks had been divided into twenty-eight phases that ranged from a nonhuman first phase to that of the fool and had represented an enlargement of an early belief that masks were what people assumed to bridge the discrepancies between their own and other people's conceptions of themselves. Nowhere does Berryman publicly acknowledge an affinity with Jung, though in song 327 Henry chides Freud for having enlightened—but misled—others. Henry insists, in echo of James Joyce, that "a dream is a panorama / of the whole mental life"; and in the next song, he refers to "his ancient brain," suggesting something like a racial recall. Berryman, however, goes only so far as to acknowledge the possibility of Freud's late work having entered his writing, especially *Civilization and Its Discontents* (1929). The comment follows a condescending description of a woman who sees Henry "corresponding vaguely to Freud's differentiation of the personality into superego or conscience, ego or façade or self, and id or unconscious" (PR, 190). Berryman adds that he did not know whether or not she was right, but that he had not begun with so full-fledged a conception. *Recovery* (1973), the poet's unfinished posthumous published novel, describes its autobiographical hero, Alan Severance, as having "been a rigid Freudian for thirty years, with heavy admixture however from Reich's early work";[11] and one assumes that if the poet understood or sympathized with Jung it was mainly through an interest in Yeats.

"The Nervous Songs," which represent Berryman's clearest approximation of an acceptance of Yeatsian masks in the early poems, are again realized so as to bring the Irish poet in line with the social concerns of Auden. Based as are *The Dream Songs* on Yeats's *Words for Music Perhaps* (1933), the lyrics depict the poet's confrontation with the twenty-eighth phase, when the physical world suggests to the mind "pictures and events that have no relation to [one's] needs or even to [one's] desires; [one's] thoughts are an aimless reverie; [one's] acts are aimless like [one's] thoughts; and it is in this aimlessness that [one] finds [one's] joy." Yeats began to compose his lyrics in the spring of 1929 after a long illness; his mood was one of "uncontrolled energy and daring." He wrote Olivia Shakespear that his "songs" were "songs," "not so much that they may be sung as that I may define their kind of emotion to myself. I want them to be all emotion and all impersonal." Later he added in another letter: "Sexual abstinence fed their fire. . . . They sometimes came out of the greatest mental excitements I am capable of." [12] "The Nervous Songs" use the same six-line stanza basic to Yeats's pieces, but with neither his compulsion to rhyme nor his inclination to add occasional refrains. The sexual appetite of Berryman's girl in "Young Woman's Song" is not the exuberance of Crazy Jane but the result of capitalism which forces one to pay £3.10 for a hat and to turn one's body into a commodity. Similarly the discrepancy between thinking and the world in "The Song of the Tortured Girl" results from Nazi torture rather than from some godly gift. If Berryman's people are to act as mediums through which new truths are made known, it will be less by any Yeatsian accident of identity than by means of an overwhelming social coercion.

At the same time that Berryman was working on the last poems of *The Dispossessed*, he wrote a number of sonnets that he later published as *Berryman's Sonnets* (1967). The poems record an adulterous affair which he undertook during the spring and summer of 1947. The works were not originally intended for public view (#47) and carry on in private the experiments with characterization and passionate syntax that are more conservatively displayed in the published volume. By basing the predicaments of the various pieces on literary as well as life circumstances, the poet begins to construct a language and syntax and view of personality whose relations to nature are blurred. Lise (or Chris, as it was probably) is always trying to break through a cloud of literary convention, jargon, textbook inversion, and alcoholic fantasy. She is variously Petrarch's Laura, Sidney's Stella, Shakespeare's young man, Anne Frank, the daughter of a Tulsa oilman, and Ilse Koch —the conventional "cruel mistress" whose function it is to make the lover suffer either requited or unrequited love. The poet, too, seems unable to determine whether he is a character in life or literary history or literature. He embarks on a comparable variety of roles, including eventually that of Don Quixote (#88), who evinces similar self-confusion in Cervantes's novel. Quixote's being a character in fiction leads Berryman finally to present his adultery as if it were fictional as well, and this approach may account for his eventually releasing the lyrics. He adds to the original 111 poems four new sonnets and a Henry-like proem that cites Jacques Maritain to the effect that wickedness is perhaps soluble in art.

Critics have been able to detect in these sonnets prefigurations of the techniques that the poet would later display in *The Dream Songs*. Hayden Carruth in "Declining Occasions" (1968) summarizes these devices as "archaic spelling, fantastically complex diction, tortuous syntax, formalism, a witty and ironic attitude toward prosody generally." But one thing that is not found here is a picaresque hero. Berryman is a serious, romantic, and passionate lover, and his attempts to deflate this image often make him resemble the cross-gartered Malvolio of Shakespeare's *Twelfth Night*. He is in life the passenger that "On the London Train" depicted, caught up in the slim chances of realizing the dream of a literary romance and pursuing that opportunity past the point of reason into regions of self-destruction. Berryman relates through Severance that the affair changed him from a social drinker who occasionally got drunk into an alcoholic: "I'd been faithful to my wife —despite heavy provocation . . . for five years. My mistress drank heavily and I drank along with her, and afterward I just kept on" (R, 12). Elsewhere William Martz in *John Berryman* (1969) records that the romance "brought him to the point of suicide, with thoughts of killing both himself and his mistress because she flatly refused to leave her husband and to marry him. His wife, who was ignorant of the affair, persuaded him to undergo psychoanalysis, and he stayed under analysis from 1947 to 1953." [13] The affair with Chris (Lise) was indeed the *crise* he refers to in sonnet 18, and alcohol hazes figure as often as the hazes of literary allusions in the work's unfolding.

What *Berryman's Sonnets* accomplishes is the temporary elimination of Auden's social consciousness, for without a clear distinction between art and nature, one is unsure what social institutions need reform. One can as easily propose, as had Williams in his late works, that it is the mind that requires change. With this removal of social consciousness, there is consequently less need to reproduce actual speech; one can as well produce artificial language, as the sonnets do, accomplishing the modern equivalent of the rejection implied in Ben Jonson's pronouncement that Edmund Spenser, "in affecting the ancients, writ no language." Berryman in "The Long Way to MacDiarmid" (1956) makes explicit this rejection, stating simply that Jonson was wrong in the matter; and presumably the confused realms that the *Sonnets* reflects demand a corresponding language that embodies previous art as well as nature. But, if one eliminates nature as the basic means of verification for thought, what becomes the new basis for credibility in art? Is it to be, as Quixote suggests, faith in the author? If so, is the author like Henry David Thoreau to write about himself because it is a subject that he knows better than anyone else? Berryman suggests as much in "The Poetry of Ezra Pound" (1949): "Yeats, another Romantic, is . . . the subject of his own poetry, himself-as-himself. Pound is his own subject *qua* modern poet." Yet Berryman will infer of Pound's poetry that the personal is not very personal: there is a "peculiar detachment of interest with which Pound seems to regard himself" as well as an "unfaltering, encyclopedic mastery of tone" that somehow offsets a "comparative weakness of syntax." Berryman designates that other master of artificial language, John Milton, "the supreme English master of syntax"[14] and even imitates him in dream song 20 ("Hurl, God who found / us in this, down / something"). All the same one suspects from Berryman's comments on Pound that the real arbiter for credibility is already the liveliness or energy that entices a reader's empathy.

The inclination not to seek verification of thought in nature seems to have been increased by the reception of *The Dispossessed*. Berryman told Peter Stitt in a *Paris Review* interview (1972): "If a writer gets hot early, then his work ought to become known early. If it doesn't, he is in danger of feeling neglected. We take it that all young writers overestimate their work. . . . I overestimated myself, as it turned out, and felt bitter, bitterly neglected." He then went on to add that "Auden once said that the best situation for a poet is to be taken up early and held for a considerable time and then dropped after he had reached the level of indifference" (PR, 179). So far as reviews of the volume go, the reception was favorable, and in 1949 he received the Shelley Memorial Award. What the volume failed to do, however, was to secure the poet a standing comparable to the one Robert Lowell achieved in 1946 with the publication of *Lord Weary's Castle* or to the position that Berryman's longtime friend, Dylan Thomas, held by virtue of poetry readings and his *Selected Writings* (1946). The bitterness allied with the disappointment over the failure of the affair the year before and its suggestion that "the old high way of love" that the poet sought was no longer possible led Berryman first to seek verification in psychoanalytical theory in his biography of Stephen Crane (1950) and then to use history in part in *Homage to Mistress Bradstreet* (1956). William Meredith in "In Loving Memory" (1973) reports that by the end of his life, Berryman's antipathy to today's "conventional manners" prompted his statement that "promiscuous honesty" was "often no more than an evasion of the social predicament." His alternative yearning for Yeatsian "decorum, even for old-fashioned manners," was not so much a return to Audenesque "social behavior" as to a "social ideal." Meredith conjectures that "at heart, Berryman was a courtly man, though usually (like most of us) he could act out only a parody of that. The forms of behavior that attracted him were as traditional as the forms of prosody." [15]

The divorce from nature that both the romance and the "bad" reception effected may well account, too, for a terror that the poet began to feel and which increased his need for alcohol. Berryman told Jane Howard that life "is a terrible place, but we have to exert our wills. I wake up every morning terrified," and she went on to comment, "Hence the whisky—under whose influence the terror seems somewhat to diminish—and hence . . . the ink and what it writes" (L, 76). The divorce certainly accounts for the poet's seeking out other alienated figures as "friends." He told Stitt of A. E. Housman, "Housman is one of my heroes and always has been. He was a detestable and miserable man. Arrogant, unspeakably lonely, cruel, and so on, but an absolutely marvelous minor poet, I think, and a great scholar" (PR, 182). Earlier he had described with a degree of wonder the fortitude of Gerard Manley Hopkins and Robert Bridges, forging ahead with their poetries despite the neglect of the reading public. But perhaps most importantly the alienation establishes a justification for Berryman's choosing to adapt a modernist view of imitation to postmodernist ends. If, for instance, psychoanalysis creates a mirror image of the self through recollection for the purposes of understanding, why not, as Yeats proposes, construct a nonself or antithetical image for such purposes? Why not use a Yeatsian mask? The purposes of dramatic monologue in writers like Jarrell and Auden do not prevent the nonself from defining the self. Playing at roles is a time-honored approved method of defining one's limits. Simply because these roles in such poets are kept within the confines of novelistic and

Freudian characterization does not necessarily exclude one's developing them along other lines. Why can't the roles be developed along the lines of style or passionate syntax alone, for, as Berryman states in "A Note on Poetry," language "permit[s] one to say things that would not otherwise be said at all; it may be said, even that [language] permit[s] one to feel things that would not otherwise be felt." [16]

Homage to Mistress Bradstreet seems to strike an equilibrium between such theories of characterization. Anne Bradstreet's character is still delineated along novelistic lines. Like the poet she is alienated from the beliefs of her day, finding her gift of poetry ignored by her husband and her sensuality forced into submission. These qualities which are presented in a conventional stream-of-consciousness technique are enmeshed in an unconventional syntax that John Ciardi in "The Researched Mistress" (1957) describes as "a rhythm so intensely compacted and forward moving as to be a communication in itself." [17] The eight-line stanza the poem assumes is again, by Berryman's own indication, a variation of Yeats's "Major Gregory" stanza; but modifications like breaking the stanza "after the short third line," having the next four-beat line lead into a "balancing heroic couplet," then truncating the stanza again, and finally widening it into an alexandrine, produce a far less stately flow. As he suggests, the stanza is "at once flexible and grave, intense and quiet, able to deal with matters both high and low" (S, 72–73). His subject, he acknowledges, is Bradstreet as a woman rather than as a poet. "The point of the . . . poem," he told Kostelanetz, "was to take a woman unbelievably conventional and give her every possible trial and possibility of error and so on, and wind her up in a crazy love affair, and then get her out of it" (K, 345). The syntax which strives for comparably extraordinary effects continues by its very rejection of the ordinary the disaffection from Auden's social consciousness that the *Sonnets* commenced.

Berryman had begun the poem in 1948, thinking it might run "about seven or eight stanzas of eight lines each" (PR, 195); but he stuck after the first eleven lines. Not until reading a 900–page typescript of Saul Bellow's *The Adventures of Augie March* (1953) was the poet able to continue. He recognized in Bellow's novel "a breakthrough . . . the wiping out of the negative personality that had created and inhabited his earlier work" (PR, 198). Augie was nothing like Bellow; he was really an antithetical rather than an objectified self, and the characterization and scope of the work suggested that a comparable achievement in poetry might be possible. Berryman began to reconceive his poem as "a continuity of individual personality" that developed by shifts of association collecting about three occasions of rebellion, each "succeeded by submission, though even in the moment of the poem's supreme triumph . . . the birth of her first child—rebellion survives" (S, 74). The first of these rebellions at fourteen is ended by smallpox, and it concerns Bradstreet's acceptance of her body; the second involves her submission to the hardships of colonial life; and the last, which prompts her imagined romance with the narrator, concerns her submission to a loveless marriage. Out of the fusion of these rebellions Berryman hoped to construct a poem that might rival *The Waste Land* (1922) by offering what *The Dispossessed* had not—a heroine whose survival is inspiring.

Berryman proposes his response to Eliot in what he likes to insist is an "historical poem," even though he confesses that "the affair in the whole middle part of the poem is not historical but purely imaginary" (K, 345). Granting this whole middle part is a temporary lapse, one may still wonder at what kind of "history" *Homage* is. The work alternately suggests that it is historical in subject and in form, a twentieth-century attempt to reproduce a seventeenth-century dialogue of body and soul; yet the poem seems ever altering facts, and the particularly Donnean intensity of the language runs counter to Bradstreet's own preference for Guillaume du Bartas and Francis Quarles. Berryman admits that his heroine "was unbelievably devoted to her husband" (PR, 195); he also describes hugging himself one night, having decided that her "fierce dogmatic old father was going to die blaspheming, in delirium" (S, 74). Alan Holder in "Anne Bradstreet Resurrected" (1969) cites other discrepancies between the poem and its major source, Helen Campbell's *Anne Bradstreet and Her Time* (1891). Berryman has Bradstreet speak when Campbell indicates that she was silent; he intensifies her desire for children; he makes her a closer friend to Anne Hutchinson than it seems she had been; and he attributes to her the deforming effects of smallpox that Campbell assigns to Lucy Hutchinson. Berryman's only allusion to her poetry is to "The Four Monarchs" (stanza 12); he was willing generally to pronounce it dull and didactic; and, indeed, the neo-metaphysical language and intensity of his voice work against the neoclassical couplet that the real Bradstreet practiced.

Holder rightly asserts that the poem is "operating on the Yeatsian assumption that the artist's nature and his production are antithetical" [18]— that the interesting figure of Bradstreet is also a dull writer; but what Holder does not consider is that Bradstreet is herself an antithetical self for the poet. The work is, as Berryman proposes, "the construction of a world rather than the reliance upon one existent which is available to a small poem" (S, 75–76). Its system of verification is one of intrarelational elements. The constructed world does not hold its content for comparison to life so much as parts of its content compare to other internal elements along lines suggested by I. A. Richards in "The Interaction of Words" (1942) and expounded by the New Critics. The work may, as Berryman contends, be the "equivalent of a 500-page psychological novel" (PR, 197); but if it is a psychological novel, it is about Berryman as well as Bradstreet. It is a novel whose action repeats that of the passenger in "On the London Train" and the speaker of Berryman's Sonnets by creating and courting an ideal love whose actual verification is doubtful and whose existence, in the case of Bradstreet, is less significant than the "peculiar energy of the language" that Stanley Kunitz in "No Middle Flight" (1957) sees resulting from a galvanization of noun and verb and crystallizing Berryman's separate imaginative world. The "essence" of this energy, Ciardi contends, is "the compression of the language to squeeze out all but the most essential syntax (as well as some of that)" so that "relatively few unaccented syllables" remain "and the resultant clustering of heavy stresses, enforced by a heavy incidence of internal pause (caesura) thrusts the poem forward."

Despite Berryman's endorsements from Robert Fitzgerald, Edmund Wilson, Conrad Aiken, and Lowell, Kunitz proposes that "the poem as a whole lacks inherent imaginative grandeur; whatever effect of magnitude it achieves has been beaten into it"; and Ciardi is at a loss to determine "whether the passion is as truly love as he asserts, or more nearly a thing literary and made." [19] To put it another way, both critics were at a loss to determine whether the delight in craftsmanship lies in the craft that makes the subject visible or obscures it. Other critics tried to determine if Jarrell was right in holding that there may be "some last heat or pressure, concentration and individualization" that turns "a photograph into a painting, a just observation into a poem." That is the position of Lowell in "The Poetry of John Berryman" (1964). Lowell says of *Homage* that "nothing could be more high-pitched, studied and inflamed. One can read it many times, and still get lost in it; with each renewal it becomes clearer and more haunting." It would also be the position that A. Alvarez in *Under Pressure* (1965) would make typical of American writing: "The movement of the modern arts has been to press deeper and deeper into the subterranean world of psychic isolation, to live out in the arts the personal extremism of breakdown, paranoia, and depression." "The Extremist artist," he went on to say in a 1966 postscript to "Sylvia Plath," "sets out deliberately to explore the roots of his emotions, the obscurest springs of his personality, maybe even the sickness he feels himself to be prey to, 'giving himself over to it . . . for the sake of the range and intensity of his art.'" Hayden Carruth would later see something ominous in the growing remoteness of a poet's moving "from a real woman, to the ghost of a woman three centuries gone, to the phantasmagoric world of 'Henry' and 'Mr. Bones.'"[20]

Ciardi's indecision has been the position of most critics who, anticipating novelist characterization and following the lead of Fitts, have found more and more that Berryman's technique calls attention to itself. James Dickey, for example, would soon be complaining that "Berryman is a poet so preoccupied with poetic effects as to be totally in their thrall. . . . His inversions, his personal and often irritating cute colloquialisms and deliberate misspellings, his odd references, his basing of lines and whole poems on private allusions, create what must surely be the densest verbal thicket since Empson's." Jarrell, who was perhaps most responsible for pointing the direction, fell into public silence, content to praise the "intelligence" of Berryman in his "Fifty Years of American Poetry" (1962) rather than consider what must have been an awareness that there may be dangers in excessive heat or pressure, that the self-consciousness of Berryman's syntax had upset the normal balance of superego and id that Jarrell championed as the goal of postmodern verse.[21] Jarrell too must have been disturbed by Berryman's choosing to stress "eccentricity" over normalcy and by his making the "eccentric" writer the hero of culture. How by excluding himself from normative behavior could the poet resolve his vision into acceptable patterns? Berryman himself recurred to one of Jarrell's favorite writers, Rudyard Kipling, for his justification: "As Kipling used to say of his stories, 'I hold them up and let the wind blow through them, and if anything's left, I publish it'" (L, 76).

Berryman took to heart, however, Kunitz's statement that *Homage* lacked "inherent imaginative grandeur"; and in accepting the National Book Award twelve years later, he wondered how he "dared ever lift [his] head and trouble the public again."[22] Yet he did, and his "survival" provides the guiding image for his hero —a survivor too. Lowell accurately observed of the situation that "it's something to create a sensation when you're over fifty" (L, 68). Most poets retire at the age when Berryman was issuing the first installment of *Dream Songs*. Nonetheless, like Henry and the American Negro whose voice he often assumes, he had stuck it out; he had proved as expert as the Black in survival. As one critic observed of the Negro, "he is familiar with death and yet somehow continually picks himself off the very floor, clambers out of the very basement of modern civilization. Supremely a victim, he escapes self-pity through joy in survival. Like the cat, he has nine lives. Henry's search is to learn to be a cat, simply to continue, as coolly as possible, to play it by ear" (L, 71). Berryman himself adds: "Well, he's very brave, Henry, in that he keeps on living after other people have dropped dead." In "Henry Tasting All the Secret Parts of Life" (1965) Meredith associates this "survival instinct" generally "with every sort of person and situation," pointing out that it includes even the madmen: three of the songs (52–54) deal directly with insanity and a number of others touch on it with familiarity, making Henry in one way a latter-day, different antithetical self than had been Yeats's Crazy Jane and Tom the Lunatic.[23]

Berryman also moves to a different structure than the basically narrative method of *Homage*. He chooses one closer to that of the *Sonnets*, again basing its stanza on Yeats's *Words for Music Perhaps*. The "original design," as he reveals in song 379, for any would-be "assistant professors become associates / by working on his works" was blurred by "strange & new outlines." He told one interviewer (in 1969) that "some of the Songs are in alphabetical order; but, mostly, they just belong to areas of hope and fear that Henry is going through at a given time." "Its plot," he went on to explain, "is the personality of Henry as he moves on in the world. Henry gains ten years. At one time his age is given as forty-one, . . . and at a later point he's fifty-one" (HA, 5, 6). In song 112 he announces: "My framework is broken, I am coming to an end," and in song 348 he suggests that opposed to "the definite hole / in a definite universe . . . Henry & his surviving friends now truly confront" oblongs "when a whore can almost overthrow a government." These "oblongs" appear to have dimensions based in some way on 7, 11, and 5, the product of the first two being the number of songs in *77 Dream Songs*, and the product of the three (385), the total number of songs in the final collection. In "Cagey John" (1968) William Wasserstrom proposes that a numerical relation exists between the epigraph from Lamentations (3:63) and the structure of the first three parts. The parts break down into groups of 26, 25, and 26 songs respectively; and, with seven exceptions, the poems are "arranged in three verse paragraphs each six lines long"; but more significant Wasserstrom restores the first half-verse to Berryman's quotation and finds that its admonition— "behold their sitting down, and their rising up"—contains the germ of the minstrel show and death-and-resurrection motifs on which the poem is principally based.[24]

The total work's division into seven parts—an initial trivium followed by an enlarged quadrivium whose final poems, 384 and 385, echo poems 76 and 77 in the first collection—enforces the over-all importance of this number in the work's organization. The number may exist as a totality; or, since the groupings can be seen as two blocks of three separated by the "posthumous" dream songs, one can argue for a breakdown of seven into a 3–1–3 principle. Seven is important in the churches, trumpets, seals, angels, stars, etc. of the Book of Revelation to which on at least four occasions (songs 10, 46, 56, and 347) Henry alludes, aside from his making Christine Keeler (in song 348) into a pale reminder of the Whore of Babylon. One would not be too far afield in viewing the

128

combined work, as certainly Henry views it, as the chaos of the
Fourth Kingdom awaiting the Second Coming of Christ. Nonetheless Berryman rightly insists that the effect of the organization is
not an Apollonian structure but a process of expunging fear that
the conclusion of the book's opening epigraph from Lamentations
(3:57) anticipates. Later the quotations from Sir Francis Chiches-
ter and Major General Charles George Gordon will confirm Berryman's fear underlying the work, which, one gathers, is like the
abyss of which Pascal speaks: one is constantly putting obstacles
at the edge of it so as not to fall in. The condition is that of "the
doomed young envy[ing] the old, the doomed old envy[ing] the
young" (190); and the unique rhetoric is meant to become a way
of escape by separating its hero from its enemy, the fallen masses
of mankind.

The "irreversible loss" which prompts the poem's action and
which Henry suffers is presented to readers in song 1 as a falling
out with a "they" who were "trying to put something over" on
him. Henry thus feels the same sort of alienation that Berryman
describes for himself, and this alienation is suggested in the sequence by a series of criminal/outsider references. The "unappeasable" huffiness that Henry is made to feel at this falling out echoes
dimly the wrath of Achilles on which the *Iliad* begins; it indicates
as well a shift, in the terminology of David Riesman's *The Lonely
Crowd* (1950), to inner-directedness. The falling out constitutes
the discovery of the other or consciousness, often through opposition: one has limits; one extends only so far and at that point
something else takes over. Henry recalls that at one time he lacked
this sense: "All the world like a woolen lover / once did seem
on Henry's side." The differentiation which is implicit in this
separation generates a process of empirical self-definition along
what William James categorizes as spiritual, social, and material
lines. The differentiation allows as well the device of Yeatsian
masks by which Berryman had earlier defined self. Anthropologists like Claude Lévi-Strauss theorize that the separation forces
a simultaneous need for language, society, and the prohibition of
incest; and in *The Dream Songs* Berryman suggests the division
has resulted in the work's "original crime: art, rime" (26).

On a spiritual plane the separation has a counterpart in Adam's fall from Grace or Lucifer's fall from Heaven, and as the sequence opens, Henry is either hiding all day, as Adam hid after eating the forbidden fruit, or he is hidden from others by the day, as Lucifer in *Paradise Lost* is hidden after his fall. The separation has a psychological oedipal counterpart in man's fall from the womb (Eden) into the world, and Henry seems in the sequence to be greatly preoccupied with his mother (songs 11, 14, 100, 117, 129, 147, 166, 208, 317, and 322) and with birth. Imaged in terms of a lost bed-partner, the separation takes on social echoes from Plato's *Symposium* and Aristophanes' parable. There, as punishment for repeated assaults on Heaven, Zeus halved the essentially primeval man, so that man since, to achieve a feeling of his original fulness, has had to seek his complement. The material separations can be seen in Henry's various attempts to become the things he admires. But the intent of such a separation is ever to find a method for dissolving back into an original unity; and, in song 380, Henry recognizes that, as the content of his outcries does not constitute recognition of a dimension outside the self but an investment of objects with self, the autobiographical mode of Wordsworth's *Prelude* (1950) is the way:

> Wordsworth, thou form almost divine, cried Henry,
> 'the egotistical sublime' said Keats,
> oh ho, you lovely man!

As Yeats had indicated, one merges with his work by relating his own subjectivity to a second subjectivity rather than by the method of science which obscures personality by depersonalizing it.

The complexity of this integration of personalities as it deals with subjectively treated literary sources and with life processes completes the work's connection with the epigraph from Olive Schreiner. Her preface to *The Story of an African Farm* (1894) outlines two methods of painting life: the first, objective or stage method, by which characters are marshalled and ticketed along conventional plot lines; and the second, subjective or life method, in which "nothing can be prophesied. . . . Men appear, act and react upon each other, and pass away. . . . When the curtain falls, no one is ready."[25] Berryman claims the second method and its underlying subjectivity for *The Dream Songs*. The method allows him to invest his hero with an admittedly prejudiced awareness of

isolation—of his being "at odds wif de world & its god" (5)—
as well as with a recognition that one method of unification
lodges not in love, as it should, but in a threatening rhetoric of
conformity:

> It is in the administration of rhetoric,
> on these occasions, that—not the fathomless heart—
> the thinky death consists. . . . (10)

It permits him also to give Henry a sense of guilt, which Henry
then measures repeatedly against crimes like murder which he
judges are greater than his:

> But never did Henry, as he thought he did,
> end anyone and hacks her body up
> and hide the pieces, where they may be found. (29)

Such investments of subjectivity demand, in turn, that readers
adjust their normal expectations and view the various and often
repetitive roles of Henry and Berryman as single impersonations
controlled and colored by discrete shifting intelligences. Neither
impersonally realized places and situations nor Yeats's fixed and
clearly defined antithetical selves occur. Divorced from Henry and
Berryman, such places and situations might be showplaces for
presenting a single subjectivity, and the outrageous biases of both
voices exist as a block to such presentations. The world one
enters is relational rather than material, and, unlike the meditative
practices of Donne, Hopkins, and others, the observations that
one encounters are meant to be irreducible and unverifiable. The
relational emphasis of this world gains credence, moreover, by a
suppression of subjective devices like motivation, rationalization,
and recall that might otherwise cement verifiable continuity in the
characters of Henry and his creator. Henry's sense of isolation,
for instance, resists union by a rhetoric of conformity based on
will (language) for a "blind" discovery which is preverbal and
which, like the ending of *The Waste Land*, "passeth understanding." Songs 155 and 242 present prefigurations of this preverbal
world in Henry's silent communications with Delmore Schwartz
and a student, and song 366 reemphasizes that "these Songs are
not meant to be understood, you understand. / They are meant
only to terrify & comfort." The resolution with Berryman when

it occurs is based on an implicit but unexpressed continuity that suggests apparent discontinuity while simultaneously embodying love.

Berryman accomplishes the sense of apparent discontinuity which such a relational vision requires by returning again to two methods of mimesis. He will at times seem to be creating an imaginary world which is self-sufficient and independent of nature. At other times, as in the elegies of "The Lay of Ike," he will make pointed reference to a real outside world. In addition to this general discontinuity, he will use a rhetoric which confuses expectation by self-consciously altering normal syntax in a number of ways. He will, for example, invert normal sentence order so that subject-verb-complement becomes complement-verb-subject ("Hard on the land wears the strong sea / and empty grows every bed"); or he will use an emphatic verb when the reader might normally expect a simple tense ("All the world like a woolen lover / once did seem on Henry's side"); or he will shift from a simple to an emphatic mood ("never did Henry . . . end anyone and hacks her body up"); or he will leave out part of a progressive verb ("He wishing he could squirm again"); or he will violate the normal expectations of subject-verb agreement ("he don't feel so"). Likewise he will shift the usage levels of his language from standard to colloquial to vulgate, in the process resurrecting archaic words like "makar" for poet, infantilisms like "thinky" for "thoughtful," and slang. He will also shift his pronoun referents from first to second to third person and from singular to plural and, as in the opening song, dissolve his own "I" into Henry's "I." Henry will also convert adjectives into nouns ("said a screwed-up lovely 23"), adverbs into adjectives ("made Henry wicked & away"), use synecdoche ("Two daiquiris / withdrew into a corner of the gorgeous room / and one told the other a lie"), and displace modifiers so that ambiguity results ("Once in a sycamore I was glad / all at the top, and I sang." Does "all at the top" describe Henry's position on the tree or does it describe his state of mind?). Still, in the case of these breaches of expectation, if the discontinuity were real, fragmentation would occur; yet it does not.

The continuity which allows this apparent discontinuity while at the same time furthering the work's sense of a "long poem" is shaped by principles of recurrence. Blocking six lines into stanzas with regular rhymes suggests an initial mechanical unity that blocking three stanzas into separate songs conveys to the whole work. The blocking creates an "imaginary score" to contain the disjunctions, much as music in actual song by its recurrence contains disjunctive verses or as any mechanical procedure tends by its approach to unify results. These "imaginary scores" are reinforced by recurrent words, images, and attitudes as well as by the central figure of Henry. Henry, who represents Berryman's most original variation on the Yeatsian mask, tends repeatedly, as had the speaker of the *Sonnets*, to historicize his plights by comparing them to other famous events in history, or to dramatize them by imagining himself in movie roles, or to fictionalize them by relating them to previous literary situations. These multiple attitudinizings and taking of roles have been compared by critics to the transformations about a single psychological type that occur in *Finnegans Wake* (1939); but, perhaps owing to the absence of motivation and rationalization, they come to resemble more nearly what Stephen Leacock in "A, B, and C" (1910) calls "the human element of mathematics." Just as these famous characters of arithmetic problems become tokens to illustrate situations that devolve into mathematics, Henry becomes a token whose situations often relate immediately to a mathematics of syntax and on occasion more remotely to life. The perpetual editorializing that prevents one from viewing Henry independently, and thus forces one to accept or reject his authority, provides no room for deep understanding.

In constructing this new rhetoric which is also to define Henry's and his interlocutor's natures, Berryman makes abundant use of Freud's theories in *The Interpretation of Dreams* (1900) and *Wit and Its Relation to the Unconscious* (1905) on the way that thought functions both in dream work and in wit work. Both dream and wit have in common that they are reactions to censorship in conscious thought, working in dreams through condensation, displacement, and transformation of the optative into the indicative ("it is" for "would it were") and in wit through condensation, displacement, and indirect expression. In dreams censorship is overcome "regularly through displacements and through the choice of ideas which are remote enough from those objectionable to secure passage through."[26] In wit, which neither compromises with nor evades inhibition, the censorship is overcome by letting the unaltered or nonsensical ambiguity of words and multiplicity of thought relations appear to the consciousness at the same time admissible as jest or rational as wit. Thus the dream songs function to allow Henry access into experience which would normally be censored. He feels that he needs this access because he is now "unmistakably a Big One" (7) and does not feel like one (184). In fact, as the songs unfold, he fears that he will not go out in a blaze of glory like Yeats, Williams, Goya, and Beethoven, that his fate should be for various reasons of worthlessness that of Delmore Schwartz, who might "remember the more beautiful & fresh poems / of early manhood" (150).

If Freud provides the method of constructing rhetoric, the particular bidirectional stress that Berryman places on language derives its existence from the writings of Pound and R. P. Blackmur as well as the practices of writers like Cummings, Roethke, and Joyce. Pound in this regard enunciates "the feeling back," and he does so along what Ernest Fenollosa called "the ancient line of advance." As early as *How to Read* (1929) Pound had connected the poet's role to the preservation of language and culture: "The individual cannot think and communicate his thought, the governor and legislator cannot act effectively or frame his laws, without words, and the solidity and validity of these words is in the care of the damned and despised *litterati*. When their work goes rotten . . . i.e. becomes slushing and inexact, or excessive or bloated, the whole machinery of social and individual thought and order goes to rot." Blackmur in contrast outlines the "advance" in terms of new or fresh idiom: "language so twisted and posed in a form that it not only expresses the matter in hand but adds to the stock of available reality." In "Olympus" (1970) Berryman describes his coming across the Blackmur quotation during his last year at Columbia (1935–36): "I was never altogether the same man after *that*." In an early essay on Cummings (1930) Blackmur had denied to that poetic experimenter the value of "fresh idiom," branding the poet's use of Freudian wit and dream work "baby-talk."[27] Berryman would appropriate the term for the language of his own dream songs as if to emphasize his respect for both figures. Roethke, who had similarly employed a dream language in *The*

Lost Son (1948) and whose work Berryman taught along with that of Yeats and Whitman at the University of Iowa in 1954, seems also to have influenced Henry's creation. Less influential than some critics would maintain is the work of Joyce. Berryman refrains from portmanteau words and translingual punning and restricts his inventions to syntax rather than neologisms.

The stress that Berryman, by means of these writers, places on the language aspects of Freudian psychology in reconceiving characterization for *The Dream Songs* appears less arbitrary and eccentric in the light of the work Jacques Lacan was engaged in at approximately the same time. Acknowledging that creative writers had preceded him in many of his discoveries, Lacan proposes an interpretation of dream work based on the linguistic theories of Roman Jakobson and the anthropology of Lévi-Strauss. Lacan views Freudian dream theory as a grammar or phonology of the mind so that psychoanalysis becomes a kind of decoding device for condensed or displaced messages rather than a method of indicating disease. Using the metaphoric and metonymic poles of Jakobson to divide language into systems either of similarity and substitution or of contiguity and connection, Lacan sees dream in Straussean terms—as a network of symbolic exchanges where relationships between the exchangers rather than actual possession of objects are important. Pathology, in fact, occurs when one substitutes for this relation between persons a relation between body images and desires to accumulate that which is intended to serve only symbolically. In the matter of identity the linguistic "I" is not the subject except as a relation and becomes for Lacan "the ego" only as it assumes a body image or "false-self." Like Berryman he identifies this body image of self with a notion of mimesis based on mirroring. The image is constructed out of a series of identifications with or oppositions to an other, and by being so constructed, it loses track of the fact that the conceptualizer or the "I" is never fully realized in the conception or, as Berryman says of himself in relation to Henry, Henry does not have the poet's advantages of supervision.

Dream interpretation becomes as a result for both Lacan and Berryman a form of masking based on syntactical translation, and Berryman is fond of relating the various structures of dreams that he has been able to determine. In song 327, for instance, he claims to have once taken a dream "to forty-three structures, that / accounted in each for each word." Jane Howard reports that another Berryman dream, perhaps the one in which "he was cast as the Pope, dispatched on a mission of critical importance to Eastern Europe to check up on a malcontent Polish cardinal," yielded "thirty-eight structures—not levels, structures" (L, 75). But, as Lacan suggests, the gap that exists in such translations between the subject and the form of his expression can never fully be resolved even by a multiplicity of structures. Speech or discourse which tries to overcome this difference merely confirms the impossibility of filling up the hole which language itself creates. Even the disjunctions of syntax to enlarge language to include new emotions lead merely to new blocks that, in Pascalian terms, act as obstacles toward that abyss of pure being. In the views of both Lacan and Berryman, one must give up this notion perpetuated by science and by poets like Eliot and Williams that through language one can become transparent and assume rather that in this world everything must be relational and that out of this social relativity must come characterization.

Thus, by reinterpreting the mutually subjective Yeatsian masks as syntactical structures, Berryman manages to do in *The Dream Songs* what Roethke never quite succeeded in accomplishing by "taking a cadence" from the Irish poet—namely to achieve identity by using a second active intelligence. Berryman needs to achieve an identity in such terms because, like Jarrell, writing had for him become a kind of self-analysis and he was put off by the determinism implicit in Freud's perpetual looking back. In song 384, when the characterization of Henry is over and the actual dissolution of personae begins, one can assume that Berryman's possession is over and that the rhetoric which was a tacit recognition of a split that inaugurated the characterization is resolved appropriately into a silence. Henry's now being one with the author eliminates any need for words, and this oneness is the "death" which Henry speaks of in song 26 as resolving his "original crime." It involves no sacrifice of emotion to thought, merely the end of a relational existence by the end of relating. As in Rilke and Roethke this resolution is along the lines of a connaturality: one merges with what one contemplates because at a deep level there is an essential unity of all existence. Indeed *The Dream*

Songs repeats the message of "Song of Myself": one learns of all life's essential unity by feeling widely, and this wide feeling can best be accomplished by resisting glib conceptualizations. Readers of Berryman's volume are asked, as they are by Whitman, to confront individually a large number of incidents. These incidents are deeply moving, both for their pathos and their humor; and they work less to delineate dimensions in character than, like the extravagances of baroque music, to enlarge a reader's sensibilities. In their themes of survival they touch on Audenesque social concerns, and in their themes of alienation impinge on the Yeatsian outsider; but mainly by their stresses on fresh idiom, they emphasize the shift from biological to human relationships. "No ideas, but in things," Williams had insisted;[28] and here Berryman adds: "No humanity, but in adequate language."

Notes

1. William Carlos Williams, *Imaginations*, ed. Webster Schott (New York: New Directions, 1970), p. 55; John Bayley, "John Berryman: A Question of Imperial Sway," *Salmagundi* 22–23 (spring–summer 1973):86; William Carlos Williams, *Autobiography* (New York: New Directions, 1967), p. 241.

2. John Berryman, *The Dream Songs* (New York: Farrar, Straus and Giroux, 1969), p. vi. All references are to this edition. Karl Shapiro, "The Death of Randall Jarrell," in *Randall Jarrell: 1914–1965*, ed. Robert Lowell, Peter Taylor, and Robert Penn Warren (New York: Farrar, Straus and Giroux, 1967), pp. 195–229. Richard Kostelanetz, "Conversation with Berryman," *Massachusetts Review* 9 (1970), 346; hereafter referred to as K and page number.

3. Peter A. Stitt, "John Berryman 1914–1972," *Paris Review* 53 (winter 1972):193; hereafter referred to as PR and page number.

4. John Berryman, "A Note on Poetry," in *Five Young American Poets* (Norfolk, Conn.: New Directions, 1940), p. 47.

5. John Berryman, "One Answer to a Question," *Shenandoah* 17 (1965–66):69, 71, 67, 72; hereafter referred to as S and page number.

6. "A Note on Poetry," p. 46.

7. John Berryman, "Waiting for the End, Boys," *Partisan Review* 15 (1948):254.

8. Jane Howard, "Lines That 'needle, wheedle, singe and scarify'," *Life* 63 (21 July 1967):76; hereafter referred to as L and page number.

9. Randall Jarrell, "Verse Chronicle," *Nation* 167 (17 July 1948):80.

10. Daniel Hughes, "The Dream Songs: Spells for Survival," *Southern Review* (Australia) 2 (1966):8; Dudley Fitts, "Deep in the Unfriendly City," *New York Times Book Review*, 20 June 1948, p. 4; Jarrell, "Verse Chronicle," p. 81.

11. John Berryman, *Recovery* (New York: Farrar, Straus and Giroux, 1973), pp. 26–27; hereafter referred to as R and page number.

12. W. B. Yeats, *A Vision* (New York: Macmillan, 1956), p. 182; *The Variorum Edition of the Poems of W. B. Yeats*, ed. Peter Allt and Russell K.

Alspach (New York: Macmillan, 1957), p. 831; Yeats, *The Letters*, ed. Allan Wade (London: Rupert Hart-Davis, 1954), pp. 758, 814.

13. Hayden Carruth, "Declining Occasions," *Poetry* 112 (May 1968):120; William J. Martz, *John Berryman* (Minneapolis: University of Minnesota Press, 1969), p. 7.

14. John Berryman, "The Long Way to MacDiarmid," *Poetry* 88 (April 1956):59; Berryman, "The Poetry of Ezra Pound," *Partisan Review* 16 (1949): 388.

15. William Meredith, "In Loving Memory," *Virginia Quarterly Review* 49 (1972):73.

16. "A Note on Language," pp. 47–48.

17. John Ciardi, "The Researched Mistress," *Saturday Review* 40 (23 March 1957):36.

18. Alan Holder, "Anne Bradstreet Resurrected," *Concerning Poetry* 2 (spring 1969):16.

19. Stanley Kunitz, "No Middle Flight," *Poetry* 90 (July 1957):245, 246; Ciardi, "The Researched Mistress," p. 36.

20. Randall Jarrell, "Recent Poetry," *Yale Review* 45 (1955–1956):124; Robert Lowell, "The Poetry of John Berryman," *New York Review of Books* 2 (28 May 1964):3; A. Alvarez, *Under Pressure* (Harmondsworth: Penguin Books, 1965), p. 185; Alvarez, *Beyond All This Fiddle* (London: Allen Lane, 1968), pp. 57–58; Hayden Carruth, "Declining Occasions," p. 120.

21. James Dickey, *Babel to Byzantium* (New York: Farrar, Straus and Giroux, 1968), p. 198; Randall Jarrell, *The Third Book of Criticism* (New York: Farrar, Straus and Giroux, 1969), p. 330.

22. John Berryman, "Acceptance Speech," 12 March 1969.

23. John Berryman, "An Interview," *Harvard Advocate* 103 (spring 1969):6; hereafter referred to as HA and page number; William Meredith, "Henry Tasting All the Secret Parts of Life," *Wisconsin Studies in Contemporary Literature* 6 (1965):31.

24. William Wasserstrom, "Cagey John," *Centennial Review* 12 (1968):338, 339.

25. Cited in Hughes, "The Dream Songs," p. 9.

26. Sigmund Freud, *The Basic Writings*, ed. A. A. Brill (New York: Modern Library, 1938), p. 755.

27. Ezra Pound, *Literary Essays*, ed. T. S. Eliot (New York: New Directions 1954), pp. 21–22; John Berryman, *Love & Fame* (New York: Farrar, Straus and Giroux, 1970), pp. 18–19; R. P. Blackmur, *Form and Value in Modern Poetry* (New York: Anchor Books, 1957), pp. 337, 312.

28. William Carlos Williams, *Paterson* (New York: New Directions, 1963), p. 14.

6

The Cycles of History: Sylvia Plath

Sylvia Plath told listeners of the BBC shortly before her death that "I am not a historian, but I find myself being more and more fascinated by history and now I find myself reading more and more about history." The remark made in October of 1962 in an interview commissioned by the Harvard Poetry Room contrasts significantly with a statement that appeared in the February issue of the *London Magazine:* "The issues of our time which pre-occupy me at the moment are the incalculable genetic effects of fallout and . . . the terrifying, mad, omnipotent marriage of big business and the military in America." She claimed to be influenced by these issues only "in a sidelong fashion. . . . My poems do not turn out to be about Hiroshima, but about a child forming itself finger by finger in the dark." On both occasions she cites the influence of Lowell's *Life Studies* (1959) in helping her come to terms with her own emotional situation and craft, noting in the Harvard interview a belief "that personal experience is very important, but . . . it should be *relevant*, and relevant to the larger things, the bigger things such as Hiroshima and Dachau and so on." [1] No reader of *The Bell Jar* (1963) will mistake the impact of Lowell's "Memories of West Street and Lepke" (1958) on the structure of the novel. As in that poem Lowell had seen his own breakdown, shock treatments, and recovery in terms of the electrocution of Czar Louis Lepke of Murder Incorporated, Plath's heroine sets her own breakdown, shock treatments, and recovery against the electrocutions of Ethel and Julius Rosenberg.

Few readers can avoid the coincidences of her interests in fall-out, militarism, and concentration camps and the public discussions of militarism and the vast literature that attended the capture and impending trial of Adolf Eichmann. Atomic bomb-testing and radioactive fallout had been issues in the 1956 presidential campaign and continued as issues until 1963 when a test-ban treaty among the Soviet Union, the United Kingdom, and the United States was signed. The economy of the country seemed increasingly to owe its stability to what President Eisenhower called a "military-industrial complex," and the dependence was threatening not only to curb freedom in the United States but also to precipitate a new world war. Fred J. Cook had developed the history and implications of this "wedding" of arms and industry for an issue of the *Nation* (October 28, 1961), and Plath cites the issue as important. She could not have missed the equally "sensational" capture of Eichmann in Argentina in June of 1960. At least three books on the capture and the life of the former Nazi were issued in 1961 from British publishers together with an account by Rudolf Hess of his activities at Auschwitz. The year also saw the release of the motion picture *Judgment at Nuremberg* in addition to lengthy controversies about the jurisdiction and legality of the upcoming Eichmann trial. Like others of her generation Plath sensed an era of non-involvement ending. Her concern with these issues would mark an emergence from "silence" into an era of political and social activism. This new era would, in turn, require new attitudes toward both her surroundings and her self.

Some of the attitudes would be adopted from older, more politically involved poets like W. H. Auden, whom she told her interviewer she was "at one time . . . absolutely wild for" and whom she imitated and whose "age of anxiety" she appropriates in "General Jodpur's Conversion" (1961). Her allusion to "Daddy" and "Lady Lazarus" as "light verse" depends greatly on Auden's introduction to *The Oxford Book of Light Verse* (1938), which had recently been reissued. Auden insists that "light verse can be serious," and he gives as its distinguishing characteristics its having been "written for performance" and its "having for its subject-matter the everyday social life of its period or the experiences of the poet as an ordinary human being." The poems of *The Colossus* (1960), she told her BBC audience, were boring: "I didn't write them to be read aloud." She opposed their lack of flow to her "very recent work" which could be spoken and which, with its "stink of fat and baby crap," dealt intimately with everyday social life. Other attitudes would be derived from Yeats, whose poetry had already influenced such pieces as "Street Song" (pre–1957) and "Tinker Jack and the Tidy Wives" (1957) and whose tower at Ballylea she and her husband, Ted Hughes, had visited that summer. She had found the tower "the most beautiful & peaceful place in the world,"[2] and later that winter she would be excited by the coincidence of her moving into a flat in a house where Yeats had once lived. But she also shared with such contemporaries as W. D. Snodgrass views of having been socially conditioned; and Snodgrass's *Heart's Needle* (1959), detailing this conditioning, was then startling readers in England and the United States.

In *A Closer Look at Ariel* (1973) Nancy Steiner describes the torpid conditions from which the generation would be aroused. "The stereotyped Smith girl of the mid 1950's was a conformist, like thousands of undergraduates there and elsewhere, before and since." In this conformity she was no different from her male counterparts in other universities, who were being groomed to develop without radical innovations those vast programs that were started after World War II. The feeling Snodgrass expresses in "Returned to Frisco, 1946" (1957)—that members of his generation were being conditioned to choose exactly what their elders wanted them to choose—was general. David Riesman in *The Lonely Crowd* (1950) complained of "other directedness," and in certain circles existential "bad faith" was cant, and it was hoped that the outward conformity that was acutely visible might be offset by individual imaginative lives. In other circles Auden's bleak predictions of "Tract for the Times" (1941) and "A Note on Order" (1941) had come to pass. His sense that if man "does not consciously walk in fear of the Lord, then his unconscious sees to it that he has something else, airplanes or secret police to walk in fear of" seemed to have been confirmed by the regimentation he feared arose "when disorder is accepted as inevitable but has reached a point where it is felt as intolerable."[3]

Richard Wilbur in "Mind" (1954) tried to neutralize the seriousness of the situation by indicating that mind "in its purest play" is able through "a graceful error" to "correct" the physical limits of the world so as "not to conclude against a wall of stone." Discussions of André Gide's "gratuitous act" became fashionable; and Rainer Maria Rilke's "unicorn" (*Sonnets to Orpheus*, 2:4), which "happened" because room was left for "the possibility that it might be," appeared in several new guises and contexts. "Reason" and "common sense," which had been the methods used to coerce acceptance by the "grey" organizational men who wander throughout Plath's poetry, were made to appear subversive. One placard of the times announced: "Be Reasonable. . . . Do it my way"; and often in Plath's early poems, her speaker chooses an imaginative life to these forces of conformity. Yet, even in the dream states that typify the poems, Plath realizes that life without affirmative systems of value is destined to end in either disappointment, insanity, or annihilation. Both the "clam-diggers" of "Dream with Clam-Diggers" (1957) and the "snowman" of "The Snowman on the Moor" (1957), for example, threaten the speaker's existence; and poems like "Recantation" (1957) advise one to "foreswear those freezing tricks of sight," just as Plath had foresworn her isolation during her sophomore year of college to "do good" at the People's Institute in Northampton "with [her] white hands." Much as Plath claimed to be little bothered by conformity, she still felt the need to "sneak in the rear door" if she was without a date on Saturday night.

During this period of non-involvement Plath had chosen to submerge her political and social interest in the mythic method of Joyce, the "vegetal radicalism" of Theodore Roethke, evolution, and the psychological oppositions of Dostoevsky. Her senior honors paper at Smith was to be a study of the double in the works of Joyce and the topic undoubtedly brought her into contact with his uses of paradigms from classical works to illuminate present circumstances and with Eliot's explanation of the method in "Ulysses, Order, and Myth" (1923). Joyce's view of history had presumed that events recur, if not exactly, with enough approximation that their patterns can be seen whole and their ends predicted by what had previously been ends. The determinism of such a view was supported by a curriculum of Great Books whose unexpressed justification was often an attempt to reduce faction by imposing a common regimen or to use history as a means to settle the future. For a student whose life seems to have been as sheltered as Plath's, these classics in translation could be deeply moving. Ted Hughes in "Notes on the Chronological Order of Sylvia Plath's Poems" (1966) asserts that, in fact, they were: "The mention of Oedipus, and the Greek Tragedians' figures elsewhere, may seem literary, but if one can take her dream life as evidence, those personalities were deeply involved in her affairs."[4]

"The Eye-Mote" (1960) and "The Colossus" (1960) affirm that her "manipulating a continuous parallel between contemporaneity and antiquity" as "a way of controlling, of ordering, of giving a shape and a significance" to contemporary history approximated something closer to the "lived myth" of Thomas Mann's "Freud and the Future" (1936) than the mechanical congruences of Eliot. The poems show her accepting what Rachel Bespaloff in *On the Iliad* (1943) terms "heroic" stature by having her speakers assume "total responsibility even for that which they had not caused." Both speakers confound classical necessity with individual choice in terms comparable to those that Auden in "The Dyer's Hand" (1955) had carefully distinguished by using *Oedipus Rex* and *Macbeth*. "Oedipus himself has no history, for there is no relation between his being and his acts. . . . In *Macbeth*, on the other hand, every action taken by Macbeth has an immediate effect upon him so that, step by step, the brave bold warrior we hear of in the first scene turns before our eyes into the guilt-crazed creature of the 'tomorrow and tomorrow and tomorrow' soliloquy."[5] The result in the first instance is pity that "it had to be this way," and in the case of *Macbeth* "pity it was this way when it might have been otherwise." In Plath's "The Colossus" there is no sense of other alternatives as the speaker accepts the task of putting back together the greatness of the ancient world, symbolized by the *Oresteia*, the Roman forum, and most importantly the Colossus of Rhodes. The impossibility of reconstructing that bronze "wonder" of the ancient world, felled in 225 B.C. by an earthquake, foreshadows the poem's concluding failure.

In converting the actions of these poems from choice to necessity, Plath invents for herself a world where the sins of the fathers are visited on children. In "The Eye-Mote" the "sin" presumably is having been born. In "The Colossus," as in "Electra on the Azalea Path" (1960), the "sin" is being overly attached to a dead father. The speakers gain by the attachment a dimension like the curse of Atreus translated into psychoanalytic complexity. Both have lives arrested by accident and beyond reparation. In "The Colossus" the speaker decides to wait no longer for the ship that brings her release, and in "Electra on the Azalea Path" she feels that she and her father have been "undone" by the long sterile attachment. These "necessary" actions contrast with the poet's earlier depiction of a father's death in "Lament" (1955). Here "the sting of bees" takes the father away and, while he otherwise triumphs over nature, one has no sense that he is the destructive hovering shade of the later poems. If these later poems are, as some critics have assumed, merely transcriptions and not the artistic reworkings of material that has been augmented, cropped, and revised to suit the occasion, one is tempted to say that Plath has become so enamored of the mythic method that she is willing to accept its principles as determinative in life as well as art. Indeed there is a sense in which like the young St. Augustine, she seems in her work to be more deeply responsive to art than to life.

Much as Plath goes to Joyce for a comprehension of displaced events, she goes to Roethke for a concept of total pattern. The *London Magazine* interview includes mention of Roethke's "greenhouse poems" as being informative, and by the time Plath collected her work into the British edition of *The Colossus*, Anne Sexton could reproach the poet about the effects. Sexton recalled "saying something like . . . 'if you're not careful, Sylvia, you will out-Roethke Roethke,'" and in "The Barfly Ought to Sing" (1966), she gives as Plath's response "that I had guessed accurately and that he had been a strong influence on her work." This "influence" settles most markedly in "Poem for a Birthday," five of whose seven sections were deleted from the American edition (1962) of the collection. Hughes dates the start of the influence as the fall of 1959 when he and his wife were at Yaddo embarking on a combination of exercise and meditation. Plath began a serious study of Roethke and read Paul Radin's *African Folktales and Sculpture* (1952), and Hughes believes the combination provided a break with her early style and "the first eruptions of the voice that produced *Ariel*." Eileen Aird sees the transition from Plath's mythic poems to this vegetal radicalism as being more direct and evolutionary. "The reference to 'Mother Medea' [in "Aftermath"] may seem over-literary, but the figures of Greek mythology appear quite frequently in Sylvia Plath's early poetry, fulfilling in a more muted way the function of historical [natural?] references of the later poetry, by providing concrete examples of pain against which the personal experience of the poet can be projected." [6]

Some of what Plath derived from Roethke he had in turn adapted from Rilke. As early as "Rilke in English" (1939) Auden had proposed the direction of the German poet's "most immediate and obvious influence." In contrast to Shakespeare, who "thought of the non-human world in terms of the human, Rilke thinks of the human in terms of the non-human, of what he calls Things." This thinking resembles not only that of children for whom "tables, dolls, houses, trees, dogs, etc., have a life which is just as real as their own or that of their parents" but also that of the African folktales Radin assembled, in which things and animals are given comparable reality. Roethke had converted to natural metaphors what was ostensibly in Rilke a notion that life and death form one complete cycle of existence and that any lesser view distorts life. For Roethke the cycle becomes that of vegetal growth, harvest, and rebirth. In poems like "Weed Puller" the root life of plants (death) becomes the underside of "everything blooming above me" (life), and in later poems of *The Lost Son* (1948), this vegetal cycle shapes an interior mind where subsurface turns subconscious and oversurface becomes superego. Without relinquishing Rilke's belief that the function of poetry is praise, Roethke expresses a view of art that is a kind of fishing "patiently, in that dark pond, the unconscious" or a diving in "to come up festooned with dead cats, weeds, tin cans, and other fascinating debris." Each poem in *Praise to the End!* (1951) was to be "in a sense . . . a stage in a kind of struggle out of the slime; part of a slow spiritual progress; an effort to be born, and later, to become something more." [7]

Both Roethke and Rilke had been able to tap into knowledges of these cycles through processes of meditation that resemble those described by Plath in "On the Plethora of Dryads" (1957) and "The Wishing-Box" (1957). Published two years before the interval at Yaddo, both works suggest that the exercises may themselves go back to earlier efforts to recover her imagination after her attempted suicide and shock treatments in 1953. Nancy Steiner recalls how at the onset of Plath's return to Smith after her breakdown, she had fears that the sharp intelligence that had made her an honors student was damaged by electrotherapy. In the course of that final year, the fears were allayed as Plath's memory returned and her control over the direction of her life solidified. "On the Plethora of Dryads" suggests that part of the exercises consisted in "starving my fantasy down / To discover that metaphysical Tree." "The Wishing-Box," which appeared in *Granta* shortly after her marriage to Hughes, tells of a wife whose present ability to dream in no way matches the imaginative drift she once had or that her husband currently exercises. In order to regain her "powers of imagination," she responds to his demands to "imagine a goblet" and to describe the goblet for him. He asks her to elaborate the description until he is satisfied that the image is palpable. She continues the recovery on her own until finally she manages to recapture in suicide the full powers that she had as a girl.

The process of imagining objects as existing before one's eyes until they assume a reality of their own is similar to what Ignatius of Loyola makes basic to his *Spiritual Exercises* and to what Louis L. Martz in *The Poetry of Meditation* (1954) describes as existing for poets like John Donne and Gerard Manley Hopkins. For Plath as for Roethke the "pond" or "slime" is created by associations that attach themselves to objects until the Sartrean-like "nausea" becomes an underworld of nightmares, and the individual psyche melts into a primal general sleep. "Johnny Panic and the Bible of Dreams" (1968) describes for readers the "sewage farm of the ages," whose water "naturally stinks and smokes from what dreams have been left sogging around in it over the centuries. . . . Call the water what you will, Lake Nightmare, Bog of Madness, it's here the sleeping people lie and toss together among the props of their worst dreams, one great brotherhood, though each of them, waking, thinks himself singular, utterly apart." Ever "since the apes took to chipping axes out of stone and losing their hair," these dreams have been accumulating.[8] In this story they end in their being burned out in the worst nightmare of all—electrotherapy. The story suggests that the fear of relapse into chaos lingered far beyond that final year at Smith, and Nancy Steiner's report on the poet's hysteria on occasions when she lost control of herself or the ability to think confirms Plath's own carefully expressed anxiety over the possible nature of the recovery—that it was only cosmetic.

Poems like "Snakecharmer" (1959) suggest the probability of a direct influence from Rilke. Olwyn Hughes acknowledges that Plath was impressed by Rilke, whose work she knew in German and had tried translating. Margaret Newlin in "The Suicide Bandwagon" (1972) cites "Black Rook in Rainy Weather" (1957) as containing obvious echoes of Rilke and other readers have seen the recurrent "pure angels" of Plath's poetry as a second direct influence. Ostensibly based on Henri Rousseau's *The Snake Charmer* (1907), the Plath poem recounts a controlled meditation similar to that of Rilke's "Spanische Tänzerin." Both poems use performers to invoke moods that are eventually disrupted. Music is suggested as a control on the Dionysian worlds that the speakers sense take over. The snake charmer rules his snakedom and the snake-rooted bottom of his mind much in the same ways that the dancer controls, with her movements, the dangerous "consuming flames" and castanets' "snake" rattle and that myth in Eliot's review controls at a further remove the disorder of contemporaneity. Ignoring this aspect of Rilke's art, Ted Hughes is willing to compare the poem's vision to that "specific vision revealed to yogis at a certain advanced stage," but the "control" makes equally discernible Plath's hesitation in accepting the unmediated "invitation of her inner world" that both "Lorelei" and "Full Fathom Five" later represent.[9]

These two sea poems seem influenced not so much by Rilke as by Loren Eiseley's *The Immense Journey* (1957) and Eiseley's positing of the naturalist's analogue to Roethke's associative regressive meditation. Eiseley speaks of a lucky "once in a lifetime" when "one so merges with sunlight and air and running water that whole eons . . . might pass in a single afternoon without discomfort. The mind has sunk away into its beginnings among old roots and the obscure tricklings and movings that stir inanimate things." In the book Eiseley discredits the belief of Sir Charles Thomson's *The Depth of the Sea* (1873) that in the layers of the ocean "was the world of the past" where "down at the bottom . . . lay that living undifferentiated primordial ooze as deep in the sea as it lay deep in time."[10] Yet the very presentation of the view could have stimulated Plath's mind to accept its substance. The speakers of both lyrics wish to abandon the shore for the life-generating depths that have fathered all existence. They fear a lack of rapport with nature that "a well-steered country, / Under a balanced ruler" might bring about. In this fear they resemble Ferdinand in Shakespeare's *The Tempest* (1611), who may have lost his father and his ties with the past but not his sympathy with water. Ariel's song on Alonso's suffering "a sea-change" allays Ferdinand's fury and passion and prepares him for the "rebirth" that will occur on the island. A similar rebirth may be suggested by the submerging and stone/seed imagery that figure in the poems.

The two lyrics are, according to Hughes, inspired by the same essay by Jacques-Yves Cousteau. The essay is most likely his "*Calypso* Explores an Undersea Canyon," which appeared in the March 1958 issue of the *National Geographic*. The article relates "fathom by fathom" the crew's dropping anchor and then lowering an undersea camera five miles beneath the ocean's surface into the Romanche Trench. Never before had man probed so deeply with anchor or camera, and the account seems specifically echoed in the title, "Full Fathom Five," as well as by the phrases "archaic trenched lines" and "labyrinthine tangle." The surprising calm which the marine biologists discovered existing at that depth may well have prompted the lines of "Lorelei": "They sing / Of a world more full and clear / Than can be," although one should not ignore the obvious sea/Death and turret echoes of Poe's "The City in the Sea" (1831, 1845). The biologists discovered several species of sea life that had not previously been known to exist, and they found other species long believed to be extinct, whose recovery constitutes a kind of rebirth. Even without evidence of any "primordial ooze" further down, the existence of this primitive world beneath the surface of the ocean invites a parallel to the human mind and the conscious/subconscious stratification of Roethke's vegetal landscape and supports the notion of the sea as an image for meditation.

The honors paper that Plath eventually did on the double—not in Joyce but Dostoevsky—would have lent to these processes of meditation an almost psychoanalytic concept of the double. The concept would be based on opposition rather than congruence. The opposition would add up either to a third figure containing both or to a cancellation of what each half-figure represents. "Two Sisters of Persephone" (1957) demonstrates how the concept would be carried into Plath's poetry in terms of a nature myth. Here the Greek vegetation goddess, whose six months on earth and six months below earth embrace an explanation of the seasons, inspires the elaboration of the poem's two girls. One, who lives indoors "in the dark, wainscotted room," is finally "worm-husbanded" without ever becoming a wife. The second, who ventures outdoors, becomes "the sun's bride," grows quick with seed, and bears a king (Perseus?). More often, however, the opposition is divorced from these Joycean overtones of myth and left as some kind of split personality. "In Plaster" (1962), for instance, divides its speaker into a "new absolutely white person" and an "old yellow one"; and it appears from what Nancy Steiner has written and from *The Bell Jar* that the poem's notion of alter personalities was present in Plath's friendships as well.

A reading of *African Folktales and Sculpture* reinforces the sense that the eruption of Plath's mature voice was not quite so improvisational as her work later became. Both "Maenad" and "The Stones" from "Poem for a Birthday" use material out of Radin's anthology in much the same way that the wife of "The Wishing-Box" begins to recover her imagination by means of movies, alcohol, and television; and the heroine of "Johnny Panic and the Bible of Dreams" explores the dreams of other people in preparation for her realizing history's consummate nightmare. In using tales like "The Bird That Made Milk" and "The City Where Men Are Mended," Plath reshapes their temporary disappearances of children (seeds) so as to discount Radin's warning that the stories not be looked at as a representation of a primitive society "belonging to the lower stages of man's development." Rather, as in the case of Thomson, she prefers to believe Charles Darwin's view of the continent as the place where apes first took on human characteristics. The view had recently been revived by "prehistorians" like Pierre Teilhard de Chardin and by such finds as L.S.B. Leakey's *Sivapithecus* (1953) and *Zinjanthropus boisei* (1959), and her acceptance of their work is not striking. Plath also seems to accept Robert Petsch's less provable position that the folktales of aboriginal peoples "are concerned exclusively with descriptions of what transpires before one's eyes and have as their ultimate purpose, primarily, the heightening of the sense of existence." The lessening of linear narrative in her writing for the

149

present tense and the quick associative dreamlike shifts that Ted Hughes terms "the improvisational nature" of the later poems owe much to the way that these folktales move. Like their narrative threads, these poems flow and turn at whim, never relinquishing their sense of immediacy and often assuming only the most subconscious links in joining incidents and images.

Nor does the stylistic influence of these tales stop merely with the matter of narrative. Plath's inability to accept institutional religions allows her to experiment with the view of man that Radin describes. "Contrary to the belief widespread throughout the world, man in aboriginal Africa is never thought of as having once possessed a portion of divinity and having subsequently lost it." The reverse is true. African myth is so geocentric that "the gods of native Africa . . . must lose their earthly constituent, their earthly adhesions, before they can become properly divine." Similarly the tales allow her to merge the wish-fulfillment fantasies of the *Märchen* proper with the human heroes of these stories whose plots derive from purely human situations. Radin infers that this difference of folktales from *Märchen* results from an "economically and politically disturbed and insecure world." "Assuredly we have the right to infer that it is largely because these people are living in an insecure and semi-chaotic world, with its loss of values and its consequent inward demoralization, that cruelty and wanton murder loom so large in many of their tales. . . . Yet to judge from the very tales where cruelty and murder are the main themes, . . . the author-raconteur felt it necessary to attach to them a clear cut moral. . . . Death is the inevitable fate of those who fail to resist disorganization, and that outward disorganization is followed remorselessly by inward disintegration." [11]

"The Manor Garden" and "Two Views of a Cadaver Room" open *The Colossus* and establish the ranges of the nature myth as it appears in that collection. Written while the poet was at Yaddo in the first months of her pregnancy, "The Manor Garden" opposes the harvest of nature to the growing foetus within the speaker. As the outer world comes to represent death, the child moves "through the era of fishes," reliving in its development the history of evolution. It will be born into a world whose sickness and dying will become "fits," and presumably the child's life, like that existence described in "The Colossus," will be one of reconstruction.

"Two Views of a Cadaver Room" repeats the theme on a more personal plane. Using the image of a dissecting room that will reappear in *The Bell Jar*, Plath juxtaposes the bodies of grown men that the medical students dissect to the foetuses that science has pickled for the same purpose—of learning how to cure sickness. By gaining knowledge from the dead, science comes to imitate in a dispassionate way the natural process of return that "The Manor Garden" describes. This imitation of nature extends to art in the second half of the poem as Pieter Brueghel's *The Triumph of Death* (c. 1562) replaces the cadaver room. The lust of the lovers in the painting's right-hand corner forms an oasis from the "panorama of smoke and slaughter" that comprises the rest of the panel. Their passion replaces the sterile atmosphere of the scientist but not with any gentler feeling.

Plath's relegation of survival (rather than suffering) to one corner of the poems seems immediately to respond to Auden's famous "Musée des Beaux Arts" (1939) as well as to the poet's own earlier indecision about her own career. She told her Harvard interviewer that "I think if I had done anything else I would like to have been a doctor." Hughes relates that "the chemical poisoning of nature, the pile-up of atomic waste, were horrors that persecuted her like an illness." Less immediately present are her responses to "the great civilized crime of intelligence" that Bertrand Russell and others were enunciating. For them civilization had reached a point where survival not comfort was its key accomplishment. Russell's "The Future of Mankind" (1950) argued three results if atomic war broke out: (1) "The end of human life, perhaps of all life on our planet"; (2) "A reversion to barbarism after a catastrophic diminution of the population of the globe"; and (3) "A unification of the world under a single government, possessing a monopoly of all the major weapons of war." [12] It appears that Plath had personally reduced the options to two: she subscribed to either a doomsday or a reversion to barbarism in which, as Radin states for Africa, an "outward disorganization" precedes the "inward disintegration." In both cases the "progress" that a war would bring about is a return of civilization to its "seed" form in much the manner that Plath describes for nature.

"The Thin People" (1959) embodies one of Plath's earliest efforts to move from this myth of nature into social and political concerns. The poem centers on an image of famished people that the speaker as a child saw in newsreels. These victims of "a war making evil headlines" had discovered "the talent to persevere / In thinness"; yet the "talent" remains expressed in the same terms that Plath's other protagonists embrace. Thinness becomes a "seed," and like seeds the thin people go from darkness into "the sunlit room" where not even forests can arrest "their stiff battalions." "The Disquieting Muses" (1959) confirms this sense that human action is "necessary" rather than "willful." The poem presents its speaker in terms that Auden reserves for Oedipus. It confounds the wishes of the godmothers of "Sleeping Beauty" with the fate woven by the Norns. The mother who would have her daughter oppose like Oedipus the fate that she has been granted is asked to accept responsibility for the suffering which she has caused the speaker to bear. In making the request, the speaker—as she does in other poems—extenuates nothing and blames the parents for everything. Fixing blame seems to be the important process in the poems that Plath wrote during and just after her classes with Lowell, and it may reflect not only his influence but the influence of Sexton as well. Yet, by the time Plath began "Getting There" (1963), fixing blame seems to be less important than purging guilt. The poem describes travel to a Nazi concentration camp in boxcars as a kind of Yeatsian "dreaming back." The trip is a purification rite, a stripping back of the shell of civilization until an infantile "purity" is reached. For Yeats the process was necessary so that the spirit could separate itself from the passionate body and be reborn in a manner very much like that of plants.

One may associate this process of "dreaming back" in Plath's poems with psychoanalysis and what Auden calls Freud's major contribution to modern thought—his treating neurosis historically —but to do so would be an error. Freud's process is a method by which the conscious comes to understand and purge itself of obsessive action; it does not promise innocence—or, as does "Lady Lazarus" (1963), superhuman status. It remains, as Auden indicates, in the area of human behavior. "Insomniac" (1961), which deals with "dream" in Freudian terms, has the night dissolve into "white disease" and "trivial repetitions" rather than the "celestial burning" of "obtuse objects" that "Black Rook in Rainy Weather" (1957) makes a forerunner of the ovens of "Mary's Song"

(1963). There the heretics and Jews are viewed in language that deliberately recalls the "sages standing in God's holy fire" of Yeats's "Sailing to Byzantium" (1927). They burn until their being made translucent comes to be equated to Christ, and the speaker like the Communion Host is killed and eaten. The "meal" is possible, Plath maintains, because the world has not had its heart consumed away. The residual heart is the oven and holocaust through which the Jews and the poem's speaker must both proceed. If supported by a source other than Yeats, the process might derive from Radin's description of the loss of earthly constituents and adhesions that man undergoes in aboriginal Africa to become divine.

Plath's objections to Freud are lengthily expounded in "Johnny Panic and the Bible of Dreams," one of two stories she wrote based on her experiences as a secretary to a Boston psychiatrist during autumn 1958. Opposed to the "dream-stopper," the "dream-explainer," and the "exploiter of dreams for the crass practical ends of health and happiness," Plath's narrator would be "that rare character, rarer, in truth, than any member of the Psychoanalytic Institute: a dream connoisseur." Dreams become her means for singling out people rather than classifying them, for as one typing transcriptions of dreams, she finds dreams more individualizing than "any Christian name." Yet the very worst dreams collectively make up her single Lake Nightmare and turn the dreamers into "one great brotherhood" of those who have witnessed "unfinished messages from the great I Am." These deeper dreams force patients "to a place more permanent" than the clinic where the narrator works. Her "psyche-doctors" thrive on conformity as they labor daily "to win Johnny Panic's converts from him by hook, crook, and talk, talk, talk." They refuse to "forget the dreamer and remember the dream" or recognize that "the dreamer is merely a flimsy vehicle for the great Dream-Maker himself." They stand for proper social behavior and present rationally what the narrator would have remain a mystery, though one is perhaps not to accept as Plath's the bleakness of the narrator's final vision. The narrator sees herself a Jeremiah willing to visualize "the slaughterhouse at the end of the track" and accept a love that is suicide.[13] One may suppose, instead, that like Lowell's "Skunk Hour" (1958), the emotions comprise "an Existential night" in which the writer reaches some point of final darkness where the one free act is suicide, and she emerges from the experience stronger and less sure.

The Bell Jar continues in a more implicit way many of the arguments that begin in the story. Freud's formulaic allegorizing of human action into Ego and Id becomes part of the "shrinking everything into letters and numbers" that provokes Esther's revulsions to physics, chemistry, and shorthand. In the novel, Joan chatters about egos and ids with Doctor Quinn whereas Esther "never talked about Egos and Ids with Doctor Nolan." Since Doctor Nolan is the successful psychiatrist and Joan the lesbian and suicide, one presumes that Freud's use here is as negative coloring. This presumption is strengthened by Esther's own statement about analysis: "I had hoped, at my departure, I would feel sure and knowledgeable about everything that lay ahead—after all, I had been 'analyzed.' Instead, all I could see were question marks." Esther attributes to electrotherapy the purging of heat and fear that make up her "bell jar." Yet, however much these attitudes toward Freud are negative, they do not offset the excitement Plath reports feeling in the "emotional and psychological depth" of Sexton's poetry or in her own view of poetry as "sensuous and emotional experiences . . . manipulated with an informed and intelligent mind." Her poems remain squarely in the psychological tradition of Auden and the generation of poets that emerged after him. Like Randall Jarrell she believes art to be "the union of a wish and a truth" or a "wish modified by a truth," but because her "truths" deal often with obsessions, her poems appear open less to what Auden's "Squares and Oblongs" (1957) designates as "man's historical order of being" than to what he calls "the natural, reversible, necessary order." The effect is to give the poetry the appearance of being written by a writer who does not care much about book publication, reputation, critical accolades, awards, or whatever, but merely, as Stephen Spender asserts, about being able to express in her best poems "controlled uncontrolledness." [14]

A hiatus in Plath's development followed the Hugheses' return to England and the birth of their daughter before the poet began in early 1962 to recover her "*Ariel* voice" with the writing of "Elm" and "The Moon and the Yew Tree." Plath had already

abandoned the methodical composition that she practiced at
Smith, "plodding through dictionary and thesaurus searching for
the exact word" to create her poetic effects. Now she wrote "at
top speed, as one might write an urgent letter." [15] "Elm" shows
her still caught up in the Roethkean systems of meditation and
correspondence between the human and nonhuman. Based on an
enormous tree that stood over the Hugheses' house in Devon, the
poem presents associations whose intent is again to "know the
bottom." The tree is "inhabited by a cry" which nightly flaps out,
"looking, with its hooks, for something to love" and which daily
terrifies the tree's existence with "its soft, feathery turnings, its
malignancy." "Incapable of more knowledge," the tree/speaker
identifies her fear as "the isolate, slow faults / That kill, that kill,
that kill." Completed shortly afterward, "The Moon and the Yew
Tree" already shows evidence of a Yeatsian influence with its conflict of religions. Originally an exercise suggested by Hughes, the
poem centers on the church and yew tree that stood opposite the
front of their home and goes beyond the simple correspondences
of Roethke to a tension between chthonic and Christian forces
similar to that of Yeats's "The Unappeasable Host" (1896). In the
Plath poem, color does most of the work of aligning forces. Those
of nature are black whereas the "light of the mind," like Mary
and the interior of the church, is "blue and mystical." Douglas
Cleverdon recalls that early in 1962 Plath was asked by the BBC to
do a radio play, and her work on the verse play may well have
set off a fresh reading of Auden, Eliot, and Yeats.

   "Fever 103°" again takes up the Yeatsian image of purging fire,
this time represented by the atomic destruction of Hiroshima.
A. Alvarez ventures that the poem may well have been spawned
by a viewing of *Hiroshima mon amour* (1959), but the popularity
of John Hersey's *Hiroshima* (1946) and the ongoing discussion
of the effects of atomic fallout in promoting the test-ban treaty
should be considered. The title is meant to convey an enormously
high temperature, and the opening word "pure" immediately sets
the work's theme. Fever is the body's method of "burning out"
impurities. Here, the fever proves as inept as Cerberus at "licking
clean . . . the sin, the sin." A vision of Isadora Duncan follows:
rolls of smoke seem to surround the speaker much as scarves sur-
rounded and strangled rather than cleansed the dancer. The image

which seems to be set off superficially by an association of the smoke with scarves is cemented by Yeats's use of the dancer in his image of dreaming back. The smoke becomes a cloud of atomic radiation covering (as it had) the inhabitants of Hiroshima and eating away everything. The radiation becomes the speaker's sin as she turns from her own thoughts to address her love. Like Christ's descent into hell, her "purging" had lasted three days and made her "too pure . . . for anyone." She is a lantern, her skin "gold beaten"; she is "a huge camellia / Glowing"; in short she is again one of Yeats's "dancers" or "sages burning in a holy fire." Her selves dissolve like "old whore petticoats" as she nears Paradise. Plath has identified the fires of the poem as "the fires of hell, which merely agonize, and the fires of heaven, which purify";[16] but it is clear that rather than discrete fires, one has, as in Yeats, a single continuous fire which begins in the agony of burning off the world and ends in "flames that do not singe a sleeve."

"Candles" (1960) suggests that the "fires" of these poems may also go back to Walter Pater, from whom scholars conjecture Yeats derived his "purging fires." Pater's entreaty in the conclusion to *The Renaissance* (1873) that one burn with "a hard, gem-like flame" is reversed as the birth of a child is seen as a hardening of lucent tallow into pearl. The hardening suggests the process of return or metempsychosis in Yeats. Metempsychosis is likewise a theme in Joyce's *Ulysses* and would figure in any study of the double in his writing, and rebirth is a theme in both of the folktales that Plath takes from Radin. Certainly the determinism and the myth of nature underlying her work encourage the concept of return, but "Cut" (1963) suggests that the "purging," as in the poetry of Rilke and Roethke, is more mystical than generative. The speaker's recounting of her slip while she sliced an onion that ended in a cut thumb defines the relationship between the personal and the racial as connatural rather than reincarnational. The plasmic structure of the blood contains within its chemical make-up a history of mankind, and the poem seems to say with its series of associations that Plath's Lake Nightmare is part of everyone's bloodstream instead of a recollection of previous existences. This statement would be consistent with Thomson's belief in a primordial ooze lying at the bottom of the sea from which all life evolved and with the use of the belief in "Full Fathom Five." The statement also suits the view in "The Manor Garden" that, as proof of evolution, the human foetus reenacts the evolutionary process as part of its growth. Finally the statement reinforces Plath's metaphor of the heart as holocaust and oven in "Mary's Song."

"Cut" begins with a comparison of the hurt thumb to a little man. The severed tip is "a sort of hinge" or "a hat," the first implying entry into something and the second conveying that the "something" may be "the head." The second possibility produces the inaugural victimizer/victim pairing of "little pilgrim" and Indian. The speaker imagines a primal scalping whose streaming blood becomes a "turkey wattle." An application of Merthiolate/ pink champagne changes the "crime" into a "celebration" and, just as one is about to deduce the "celebration" is the first Thanksgiving, the speaker seizes on the fact that blood is made up of millions of red and white corpuscles to convert the occasion into the American Revolution. She now addresses the thumb as her "Homunculus," telling it that she has taken a pill—probably an aspirin—"to kill / The thin / Papery feeling." The "celebration" has thus become a "high" that must be treated before it turns into a hangover. Coevally the juxtaposition of "homunculus" and "pill" sets off a sense of abortion that may have begun earlier with "turkey." *The Bell Jar* describes the male genital organ as "turkey neck and turkey gizzards," and in the development of medicine, homunculus preceded sperm as a theory of impregnation. Plath uses the word again in "Oregonian Original" (1962) to refer to Punch, and here she may simply mean "little man." From the remainder of the poem, however, one senses that if she does, she means a "little man" like that of "Gulliver" (1965) who comes with "petty fetters" and "bribes." The thumb becomes her "saboteur," a "kamikaze-man," and a member of the Ku Klux Klan. When it sees the pulp of its heart (life) is to become paper (art), the homunculus commits suicide, leaving only the "trepanned veteran" whose scar suggests a lobotomy. What remains at its departure becomes a Yeatsian husk, "dirty" with the numbness of a "stump."

At this point George Steiner's remarks about the poet's uses of concentration camps become relevant. In "Dying Is an Art" (1965) he maintains that "perhaps it is only those who had no part in the events [of the death camps] who *can* focus on them rationally and imaginatively; to those who experienced the thing, it has lost the hard edges of possibility; it has stepped outside the real." Steiner marvels that "the dead men cry out of the yew hedge" and proposes that the poems constitute "an act of identification, of total communion with those tortured and massacred." But he wrongly supposes that the act of identification for Plath involves a radical reconsideration of the whole question of "the poet's condition and the condition of language after modernism and war." Her adaptation of the strategies of Yeats's dreaming back does not constitute a response to T. W. Adorno's dictum that there will be "no poetry after Auschwitz." Instead it suggests that the way she handles "the poetics of terror and mass-murder" in her poetry is to return to her earlier mythic style.[17] She reaches an understanding of man's inhumanity not by looking directly at Auschwitz but by looking at its atrocities in a continuous parallel with Yeatsian myth. This myth had led the Irish poet to a passive acceptance earlier of fascism when he saw the movement as the next state in his cycles of history. Plath, too, is led in the poems to minimize the horror of the occasions by seeing the ovens as a place for moral tempering. The Jews emerge as passive victims of a Zeitgeist meant to be as coercive as the drug that *The Bell Jar* describes being administered to women about to give birth. As those women "would go straight home and start another baby," the victims, like Job, expect to "emerge as gold" from the testing (23:10). Their suffering, as a Job's comforter might add, is proof of their guilt; and no other explanation need be given.

If these cycles of history are not determined by human choice, one may wonder exactly where Plath's activism begins. Her reviews, written at the same time as the poems, are militant. A General Jodpur can be thrown from a runaway horse and, in his walk back to camp, have a complete change of heart; tyrants can be tamed; and in *The Emperor's Oblong Pancakes* an emperor can end his insistence on oblongity in the world. By analogy Plath can strike out against the poisons "fisting themselves in the upper atmosphere," "the crisis of identity" that two "leaning Stonehenge shapes of parents" impose on "the ego-balls" of their children, and the self-righteous airs of Lord Byron's wife.[18] But as one nears the central vision of the poetry, freedom becomes less apparent and one suspects a hierarchy at work similar to that which the narrator of "Johnny Panic and the Bible of Dreams" defines for dream. Political action is possible within Plath's cycles of history only insofar as one chooses what the Zeitgeist allows. As with Hegel, Auden, and Elizabeth Bishop, "freedom is the knowledge of necessity," and necessity for both victimizer and victim is identical: the creation of a super race in an ongoing evolutionary process. The Nazis become "gods" by persecuting the Jews, and the Jews become "gods" by suffering the persecution. The two roles stand as thesis and antithesis in a relationship that Yeats describes as self and mask.

Thus "Lady Lazarus," which begins the reversal from passivity, does not in any way alter the conditions of the cycle. Her admission that she has "done it again" may make her brushes with death seem willful, but the victim of her action is likewise herself. She may be "a walking miracle," but her sense of herself as a lamp recalls both the purging Yeatsian flames and the lampshades that Ilse Koch made from the skins of prisoners at Buchenwald. Hitler's purification may again initiate the person's dreaming back, but by the end of the poem she is equally Hitlerian. She promises "to eat men" in the same way that her selves have been consumed. Much as had the fasting of Franz Kafka's "hunger artist," her dyings have become a spectacle for "the peanut-crunching crowd," and one suspects that she is impelled toward death for the same reason that he is impelled toward hunger; she cannot find anything she wants to live for. Nonetheless her art has acquired commercial value. Although she is still "the same, identical woman," one must now pay "for a word or a touch / Or a bit of blood." Preserving the theme of Nazi persecution, she addresses her persecutors as "Herr Doktor" and "Herr Enemy," claiming to be their "opus," a "pure gold baby" ready to begin again. Powerful reminders of Hitler's "final solution"—"A cake of soap, / A wedding ring, / A gold filling"—have been left among the ashes from her dreaming back. Yet the new purity that she gains has accomplished exactly what Alfred Rosenberg had imagined for the German race: a superman who can challenge "Herr God" and "Herr Lucifer" by having gained self-discipline. She has, in effect, undergone the dehumanization that Radin finds common in aboriginal African deities, although "Brasilia" (1963) once more binds the dreaming back to Nietzsche and Germany by referring to its survivors as "super-people."

The dialectic of wills that is implicit in "Lady Lazarus" is expanded in "Daddy." He is the "Herr Doktor" of the previous poem, but the speaker is far less willing to remain his "opus." Plath describes her condition as being that of "a girl with an Electra complex. Her father died while she thought he was God. . . . Her father was also a Nazi and her mother very possibly part Jewish." The two strains have married in the daughter into a kind of paralysis, and at the poem's beginning she is rejecting the bonds that the father places on her, imaged as a shoe. By her resistance the girl suggests that she may be rejecting Yeatsian history and its passivity as well, but Plath indicates an action like that of the father in Yeats's *Purgatory* (1939). Much as he murders his son in a reenactment intended to expiate a previous parricide, Plath's figure is compelled "to act out [her] awful little allegory . . . before she is free of it." [19] The paralysis, which has kept her infantile, is reflected in both the nursery-rhyme rhythms and her self-image as "The Woman in the Shoe." She has never been able to fix upon or speak to her father, and the poem begins by detailing the failures in Massachusetts, Germany, and Poland. The result has been an absence which the concentration-camp imagery converts to a guilt or torture. She finds herself bounded by barbed wire and senses that she may have been brought into her present circumstances by some railway journey. There is no doubt that here and there Plath's own emotions have entered the poem, but what one has is not pure autobiography so much as another Yeatsian dreaming back to throw off the husk or passionate body for a pure existence.

The connection between the failure at communication and barbed wire is explained in *The Bell Jar*, when Esther speaks of picking "up a German dictionary or a German book, the very sight of whose dense, black, barbed-wire letters made my mind shut like a clam." [20] The poem's speaker admits to being "like a Jew" and having a "gypsy ancestress"—two races signalled by Hitler for extermination. Her father turns Luftwaffe (Hermann Göring), bureaucrat (gobbledygook), and panzer-man (Erwin Rommel). His brutishness becomes like Marco's "woman-hating" in *The Bell Jar*, a basis for attraction. The imagery again shifts as the poem becomes more confounded with the author's life and the father figure takes on the role of teacher. Clefts settle in the chin rather than his foot; nonetheless he is the devil as coercions of school and the speaker's attempt to get back to him at ten and twenty attest. His having reduced her to a nursery-rhyme character is now matched by her reconstructing this once God-turned-super-human as an imitation man. He is a voodoo doll to which the speaker has wedded herself. It is this wedding that is negated as the dreaming back ends and the speaker prepares for a final separation. She has disposed of two—the creator/father and the parasite/vampire—fused beneath a stake that she has driven into the creature's heart. Freed finally from these constrictions, she and the villagers relax; but it is a relaxation made possible by her assuming a brutality that equates her with him and thus makes her of one cycle with him and superhuman as well.

Because of the reference to it in the Harvard interview, "The Swarm" (1963) must be included among these other historical poems. Yet it seems by any measure the least historical of Plath's final works. It depicts a struggle for survival between nature and the "men of business," variously imaged as a swarm of bees and beekeepers and as Napoleon's armies and the victors of Waterloo. The poem's equating bee-swarms to swarming troops may be meant to convey the natural/cyclical process of the great events of history, managed because of their subconscious and impulsive character by the ontogenetic exploitative superego. Nature produc-es hives and honey while the "grey" beekeepers who exploit them produce the "new mausoleums" of ivory. Nature also promises in the end to make temporary the reign of the mind in a teleology that echoes C. S. Lewis's *The Abolition of Man* (1947). There Lewis had explained man's attempts to control nature as deriving from his belief that he is the result of a natural accident and consequent-ly may be destroyed by accident as well. To avoid this end, man has divorced himself increasingly from nature and the divorce has been dangerously injurious. The opposition in Plath's case seems less preoccupied than she normally is with "purging," and the tension may go back for its paradigm to either the double of Dos-toevsky or the self and mask of Yeats. The selection of Napoleon may well have been provoked, as Plath indicates, by her reading. In April of 1962 she reviewed a life of Josephine by Hubert Cole and tended to see what was to become her own marital situation reflected in Josephine's separation from Napoleon and the comfort that her two children brought after the divorce.[21] Napoleon figures, too, in Lowell's *Imitations* (1961) as well as *Life Studies*.

Finished during the week before her death, "Edge" (1963) turns from these willful acts to "the illusion of Greek necessity." Clytemnestra's prophetic dream of her own destruction by Orestes seems to have inspired the imagery of Plath's "perfect," childless woman. "Perfection," as she noted in "The Munich Mannequins" (1965), is, like the angels of Rilke's *Duino Elegies*, "terrible[;] it cannot have children." Nor can it in Plath's mind allow even a possibility of things to exist and consequently for Rilkean unicorns to be. Instead the woman folds possibility back into herself much as a rose closes its petals. The process is the reverse of that described by E. E. Cummings in "somewhere i have never travelled," a poem read aloud by Esther to her boyfriend in *The Bell Jar*. The moon looks on, suggesting the cycles of its own waxing and waning as the menstrual cycle. The poem seems to be saying that one is killed as much by one's dreams of perfection as by any other means. In saying this, "Edge" echoes so many of the poems whose dreams of accomplishment terrorize the speaker, often as imagined father figures but as mother figures too. As parents destroy the possibility for their children to live and often destroy their children by trying to force them to live out parental aspirations, so also children destroy themselves in order to realize their parents' hopes or they destroy their parents in order to be themselves. Technology which has speeded up the process of change has also made this "generational conflict" more visible and intense. There seems to be no way out of this "bad faith" which is recurrent and hence natural, reversible, and nonhistorical.

Instead, if one is to grant relevance to Plath's cycles of history, one grants it on the same terms that Auden grants history to Yeats —as a conflict between Reason and Imagination, objectivity and subjectivity, and the individual and the masses rather than between good and evil will, integrated and diffuse thought, and personality and the impersonal state. Without citing Auden directly or mentioning Yeats, Joyce Carol Oates in "The Death Throes of Romanticism" (1973) objects to Plath's work in exactly these terms. Oates finds Plath's battle between Reason and Imagination "a suicidal refusal to understand that man's intelligence *is* instinctive in his species." Plath's quarrel between objectivity and subjectivity becomes an "'I' that is declared an enemy of all others" and her preference for the individual over the masses productive of "a limited vision" that believes itself unquestioningly *the* correct "mirror held up to nature." Oates also objects to the passivity of Plath's victims, calling her "dreaming back" a regression into infantilism. Nevertheless Oates is willing to see deeper than the visions of feminist critics who wish merely to make Plath a martyr for female oppression and who would limit the seriousness with which she undertook other areas of persecution and the total change that would be needed to offset her objections. Like Esther in *The Bell Jar*, once Plath realized the monotony of repetition, she "wanted to do everything once and for all and be through with it." [22] Part of the dilemma of her poetry is that, in sensing the repetitions of life, she could neither acquiesce nor provide alternatives for them.

Nancy Steiner remarks that Plath "could not guess that society would ever change; she seemed to see the taboos and tensions of her background as permanent conditions that could never be substantially altered." The sense is already present in the poems that Plath published as a high-school student in *Seventeen* and the repetitious villanelles that seem to typify her undergraduate writing at Smith. Steiner opposes this attitude to other students who could flit "excitedly on the first wave of a new and radical movement, like a prophet who could see ahead into the '60's and '70's." [23] By accepting the backward glance of recurrence rather than the forward look of the industrial imagination, Plath could only move into a world that would become increasingly hostile to innovation. Nor could the psychological ideal that had sustained Auden and the generation of poets before her be any more comforting, for the very rationality of the Freudian approach had produced a conformism and threatened to destroy faction through coercion. Nonhistorical and nonrational approaches would have to be tried if poetry and politics were to recover some of the power to overcome the limitations of self that Freudian thinking had produced. It remained for other poets to rediscover ways of opening up this closed world with visions aided by surrealism, dada, deep imagery, technology, and the principles of natural science.

Notes

1. Sylvia Plath, *The Poet Speaks*, ed. Peter Orr (London: Routledge & Kegan Paul, 1966), p. 169; Plath, "Context," *London Magazine* 11 (February 1962): 45–46; Orr, pp. 169–70.

2. W. H. Auden, Introduction to *The Oxford Book of Light Verse* (1938. Reprint Oxford: Oxford University Press, 1962), p. ix; Orr, p. 170; quoted in Lois Ames, "Sylvia Plath: A Biographical Note," *The Bell Jar* (New York: Bantam Books, 1972), p. 213.

3. Nancy Steiner, *A Closer Look at Ariel* (New York: Harper's Magazine Press, 1973), p. 35; W. H. Auden, "Tract for the Times," *Nation* 152 (1941): 25; Auden, "A Note on Order," *Nation* 152 (1941): 131.

4. Ted Hughes, "Notes on the Chronological Order of Sylvia Plath's Poems," in *The Art of Sylvia Plath*, ed. Charles Newman (Bloomington: Indiana University Press, 1970), p. 190.

5. T. S. Eliot, "Ulysses, Order, and Myth," *Dial* 74 (1923): 483; Rachel Bespaloff, *On the Iliad*, trans. Mary McCarthy (New York: Harper Torchbooks, 1962), pp. 73–74; W. H. Auden, "The Dyer's Hand," *Listener* 53 (1955): 1064.

6. Anne Sexton, "The Barfly Ought to Sing," in *The Art of Sylvia Plath*, p. 178; Hughes, p. 192; Eileen Aird, *Sylvia Plath* (New York: Barnes & Noble, 1973), p. 27.

7. W. H. Auden, "Rilke in English," *New Republic* 100 (1939): 135; Theodore Roethke, "Open Letter," in *Mid-Century American Poets*, ed. John Ciardi (New York: Twayne Publishers, 1950), pp. 67–68.

8. Sylvia Plath, "Johnny Panic and the Bible of Dreams," *Atlantic Monthly* 222 (September 1968): 55.

9. Margaret Newlin, "The Suicide Bandwagon," *Critical Quarterly* 14 (1972): 376–77; Hughes, p. 189.

10. Loren Eiseley, *The Immense Journey* (New York: Vintage Books, 1959), pp. 16, 31, 33.

11. Paul Radin, *African Folktales and Sculpture*, Bollingen Series 32 (New York: Pantheon Books, 1952), pp. 1, 12, 4, 9.

12. Orr, p. 172; Hughes, p. 190; Bertrand Russell, "The Future of Mankind," *Points of Departure*, ed. Arthur J. Carr and William Steinhoff (New York: Harper & Brothers, 1960), p. 589.

13. "Johnny Panic and the Bible of Dreams," pp. 54–55, 58.

14. *The Bell Jar*, pp. 29, 183, 199, 176; Orr, pp. 168–69; Randall Jarrell, *A Sad Heart at the Supermarket* (New York: Atheneum, 1962), p. 26; W. H. Auden, "Squares and Oblongs," in *Language: An Inquiry*, ed. R. N. Anshen (New York: Harper & Brothers, 1957), p. 174; Stephen Spender, "Warnings from the Grave," in *The Art of Sylvia Plath*, p. 200.

15. Nancy Steiner, p. 43; Hughes, p. 193.

16. Douglas Cleverdon, "On *Three Women*," in *The Art of Sylvia Plath*, p. 227; quoted in A. Alvarez, "Sylvia Plath," in *The Art of Sylvia Plath*, p. 62.

17. George Steiner, "Dying Is an Art," in *The Art of Sylvia Plath*, pp. 217, 216; George Steiner, "In Extremis," *Cambridge Review* 90 (1969): 247–48.

18. Sylvia Plath, "General Jodpur's Conversion," *New Statesman* 62 (1961): 696; Plath, "Oregonian Original," *New Statesman* 64 (1962): 660; Plath, "Suffering Angel," *New Statesman* 64 (1962): 828–29.

19. Quoted in Alvarez, p. 65.

20. *The Bell Jar*, p. 27.

21. Sylvia Plath, "Pair of Queens," *New Statesman* 63 (1962): 602–3.

22. W. H. Auden, "Yeats as an Example," *Kenyon Review* 20 (1948): 181–95; Joyce Carol Oates, "The Death Throes of Romanticism," *Southern Review*, n.s. 9 (1973): 508, 506, 502; *The Bell Jar*, p. 105.

23. Nancy Steiner, pp. 78–79.

7
The Poetics of Impediment: Elizabeth Bishop

That the seemingly modernist poetry of Elizabeth Bishop should be universally welcomed by postmodern poets illuminates not only a different kind of postmodernism but also the complexity of her own work. Like W. H. Auden's early poetry, which provided the model for the new style, her work abounds in "forthright statement, in which words are in general used denotatively" and images and metaphors bristle "from the exciting exactness with which they apply to experience." Occasionally, as Anne Stevenson proposes in *Elizabeth Bishop* (1966), there is Auden's "erudite colloquialism." The lyric refrain of "Varick Street" offers one instance. Moreover stories like "Then Came the Poor" (1934) contain the same attacks of Auden's Marxist phase on the uselessly idle rich, but she is far more skeptical than he is about the benefit of proletarian revolution. Poems like "The Man-Moth" (1936) with its continuity of all life and evolution by chance out of a printer's error convey an implicit Darwinism that may have prompted Randall Jarrell's listing it first among what he cites as "her best poems." This Darwinism continues into such poems as "Night City" (1972) and beyond. But the stress Jarrell and others place on the psychological appears to be the point where most attempts to link Bishop to postmodernism founder. Most critics are willing to go along uneasily with James G. Southworth's statement that, "except for some ten poems," Bishop's poetry "is as objective as poetry can well be." [1]

The consciousness of her control, the conjectural nature of her vision, and her intellectual clarity connect Bishop to Marianne Moore, E. A. Robinson, Wallace Stevens, and "the generation of poets which flourished after World War I." She has praised Moore for her "completely accurate" descriptions and ability to "give herself up entirely to the object under contemplation" and to "feel in all sincerity how it is to be *it*," and she has consistently kept enough details of her life confused or private in order to prevent Freudian interpretation. To offset these resistances to personal imposition and applied psychoanalysis and to allow a determination of her own commitment to what "It All Depends" (1950) calls "the sea" and "the very life" of poetry, a view of denotative syntax like that developed in John Crowe Ransom's two-part essay "Poetry" (1947) is useful. Writing of what he calls "precious objects," Ransom shows how by increasing the density of detail and "impeding" the reader, poets like Shakespeare are able to assert the value of what is being described. Often these objects are, as Ransom points out, familiar yet "always capable of exhibiting fresh aspects." They are comparatively absolute and inviolable, and their very lack of change coupled with familiarity allows the poet to spend more affective time on them than on equally familiar objects which are intended for use. Yet his affection uses no overtly emotive language, and critics of Bishop's writing who find little or no mannerisms and still are unable to accept a view of objectivity are, in effect, responding to the presence of such emotions.[2]

Her tributes for various dead friends and her three Nova Scotia stories convey in contexts that are often more revealing than the poems the basic Imagist attachment of emotion to objects that informs her thinking. In "Gregorio Valdes, 1879–1939" (1939) she states of Valdes's talent: "When he copied, particularly from a photograph, and particularly from a photograph of something he knew and liked, such as palm trees, he managed to make just the right changes in perspective and coloring to give it a peculiar and captivating freshness, flatness, and remoteness." She describes a painting of her rooming house that he did. She had asked him to put more flowers and a Traveller's Palm in the work, and later, showing her a sketch of the palm, he apologized "because the tree really had seven branches on one side and six on the other, but in the painting he had given both sides seven to make it more symmetrical." Coming home one evening, she saw the finished work on the veranda: "In the grey twilight they seemed to blur together and I had the feeling that if I came closer I would be able to see another miniature copy of the house leaning on the porch of the painted house, and so on,—like the Old Dutch Cleanser advertisements." Her piece on Flannery O'Connor (1964) represents as tokens of affection a similar immersion in familiar objects as well as an attentiveness by the ailing fiction writer to the details of a "cross in a bottle" that Bishop sent her. "An Inadequate Tribute" (1967) extends this wedding of emotion and detailed object to Jarrell by connecting him to a part of Cape Cod and a dazzling bright day.[3]

In each of these pieces her ability to recall accurately, vividly, and discretely is connected to affection, repossession, and individuality as much as was Valdes's ability to copy. Each person is identified with a discrete, inviolable world, much as in mnemonics an object to be recalled is associated with a precise token or commonplace. The blurring of these tokens or places leads to lapses and haziness of memory, a crumbling of the "rocklike" and "perfect" appearance of remembered things. In this need of precise recollection, the process of recovery resembles that yearning for fixity described by Robert Lowell in "91 Revere Street" (1955): "Major Mordecai Myers's portrait has been mislaid past finding, but out of my memories I often come on it in the setting of our Revere Street house, a setting now fixed in the mind, where it survives all the distortions of fantasy, all the blank befogging of forgetfulness. There, the vast number of remembered *things* remains rocklike. Each is in its place, each has its function, its history, its drama. There, all is preserved by that motherly care that one either ignored or resented in his youth. The things and their owners come back urgent with life and meaning—because finished, they are endurable and perfect."[4] The process also resembles what Gaston Bachelard designates "reveries of childhood."

In *The Poetics of Reverie* (1960) Bachelard speaks of the "indelible marks" that "the original solitudes"—those of childhood—leave on certain souls. He associates such sensitizing action with "poetic reverie" in which one can relax his aches. In Bishop's case these reveries would have much to do with her early years, spent with her grandparents in Nova Scotia and with her aunt in Boston where, as Stevenson indicates, ill health kept her from attending school regularly. "Instead, she spent long, solitary winters in bed, reading. Her passion for books and for music dates from this period (she was about eight) when, sick and without friends her own age, she began to write poems and to take piano lessons." Bishop's father died eight months after her birth and her mother never recovered from the shock of his death. Stevenson leaves open whether the mother's "nervous collapse and subsequent insanity were entirely the result of her husband's death or whether her disease was an affliction of long standing. . . . The tragedy remains. At the age of eight months Elizabeth Bishop lost, in effect, both parents." Her life in Nova Scotia with her maternal grandparents lasted until she was six; then she spent a year in Worcester, Massachusetts, with the paternal grandparents, until she went to live more or less permanently with her Aunt Maud in Boston. She returned to Nova Scotia summers afterward until she was thirteen.[5]

"The Baptism" (1937) and "Gwendolyn" (1953) show how Bishop's writing connects the transience of this early life to objects. Both stories have identical small-town settings that would seem to resemble the village where the poet spent her early childhood, and except for different narrative points of view, both may derive from the "novel about family life in a Nova Scotia village" that she told the editors of *Magazine* (1934) she was writing. Townsfolk divide into Baptists and Presbyterians, and in the first story the youngest of three sisters decides to join the Baptist congregation in preference to the Presbyterian church that her older sisters belong to. Central to the story which deals with religious despair and the growing insanity of the young girl is the association of death and flowers. The association begins when Mrs. Peppard's conversation moves from the death of "her sister's baby" to a discussion of begonias, and the link recurs in the midst of a vision where lamp smoke rises to the ceiling and smells "very strong and sweet, like rose-geranium." Finally the girl's death shortly after her baptism enlists the gift of "a beautiful plant . . . from the city, a mass of white blooms" along with the townsfolk's cut red, white, and pink geraniums. "Gwendolyn" relates the death of a second young girl from diabetes and, in doing so, associates the frail condition of the dying girl's appearance to that of an unnamed doll that once belonged to the narrator's Aunt Mary.[6]

"In the Village" (1953) recalls the return of the poet's mother to Nova Scotia "in the hope that, in familiar surroundings, she might recover."[7] Instead the visit produced her final breakdown, and she had to be put in a mental hospital in Dartmouth, Nova Scotia. Told as an evocation of that summer with its various noises of the mother's scream, cow flop, the bell at Mealy's candystore, the clanging firebell, and the blacksmith's clang, it recounts what memories the poet may have preserved of that experience. In it, as in Auden's "Musée des Beaux Arts" (1939), suffering "takes place / While someone else is eating or opening a window or just walking dully along." The mother's suffering is incomprehensible to the daughter; the two aunts who try to make things easier cannot. The situation is a variation of that described in "The Baptism," including some of the same townsfolk like Mrs. Peppard, except now the three girls have parents who make their life less isolated. What is established by the story is the relic nature of the poet's most primal needs. The proof of her parents and their love for her is very much tied up with the same objects Bishop describes being unloaded from the crates and boxes that have been shipped from Boston. Things become significant because they are related valuably to the past; but, as "The Sea and Its Shore" (1937) maintains, even this relationship cannot long withstand erosion. In time the flow of life like that of the sea will prove more immediate, and with the eventual dissolution of this immediacy, the value of such relationships will reemerge diminished. Paler they endure to represent in later life the inaccessible place where one would like to live.

"The Sea and Its Shore" speaks directly to these matters of survival and erosion. The story presents art as a temporary extension of life. Edwin Boomer, whose job it is to keep a stretch of beach free from papers, collects the more interesting scraps he uncovers. Eventually he comes to see the beach as an expression of print, but Bishop notes: "The point was that everything had to be burned at last. All, all had to be burned, even bewildering scraps that he had carried with him for weeks or months. Burning paper was his occupation, by which he made his living, but over and above that,

he could not allow his pockets to become too full, or his house to become littered." Thus this "most literary" man whose desire was to rescue some print from destruction by nature finds himself aiding nature in its laws. The categories under which he classifies information prove finally irrelevant, and what enjoyment he derives from his bonfires produces no sense of joy at their inevitability.[8]
It is easy enough to link the story to both the categories of Bishop's own writing as well as the attitudes that must have resulted from her having lost her parents and maternal grandparents at an early age. That Boomer's name should so closely resemble Bulmer, the name of her maternal grandparents, is perhaps no accident—or that her poetry should convey such seriousness in its recovery of events and objects while at the same time evincing a lack of seriousness about the durability of art. Nowhere does one get the sense that she is writing for more than herself or that she sees the content of life any differently from Boomer—as matter about herself, about people whose lives catch her fancy, and about what seems bewilderingly inexplicable.

In all these prose pieces there is a particular emphasis upon labor—whether the work is the care that Valdes puts into his painting or the affection O'Connor feels at noting that "the rooster has an eyebrow" and the altar cloth is "a little dirty from the fingers of whoever cut it out." Jarrell is seen on the beach "writing in a notebook," and both the dressmaker and blacksmith of "In the Village" are saved by their labor from deep involvement in the sorrows of the house. Even Boomer is rescued from being overwhelmed by the paper he collects by the necessity of burning it as part of his job. In contrast the rich of "Then Came the Poor" are contemptible because they are idle: they cannot be useful. One might connect this work ethic to the poet's New England–Nova Scotia background and her Puritan past or suggest, as she does in her *Shenandoah* interview (1965), that it is related to the socialist temper of the thirties: "Politically I considered myself a socialist, but I disliked 'social conscious' writing. . . . I was all for being a socialist till I heard Norman Thomas speak; but he was *so* dull. Then I tried anarchism, briefly."[9] Nevertheless it represents that same attitude of "going on" which Auden's "Musée des Beaux Arts" will later convey; the ploughman of Pieter Brueghel's *Landscape with the Fall of Icarus* cannot stop his work to watch the

171

boy's falling out of the sky; a large part of life must go on working as it always has.

Aesthetically what the emphasis on labor does is to promote literary labor as a value, allowing form, as Roland Barthes in *Writing Degree Zero* (1953) suggests, to become "the end product of craftsmanship, like a piece of pottery or a jewel." The purpose of such labor is to contain the tension described by "The Sea and Its Shore" as the erosion of art by life and reinterpreted along Freudian lines in Robert Lowell's "Thomas, Bishop, and Williams" (1946) as a conflict between the death urge (the sea) and civilization (the shore) or, as Sherman Paul in *Hart's Bridge* (1973) is willing to apply it to Hart Crane, the strong tension between the desire to return to childhood and the need to escape that childhood. In Bishop's case the effort may derive from the naturalists' belief in man's evolution from the sea and hence from his struggle to preserve the element he has achieved. Her own depictions have led occasionally to an artificially baroque love poem but more often to an equally conscious stylization of experience or technique of mapping experience that greatly resembles the mapping in the opening poem of *North & South* (1946). At times, as in "Chemin de Fer," the stylization moves into overt formalism but more often it merely tracks. "Maps," as Prince Modupe relates in *I Was a Savage* (1958), "are liars. . . . The things that hurt one do not show on a map." The "airy and easy sweep of map-traced, staggering distances" belittles the journeys that one makes on tired feet. Modupe was to learn from showing his father a map that "the truth of a place is in the joy and the hurt that come from it. . . . With my big map-talk, I had effaced the magnitude of his cargo-laden, heat-oppressed treks." Bishop's journey outward from the emotions of childhood begins with "The Map," and it does so, however obscurely, in terms earned from that childhood.[10]

Among the earliest poems the poet has seen fit to keep is "The Map," which anticipates her own love of travel as well as the predilection for travel books that Lucy in "The Baptism" and the narrator of "In the Village" display. The poem's first observations of Newfoundland and Labrador suggest a starting point in Nova Scotia as the viewer's eye moves eastward toward Norway. The map, as the metaphors of blossom and fishtank convey, represents an outlet for the speaker as exciting and consuming as those hobbies given to children, for the printer, in running the names of sea-shore towns out to the sea and of cities across neighboring mountains, is said to experience "the same excitement / as when motion too far exceeds its cause." Moreover, just as the narrator can imagine stroking the lovely bays, the "peninsulas take the water between thumb and finger / like women feeling for the smoothness of yard-goods." The feel of both is for the unfinished or what can be worked on. This "unfinished" quality as it applies to land and sea occupies the opening stanza. There the poet wonders if the land lies in the sea or merely draws the sea about it like a cape. Are the shadows growing into the sea or withdrawing from it? She concludes that the land does the "investigating." Mapped waters are quiet and self-contained. In coming to this realization, she wonders whether the colors given to land are assigned or earned since "topography displays no favorites." Echoing the opening of Robert Frost's "West-running Brook" (1928) and its depiction of how that brook got its name, Bishop ends by stating: "More delicate than the historians' are the map-makers' colors."

Frost's poem had dealt as well with contraries as a vehicle to identity, but he treated the problem in historical terms. In Bishop history disappears to be replaced by a denotative flatness. What impresses one immediately about this flatness is the femininity of the speaker. The emotive adjectives are deliberately feminine —"fine tan sandy shelf," "moony Eskimo," "lovely bays"—but equally feminine are the occupational metaphors—flower gardening, caring for fish, dressmaking, and finally map coloring. Norman J. W. Thrower, in *Maps & Men* (1972), notes: "It later became the custom to hand-color the prints of engravings, . . . a practice that prevailed until the end of the nineteenth century. Understandably, map coloring became an important activity in various cartographic centers, and ladies, sometimes those socially prominent, often engaged in this work." [11] Thus the poem iterates the tension between land and sea that "The Sea and Its Shore" codifies into a conflict between the artist and life and, as that work established art as a temporary rather than permanent thing, so too does the poem convey the fragility with the word *delicate*. In the absence of a formal meter or line, its rhymes show a stylization rather than a formalization—something designed to resemble the formal but somehow not itself formal much as maps, by excluding the joys and pains of actual experience, stylize landscapes by bending not to the abstract rules of geometry but to the natural contours of the subject. The very adjectives and metaphors which act to impede the reader establish the value which has been attached to the incidents.

Bishop's oft-noted ability to make her subjects interact with one another as well as speak back to her is conveyed in the images of the peninsula feeling water and Norway's becoming a hare. Like Theodore Roethke, Bishop is a dramatic poet not because she impersonates but because she waits until objects speak to her, which they must do in a mnemonics system. The purpose of mnemonics is to call back with such vividness that whatever is recalled resumes mentally the life it once had. In Christian mnemonics or meditation, memories of God, Christ, or the saints are called up by means of icons, relics, and tokens. In the *Shenandoah* interview the poet states that she became aware of such an approach while she was still at Vassar when reading an essay on the baroque sermon in preparation for a paper on Gerard Manley Hopkins. One of the scraps of paper Boomer picks up two years later concerns mnemonics. It lists experiences which weaken the memory. This waiting for objects to speak relies, in addition, on a concept of connaturality like that Bishop posits for Moore, a sense that the depth of things and the depth of self are united in some way and can speak to one another. The divisions between man and nature made by traditional religions along lines of man's having a soul and by evolutionists along the necessity for man to distance himself from his origins are, consequently, held in abeyance, although what seems to be evoked in Bishop's poems are less ecstatic states than the observations of a girlhood which, having been lost, seems more edenic than the writer's current state.

"The Imaginary Iceberg," which comes next in the volume, speaks more directly to the matters of the division between man and nature. Its contrast of manmade ship and naturally formed iceberg as vehicles of motion leaves no question of the speaker's preference. Icebergs make both technology and art "artlessly rhetorical"; they move the soul, being, like it, self-made "from elements least visible." One has conveyed by these "obscure" elements a response of what is deepest in man (his soul) to what is deepest in sea life (the iceberg) with a suggestion that is almost naturalistic: that the soul is not God-given but is created by a process similar to that which creates the iceberg. The suggestion is perhaps more a function of the metaphysical style than of theology, although Bishop admits to being "not religious" despite her pleasure at reading various religious poets. Moreover, as the title conveys, the subject is an "imaginary" rather than real iceberg. In this the poem may derive from Stevens. Bishop acknowledges that he was the contemporary poet who most affected her writing while she was in college. Stevenson ventures that the rhetorical questions of "The Map" may well be influenced by "Sea Surface Full of Clouds" (1924) and that the emphasis on the imaginary is in keeping with the "unfinished" stresses of "The Map" as well as what critics have seen as Stevens's view of the imagination. Joseph N. Riddel in "Stevens on Imagination" (1971) notes that for Stevens, "only mind, the unreal, can name and thus conceive beginnings and the order and direction they imply. Only mind can speak of history and form, because mind has created history and form as the space of its being." [12] Like Bishop's iceberg, mind succeeds the world or things as they are in the order of creation, but by its nature becomes essential to the real.

The poems, however, which enlarge upon the notions of history in "The Map" and the travel reading of the poet's youth, are not in *North & South*. They are "At the Fishhouses," "Cape Breton," and "Over 2000 Illustrations and a Complete Concordance" from *A Cold Spring* (1955). Set again in Nova Scotia at a convergence of sea and shore, "At the Fishhouses" describes a chat with an old man who was a friend of the speaker's grandfather. Like Lucy in "The Baptism," this speaker is later revealed to be "a believer in total immersion" and the singer of "A Mighty Fortress Is Our God," listed in the tale as a favorite hymn of Lucy's sister Flora. But most importantly the poem repeats the notions of the world as "flowing and drawn," knowledge as "historical, flowing and flown," and the poem as a mnemonic recollection: "I have seen it over and over, the same sea, the same, / slightly, swinging above the stones, / icily free above the stones, / above the stones and then the world." This late announcement of the poem as recollection gives emotional content to what otherwise might be a belabored silvery description of a cold evening in which an old man sits netting among five fishhouses. His casual talk of "the decline in the population / and of codfish and herring / while he waits for a herring boat to come in" anticipates the diminishing catch of her mental world at the poem's close. The fixed nature of the opening as "cold dark deep and absolutely clear" in its recollection of the sea becomes eventually what "we imagine knowledge to be." Cape Breton, a short distance off from the fishhouses, forms the setting of a second of the poems. The piece is again deceptively descriptive, and again the detail functions as a repossession of the island and betrays the emotional nature of the content. Sea and land are once more in opposition as the silken water "weaving and weaving" to disappear "under the mist" is opposed by the man "carrying a baby" who disappears into a meadow whose poverty is "a snowfall of daisies." The metaphysical statement is that life goes on as ever.

Just as "At the Fishhouses" and "Cape Breton" may be regarded as reflections of Bishop's desire to return to childhood, "Over 2000 Illustrations and a Complete Concordance" reflects the attempt to escape that childhood by realizing its fantasies of escape. The poem has been compared to Charles Baudelaire's "Le Voyage," but it is in light of Bishop's own conflicts that its description and movement can better be seen. The poem depicts a world traveler looking back on the illustrations of her girlhood that inspired her to travel. The book containing the illustrations is like that of "The Baptism." There the isolated sisters are said to have gone "through a lot of old travel books that had belonged to their father. One was called *Wonders of the World;* one was a book about Palestine and Jerusalem. . . . Lucy grew excited over accounts of the Sea of Galilee, and the engraving of the Garden of Gethsemane as it looks to-day brought tears to her eyes. She exclaimed, 'Oh dear!' over pictures of 'An Olive Grove,' with Arabs squatting about in it, and 'Heavens!' at the real, rock-vaulted Stable, the engraved rocks like big black thumb-prints." "In the Village" also speaks of "gilded red or green books, unlovely books, filled with bright new illustrations of the Bible stories" that "drummers sometimes came around selling." [13] In either case the traveler's return to such illustrations is to note a difference from the "serious, engravable" nature of the pictures and the often tawdry realities of the travel. The poem ends with a picture that was not realized—a Nativity's image of domesticity, "a family with pets." The traveler suspects that this picture might have satisfied the child looking at it, rather than have acted, as had the other illustrations, as a lure to disappointing adventure. The poem is undoubtedly indebted to Baudelaire's depiction of the disappointment of travels as compared to imaginary voyages, but how personal and poignant the ending becomes in Bishop's context. The familiar "family with pets" that she never had occurs in the same reveries that produce the desire for travel.

In pursuing the perfect journey, the poem echoes the problems of "In Prison" (1938) and its search for a "true place in the world." The narrator of this story finds that his "proper sphere" is a prison. He desires imprisonment as much as the speaker of "Over 2000 Illustrations and a Complete Concordance" desires travel and with comparably exacting expectations. His prison must contain "a view of a court-yard paved with stone," permit the reading of "one very dull book. . . , the duller the better," and indulge his wish to use the walls of the cell for writing. The prison must also allow him to dress a little differently from the other prisoners and to form a friendship with "an important member of prison society" that will eventuate in the narrator's becoming "an *influence*." But most importantly, like the later poem, there is a final confusion between choice and necessity. The narrator who wishes to believe the Hegelian view that "freedom is knowledge of necessity," must restate the story's premise that "this way is the only logical step for me to take": "I mean, of course, to be acted *upon* in this way is the only logical step for me to take." [14] However much one wishes to claim "necessity" in Bishop's writing, matters of choice intrude: stimulated by childhood books to visit various places, her travelers decide what places to visit. Like Baudelaire's voyagers, however, they cannot choose what they will find. Only in the imagination is the universe ever equal to one's desire: realizations always entail adjustments to the real.

Written as a satire on the narrator's presumption of "necessity," "In Prison" anticipates responses to travel that recur in much of Bishop's poetry. Either the traveler accepts the excitement and novelty of new environments just as the "prisoner" refrains from imagining the contents of his "one dull book," because to do so would "spoil the sensation of wave-like freshness" that he hopes will accompany the book's being handed him, or the traveler willfully represses other environments so that he may accept wholly one place, again much as the "prisoner" discovers that he "could 'succeed' in one place, but not in all places" and protests against ambiguous positions. Critics are right to ally such a prison to the house of "The Sea and Its Shore," the fairy palace of "Jerónimo's House," and finally to the jar which in "Anecdote of the Jar" (1919) Stevens places in Tennessee to "make the slovenly wilderness / Surround that hill." All are shelters "not for living in, for thinking in." The function of each is to provide a temporary stay against confusion—a stay often requiring mental journeying if not the physical journeying that critics like Stevenson are willing to pronounce is the poet's major preoccupation. These places consequently provide the perfect models for the arrangements of detail that in turn the formal arrangements of art emulate, but none becomes so overwhelmingly central that critics may speak of obsession either in what she seeks to recover or in her attitude toward its eventual diminution. The loss of value in one object will merely allow the investment of value in a second.

Nowhere is this change of value more evident than in the recent "Crusoe in England" (1971). The speaker of the poem has lost his attachment for England by having been castaway on an island and, by being returned to England, the "living soul" that his island flute, knife, shrivelled shoes, goatskin trousers, and parasol possessed. These objects still have some value as his own reverie and as a request from the local museum-keeper attest. In this new telling of Daniel Defoe's novel, creativity becomes the means of re-investment. Crusoe mentions Greek drama, beds of irises, and philosophy in language that is sometimes openly sentimental. He misses his "poor old island" and "miserable, small volcanoes," and he admits to giving way often to self-pity, arguing that "'pity should begin at home.' So the more / pity I felt, the more I felt at home." He is, at the same time, interested in accepting some kind of duty, and he achieves in his friendship with Friday the equivalent of a friendship with "an important member of prison society" that "In Prison" mentions. His becoming "an *influence*," however, is ended by Friday's death from measles. Friday's being male, moreover, limits the urge toward futurity that the poem identifies with duty to rude artifacts, since the urge cannot be served in biological propagation. Art thus becomes some kind

of adjustment to Necessity. The speaker's inability to accept
either the judgment of the museum keeper or the death of Friday
counters a self-definition comparable to the affirmation that self-
pity allowed on his island home. Self-definition now comes from
reverie and drawing "vast generalizations, abstractions of the
grandest, most illuminating sort, like allegories or poems." [15]

Bishop's greatest achievements in her early collections have
been in poems that willfully repress the past in order to focus on
one time and place and hence that avoid nostalgia. "The Man-
Moth," "Roosters," "The Weed," and "The Fish" from her first
volume all present situations that are so vividly and meticulously
drawn that they prevent one's withdrawal into the past. The first
concerns a fantasy creature who, like man, inhabits the city and
who "must investigate as high as he can climb." His home is the
subway tunnels. On rare occasions he visits the surface, thinking
the moon "a small hole at the top of the sky / proving the sky
quite useless for protection." Everywhere he seems to be challenging death or an *in extremis* condition from which he "falls back
scared but quite unhurt." On the basis of this challenging Lowell
sees the poem as concerning a "death desire" [16] and other critics
think it is about evolutionary progress. If caught, the man-moth
will try to palm his sole possession—a tear—which he will relin-
quish to his captor if that captor is watchful. The tear is "cool as
from underground springs and pure enough to drink." In this, the
tear complements and opposes that of "The Reprimand" (1935)
in which teardrops are seen as the eye's equivalent to the tongue's
sighs, eye's "deepest sorrow." In "The Man-Moth" this sorrow
becomes a moral for man's ambition and its consequences. Again
set up in what appears to be six eight-line stanzas, the poem realizes no formal shape, merely the semblance of form. The very
density of ordinary detail lends the work a sense of reality that
phrases like "a temperature impossible to record in thermometers"
heighten into dream.

"Roosters," in contrast, represents an awakening from sleep. It
moves from a predawn "first crow of the first cock" to the emergence of the sun which renders the crows "almost inaudible." The
cries which announce an end of night affect first hens, then sleeping wives, and then the history of man, coming to symbolize fall
and redemption before they give way to sunlight. Written in triple

rhymes to suggest either the number of cock crows accompanying Peter's betrayals of Christ or the number of those betrayals, the pattern of each triplet is a sequence of lines whose length increases and where rhymes may occur between stressed and unstressed syllables. Here the ranging sweep of the sentences catches one in detail much as if one were surveying a vast area before the vision begins its equally vast sweep through time. The bird's combativeness, leading to its death, is balanced by Peter's sin, which typifies the ability of man to earn redemption. In effecting this parallel, live roosters transform into "a new weathervane / on basilica and barn," as art which like Peter may be equally untrue to life but may, all the same, prolong life's message. Tears are again part of the transformation as Peter's tears become glaze on a rooster's sides and spurs. Returning to the present in the final five stanzas, the poem pits rooster against sun, with the sun assuming aspects of the earlier triumphant rooster, God, and Peter. The poem ends with the sun climbing into the barnyard, "following 'to see the end,' / faithful as enemy, or friend." Thus "the gun-metal blue dark" echoed in "the gun-metal blue window" which begins the poem initiates a series of correspondences between the boundless and the bounded that in time cluster about images of war, conflagration, and commemoration.

"The Weed," which Bishop acknowledges "is modelled somewhat on [George Herbert's] 'Love Unknown,'" offers another dream-vision. A weed is seen growing through the heart of the dreamer who suspects that she is dead. The weed splits the heart much as weeds create cracks in stone, releasing in the act a flood of water. Each drop of water contains "a light, / a small, illuminated scene," and the river that the drops comprise is said to "carry all / the scenes that it had once reflected," much as a memory house contains in its separate compartments devices for minute and vivid recollection. Queried by the dreamer about what it was doing there, the weed responds that it grows "but to divide your heart again." In the Herbert poem the ordeals of the heart are turned into benefits: the cleansing in the font, the softening in the furnace, and the sensitizing by means of thorns are attempts to mend what the possessor of the heart had marred. Here the heart has obvious links to the process of memorization, "of learning by heart," as well as to loving: both activities tend to preserve the inviolability of their subjects. The splitting into two and possibly into four suggests the beginning of a concept of love similar to that proposed by Aristophanes in Plato's *Symposium*. There primal man was seen as twice the person man is now, and God's halving him was the reason for love and man's currently seeking his other half. The split has left within him an image of completion as fixed and indelible as that which seems to motivate Bishop's poetic reveries. The heart's being halved and quartered would presumably lead it to seek out its other half or its parts in an action comparable to that described by the Greek playwright.

As if to affirm this action, poems of complementarity abound in Bishop's *Complete Poems* (1969). They range from "The Gentleman of Shallot," a man who sees his bilateral anatomy narcissistically as reason to believe a mirror inhabits his spine and who, should the mirror slip and break, is willing to be quoted as saying "Half is enough," to the hermit of "Chemin de Fer," who wants his actions echoed. At one time Bishop announced that she was working on a verse translation of Aristophanes' *The Birds*, and her interest in Aristophanes may account for the particular myth of love that she selects as well as for her sense of the bizarre, though this second may derive more rightly from the writings of Franz Kafka. What is most striking about "The Weed" is not the bizarre but the poem's possible debt to Emily Dickinson—the decision to realize its message by means of the most humble of messengers, a weed. The minuteness with which the probing growth of this weed is described lends the poem its vividness and mystery despite a feeling that the whole is labored, emblematic, and baroque. One simply forgets Herbert or Dickinson when Bishop relates of the weed that "It grew an inch like a blade of grass; / next one leaf shot out of its side / a twisting, waving flag, and then / two leaves moved like a semaphore. / The stem grew thick." Similarly one thinks of the techniques of a naturalist when she describes "the nervous roots" reaching to each side; "the graceful head / changed its position mysteriously, / since there was neither sun nor moon / to catch its young attention."

The theme of pain, once more suggested by tears, preserves the centrality of feeling in Bishop's work. Tears also occur in "Chemin de Fer" and the fourth song in "Songs for a Colored Singer." In the first poem the pond across which the hermit fires his rifle is seen as "an old tear / holding onto its injuries / lucidly year after year," and one suspects that "injuries" may account for the lack of echo in the poem. The falling leaves of the Negro song àre compared to "tears when somebody grieves" and become seeds from which "faces" like memories grow, again conveying the recollective nature of Bishop's technique. To see the world as tears or as prompting or resulting from tears seems to promote the world as necessary betrayal, irritation, loss, and pain against which, as "The Weed" suggests, one ought not to become hardened and yet for which betrayals, as "Roosters" indicates, one must atone. Thus, like most of the other postmodernists, her primary approach to experience is psychological rather than philosophical—although one might see her decision to endure despite inevitable losses as a kind of stoical acceptance. Her "*elend*" or wretchedness is no different from that described by Jarrell's "Seele im Raum" (1950), just as the conclusions of her journeys "in / No destination we meant" are no different from that of his "On the Railway Platform" (1939). Even her understanding "that the wickedness and confusion of the age can explain and extenuate other people's wickedness and confusion, but not, for you, your own" [17] is postmodern: it is not only what Jarrell makes true for Auden and Rudyard Kipling but what he makes typical of his generation.

Yet, much as these poems exist by a kind of suffering, "The Fish," whose "fine rosettes of lime" owe to Hopkins's "rose-moles all in stipple upon trout" and whose climax may derive from Mallarmé's "l'azur, l'azur, l'azur, l'azur," offers ostensibly a "fish story": it is a yarn about the proverbial catch "that got away." The poem which delineates the time between the supposed catching of a "tremendous fish" and the narrator's letting it go displays what is perhaps Bishop's most calculated use of detail. The only basis for one's believing that the fish was caught is her ability to describe it minutely. How can one doubt the existence of a fish whose brown skin hangs here and there "in stripes / like ancient wallpaper" and whose pattern of darker brown is also "like wallpaper: / shapes like full-blown roses / stained and lost through age"? Or for that matter why should one question a creature "infested / with tiny white sea-lice" and trailing in glory "rags and green weed"? Yet the detail of such externals is no more reliably expressed or is no more credible than the confessed imagined "coarse white flesh / packed in like feathers" or "the dramatic reds and blacks / of his shiny entrails / and the pink swim-bladder / like a big peony." One simply presumes, as with any good teller of fish stories, that she caught the tremendous fish without having engaged in a fight and looked into its eyes and that the consequence of this look made her throw the fish back.

The obliviousness of the Hopkinsish eyes, "the irises backed and packed / with tarnished tinfoil / seen through the lenses / of old scratched isinglass" offers some clue to the speaker's action. It resonates against the lack of struggle accompanying her landing the fish and suggests that the experience may have disappointed her, much as the traveler of "Over 2000 Illustrations and a Complete Concordance" had been disappointed with travel. The disappointment seems to explain why the "five old pieces of fish-line" which hang from its lips are "like medals with their ribbons / frayed and wavering." No such heroic counterstruggle has occurred here, and the victory which begins to fill up "the little rented boat" has, at least on her part, been made empty. Yet, by virtue of an engine's oil spill, a rainbow parodying God's restoration of dominion to Noah occurs; and the illumination of this rainbow, brought about by accident and technology, becomes the immediate cause of her letting the creature go. This final act may be as perverse as the fish's wanting to be caught, or it may suggest, as evolutionists like Alfred Russel Wallace propose, a transference to machine and tools of what in animals takes place through evolution of body parts. Man's dominion is again (as it was in "The Man-Moth" and "The Imaginary Iceberg") wryly evolutionist. But the effect of her letting the fish go may not merely function to explain to others "how it got away"; it may also work to emphasize the importance of detail as a basis for understanding.

The stylization of content, the suppression of pity, and the attention to detail in all these poems led Jarrell to say of her first collection: "Miss Bishop's poems are almost never forced; in her best work restraint, calm, and proportion are implicit in every detail of organization and workmanship. . . . Her work is unusually personal and honest in its wit, perception, and sensitivity—and in its restrictions too; all her poems have written underneath, *I have seen it*." He was to add in a review of her second volume (1955): "They have a sound, a feel, a whole moral and physical atmosphere, different from anything else I know. . . . They are honest, modest, minutely observant, masterly; even their most complicated or troubled or imaginative effects seem, always, personal and natural, and as unmistakable as the first few notes of a Mahler song, the first few patches of a Vuillard interior." Bishop seems to have reacted favorably enough to the earlier criticism that, in 1957, when she published her translation of *The Diary of "Helena Morley,"* she used a variation of the statement to praise the author. Citing Hopkins's comment in regard to Richard Dana's *Two Years before the Mast*, she says of the diary: "That, I think, is 'the charm and the main point' of *Minha Vida de Menina. . . . It really happened;* everything did take place, day by day, minute by minute, once and only once, just the way Helena says it did." [18]

If some of these poems succeed by willfully excluding the past and necessity, other poems in the same volume show the presence of necessary behavior. "Florida," for instance, despite its being "the state with the prettiest name," cannot prosper without the intense struggle for survival that necessity demands. The alligator has five distinct calls: "friendliness, love, mating, war, and a warning." Hence the exuberance which critics like Stephen Stepanchev see in certain poems as "irrelevant" becomes irrelevant only because of the lack of choice. Stepanchev can see the effect accurately enough but cannot perceive the cause: "It is as though Miss Bishop stopped along the road home to examine every buttercup and asphodel she saw. The images are dazzling; they call attention to themselves like ambitious actors in minor roles; but they contribute very little to the total effect." [19] To make these examinations contribute to a poem's total effect is to deny precisely their necessity in life. "Seascapes" similarly presents a "heavenly" scene as a moving narrator might see it and contrasts the vision to the hell that a stationary "skeletal lighthouse" has. Here, though mutually exclusive, both points of view seem equally fixed by necessity. Necessity also figures in as a minor theme in "Roosters," where it is represented as a struggle for survival, and in "The Fish," where it is seen in the evolutionary progress.

Equally interesting as these travel poems, which can be divided like Boomer's scraps into matter about one's self and about what seems bewilderingly inexplicable, are poems about people whose lives catch the poet's fancy. Early poems like "Cootchie," "The Prodigal," and "Faustina, or Rock Roses" lead into later works like "The Riverman" and "The Burglar of Babylon" to form a body of poems which is based on attention not to detail but to a corresponding uniqueness of human personality that often repeats in human terms what is going on in the natural world. "Cootchie," for example, speaks to the same problem of art that "The Map" had. It describes Miss Lula's black servant, going "black into white . . . below the surface of the coral-reef." The same light-house that earlier appeared in "Seascape" will search "land and sea" for someone else and will dismiss Cootchie's grave as trivial. The dismissal contrasts with the efforts of Miss Lula to commemo-rate her servant with "melting" pink wax roses. "Cootchie" may be based on a Baudelaire poem—"La Servante" in which an old servant is recollected. The poem leads directly into "Faustina, or Rock Roses," a second poem concerning service, which moves beyond the sentiments of Baudelaire to ally the matter of service with that of necessity.

This second poem about a dying woman, her servant, and a visitor prompts the visitor to question whether death is "freedom at last" or "the very worst, / the unimaginable nightmare." The visitor concludes by wondering of the origin of things: "whence come / all the petals" of the world she inhabits. The bed containing the sick woman is described earlier in rose imagery; and roses have, in the course of the poem, become confused with the servant: hence the word *or* of the title. The visitor's roses are only part of the work's elaborate pattern which may be inspired by the rose imagery of Dante's *Paradiso*. Faustina seems saved from the crazi-ness of the house and bed by an unquestioning devotion to work, by the kind of Sisyphean effort that Albert Camus calls the absurd and which runs through much of Bishop's writing. The intriguing voice of the poem is that of the voyeur-speaker. She seems both separated from the visitor, who is described in third person and yet involved: "The eighty-watt bulb" is said to "betray *us* all, / discov-ering the concern / within *our* stupefaction." Later the "acuteness of the question" of man's origin re-creates an image of Satan and Judeo-Christian evil with "a snake-tongue flickering," blunting, proliferating "*our* problems" (italics mine); but one is at a loss as to precisely when and how the third-person visitor becomes a first-person narrator. The poem seems to suggest that not even spectators can divorce themselves from the necessity of nature's laws.

Yet, if "Faustina" speaks of necessity with its parodic Dantean roses, "The Prodigal" speaks with equal power of filth and matters of choice. Realized in two sonnets, it depicts the personal hell of an alcoholic who finds himself often recovering from drunkenness in a pig pen and who finally does "make up his mind to go home." Occasionally the sun "glazing" the barnyard mud with red seems to reassure him, and occasionally "the lantern" casts a religious glow, but "shuddering insights, beyond his control" force him beyond these suggestions of art and religion. He decides to leave, and his decision lies clearly within the realm of choice. In this instance "home" seems to mean by the poem's title the alcoholic's origins, though one is never certain if they are a state of nonbeing or a place. One is almost certain, on the other hand, that the pig pen is meant to suggest worldly existence and that, like "Cootchie" and "Faustina," "The Prodigal" is intended to reflect actual observation more than literary antecedents. "The Riverman" and "The Burglar of Babylon," in contrast, are derivative and form, thereby, equivalents of the "found statements" that Boomer occasionally comes upon. Bishop relates that details of "The Riverman" come "from 'Amazon Town,' by Charles Wagley" and that "The Burglar of Babylon" is "a true story, taken from the newspaper accounts." She "made only two minor changes in the facts." [20] Thus the origin of these character poems, like the subjects of the nature pieces, raises problems of choice.

Written in free verse, "The Riverman" seems to derive from the same mixture of folktale and fact that typified "The Man-Moth." Its speaker wishes to become a witch doctor, and he believes that he has been spoken to by the river dolphin and has been given presents by the water spirits. By his initiation it is clear that he has not selected the vocation but rather that the dolphin has selected him. The night setting and the man's nakedness are both suggestive of the libidinous impulses that motivate his actions. In addition his going down into the river is a reversal of the action of most of Bishop's progressive protagonists who, if anything, move inland and away from water. The parallel between the man's house on shore and the mansion beneath the water is clear, as is the mirror imagery which, by its insistence on pristine reflection, comments on the pattern of complementarity that has been evolving in her work. Yet the imitation of prescientific thinking seems less her own than had been the thinking of "The Man-Moth." Nothing here suggests a parable for man's will, as had the earlier poem. Instead what the poem and its version of "total immersion" imply is the power of the irrational over civilization, and in that regard the work perpetuates her view that all the products of man will erode. Perhaps, as with other writers of her generation, the source for such a view is Freud's *Civilization and Its Discontents* (1929), but it need not have been. The view is implicit in Elizabeth Bishop's notion of art as temporary, and it explains why she is able to reject the evolutionist's optimism about the future of man based on his ability to construct tools and systems.

"The Burglar of Babylon" repeats this struggle for existence between the lawless (libido) and the law (superego). Like the poor, its criminal cannot go home again once he has been to Rio. This "home," like the Prodigal's, is never specified, for presumably the criminal is from Rio. His removal earlier to a penitentiary has temporarily separated him but in no way has changed that fact. The separation has, on the other hand, made it imperative that he risk death to see again "his auntie, / who raised him like a son." The reader is thus faced with an existential dilemma: the "home" of the burglar becomes, as with the poet and the alcoholic of "The Prodigal," an origin either worldly or otherworldly that is unrecoverable; and his return and pursuit by the police, who shoot their leader by mistake before killing him, end unexpectedly. His aunt cannot understand why he turned criminal, and others do not know why he was so inept that he "got caught six times—or more." The poem ends darkly: the police are "after another two" criminals who are supposedly not "as dangerous / As the poor Micuçu," but one wonders about the self-destructiveness and self-hate that must underscore Micuçu's actions and beliefs. Why else would he have failed so consistently at his crimes? The ending in a failure to secure all the criminals and, hence, to conquer the irrational drive recalls the failure earlier by art in "The Sea and Its Shore" to achieve the same control. The poem by this failure reinforces the themes of loss and pain that comprise much of Bishop's vision. To heighten this failure of containment, the poet chooses a formal genre, the ballad, a form historically allied with tales of outlawry.

Among the most winning of the character poems is "Invitation to Miss Marianne Moore." Based loosely on Pablo Neruda's "Alberto Rojas Jiménez viene volando," it forms an invitation to the older poet to spend a day with the speaker, talking, shopping, and visiting. In the Neruda poem the dead Jiménez comes flying on one of the paper birds that it was the hobby of the dead writer to construct. Jiménez is first located among the decaying dead. From here he begins his journey over living scenes until he reaches Neruda "sin sombra y sin nombre, / sin azúcar, sin boca, sin rosales." For Bishop, Brooklyn becomes the place where the poet is "buried" and whose smells and hellish "clouds of fiery chemicals" must be overcome. She too must traverse the "live world" of the East River and its "whistles, pennants, and smoke" to join the speaker. But, as ever in Bishop, the poetry that Moore writes and that critics like Wallace Fowlie say bestows immortality on writers[21] is here seen as transient: "dynasties of negative constructions / darkening and dying" despite a "grammar that suddenly turns and shines / like flocks of sandpipers flying." The effect of this brilliance among the dying is compared to a brief "light in the white mackerel sky, . . . a daytime comet."

The poem's basic stoic position—a struggle toward life in the face of inevitable destruction—is depicted in "The Sea and Its Shore" and is repeated in Bishop's remarks about the dying Flannery O'Connor: "Something about her intimidated me a bit: perhaps natural awe before her toughness and courage; perhaps, although death is certain for all, hers seemed a little more certain than usual. She made no show of not living in a metropolis, or of being a believer, she lived with Christian stoicism and wonderful wit and humor that put most of us to shame." In "Invitation" the wit of both Moore and Bishop in the face of inevitable, although not imminent, death converges in the description of the older poet as a fairy godmother:

> Come with the pointed toe of each black shoe
> trailing a sapphire highlight,
> with a black capeful of butterfly wings and bon-mots,
> with heaven knows how many angels all riding
> on the broad black brim of your hat. . . .

With such wit, it seems almost inevitable that a few critics should find the poem "whimsical bravura" and "priceless" and that they should pay less attention to the battle against self-pity which is also part of the vision.[22]

The same preoccupation with the transience of art recurs in "Santarém" (1978), except here inevitable destruction gives way to taste. The speaker's admiration for a wasps' nest contrasts with a fellow traveler's pronouncement that it is an "ugly thing." Naturalists have described how natives with machetes "obtain the whitish, tough-cartoned nests of *Chartergus* for sale to Europeans as curios."[23] In the poem the harvested nest opposes the human community and its various divisions of labor, recalling Darwin's earlier worry over specialization among insects and his defenses against critics who argued that only God could be so ingenious as to grant insects the power to construct such efficient and perfectly shaped cells. Traffic divides into dories, stern-wheeler, side-wheelers, dugouts, and river schooner. Thus technology is again made part of man's natural instincts, and art is only one more kind of technology or, rather, a relic of what once was functional. As in other Bishop poems, art is achieved by going backward to "that conflux of two great rivers"—childhood wish or "the Garden of Eden"; and in almost dialectic fashion, the poem's cathedral like the poem itself arises out of an effort to transcend that mental journey and its discovered oppositions of "life/death, right/wrong, male/female." Like the experienced cathedral and the priest's home, art is not immune to natural disaster, though like the priest, one may be away when destruction comes. The very nature of the residue and recovery of the poem's vision, moreover, links it to "Crusoe in England" and the concerns of technology and travel that mark "Imaginary Iceberg," "The Map," "Over 2000 Illustrations and a Complete Concordance," and the Brazil section of *Questions of Travel.*

Bishop's decision in 1951 to live in Brazil leads to a lessening in *Questions of Travel* (1965) of the struggles for existence that underscore most of the early poems. As both "The Riverman" and "The Burglar of Babylon" imply, the major effort here is against time, as if temporary survival has already been assured and must now be protected. Thus the travelers of "Arrival at Santos" and "Questions of Travel" have a sense of their own being at the onset, and the poems relate their defenses against the "answers" which life will offer to "immodest demands for a different world." One must be careful of the boy with the boat hook, the customs officials who may seize the "bourbon and cigarettes," and the frailty of postage stamps which threaten to come off letters and make them undeliverable. Therefore one heads away from the coast where earlier Bishop's major conflicts had been situated. He moves toward the interior where, as he is asked in the title poem: "Is it lack of imagination that makes us come / to imagined places, not just stay at home?" There the journey proves disturbing with its many waterfalls and crowded streams rushing rapidly to oblivion in the sea. Is the purpose of the interiors (civilization) to return one to barbarism (the sea)? Are writers like Giambattista Vico and Norman O. Brown right in their views of history? Is the enormous effort of such travel into the interior ultimately to be wasted? If so, her speaker asks, what drive in man compels him to see these sights for, despite the effort, he would surely regret having missed them? She concludes that knowledge of necessity is never clear: "The choice is never wide and never free."

Like the man-moth's struggle to "investigate as high as he can climb," man's thirst to realize what he imagines becomes in these late poems a mystery, a part of man's nature that is made more visible for readers by a change in the poet's intent to keep one from withdrawing to the past. Stevens in "Peter Quince at the Clavier" (1915) had seen that mystery. He proposed that unrealized concepts give way to new concepts, but those given body are preserved by memory: "Beauty is momentary in the mind . . . / But in the flesh it is immortal." Experience becomes important in itself because of its memory value and, by the durability of recollection, replaces the importance of conceptualization. This is Bishop's position in "The Sea and Its Shore," and in his discussion of "precious objects," Ransom touches on the psychological nature of this replacement as it might affect poetry. He sees poets who use a quantity of such objects as appealing to sentiment rather than to sensibility and as ignoring that special public which is conditioned to react immediately to the significances of what the poet celebrates for the larger public that needs to experience what is being described before it can react. In the case of Bishop's work, life's final uncertainty and the sometimes self-pitying acceptance of annihilation demand an emphasis on experience as the only reality and a special willingness by readers to accept the often cross-grained nature of that experience. When her vision was couched, as in the early poems, in a complex texture that counteracted the sentimentality, acceptances were easier. M. L. Rosenthal rejected her occlusions early, and in *The Modern Poets* (1960) he dismisses a large part of her work as sentimental, and critics like Nancy McNally have stressed the pain and ugliness of what is being depicted.

Something other than mere sentimentalism is again working in these late poems. Certainly Bishop's response to the false prettiness of Fowlie's *Pantomime, A Journal of Rehearsals* (1951), confirms that the ugliness of many of her recollections is, as Jarrell points out, part of the original experience. "My own first ride on a swan boat occurred at the age of three and is chiefly memorable for the fact that one of the live swans paddling around us bit my mother's finger when she offered it a peanut. I remember the hole in the black kid glove and a drop of blood." [24] Yet the continuing emphasis on labor in her writing keeps her from indulging excessively in feeling for its own sake. "The Armadillo" with its final echo of E. A. Robinson offers the clearest argument in these late pieces against her using "precious objects" merely for sentimental emphasis, though something might be said, independent of the poems, for an imagination that recurs consistently to the unpleasant events of her life. All the tears of her poetry may be meant to evoke an awe from the reader similar to that awe which she expresses for O'Connor. If not sympathy for her sensibility, then some kind of admiration for her having withstood the disappointments is being sought and sought on terms not of accomplishment so much as service. But the poems seem to be echoing more importantly Juvenal's advice in Satire x that, if one would be happy, one must want less. Man has been conditioned to think self-indulgently, and his self-indulgence must be curbed.

The situation of "The Armadillo" is not appreciably different from situations that one meets in the poetry of Robinson or Frost. Existence is seen lying between an origin that has been abandoned and perhaps cannot be known and a purpose which is equally unknowable. Yet Robinson would argue by example that the ensuing destructiveness of an Eben Flood or Miniver Cheevey or Richard Cory, being suicidal, does not destroy others; and Frost would make the situation an occasion for his speaker's taking stock. In contrast the celebration of the Bishop poem is widely ecological. The illegal cometlike balloons which are loosed into the landscape manage to threaten and harm the animals, just as man wherever he has settled has threatened the balance of nature and the existence of wildlife. The point of the poem is opposed, as a consequence, to Robinson's utilitarian posture and Frost's quiet contemplation. No man does injury merely to himself or acts entirely toward his own ends. Man's accomplishments may rise toward sainthood and seem, once up in the sky, like stars or planets; but the consequences still descend to do damage to owl nest, armadillo, rabbit, and, hence, other men. Thus the question raised early by "A Large Bad Picture" as to whether the ends of man are determined by "Commerce or contemplation" is turned into a nonquestion. The vital question becomes one of interrelation and a determination of how best the present may preserve for the future what already exists. In such a world shut off from certitude and salvation, one's options become Micuçu's or Flood's; one either tries to recover childhood or its primitive equivalent—a world before man began to impose his egotistical will—or one resorts to isolation, self-pity, drink, and eventually suicide. Bishop makes clear that, for all the exceptional experiences that she has had and dwells upon in her work, she desires the return.

"Manners," "Sestina," "The First Death in Nova Scotia," and "Sunday, 4 A.M." from *Questions of Travel* as well as the late stories, "Gwendolyn" and "In the Village" exemplify this return. They complement the move to a more primitive Brazil with a return by the poet mentally to her origins; the move is equated not with any theological or evolutionary system but with her early life. In bringing her work back to a world determined by others and to childhood as the completion of self, Bishop is least protected against a charge of sentimentalism. "Manners" simply and nostalgically describes her grandfather's lesson in "good manners." "Sestina" recounts in equally sentimental terms a rainy day spent with her grandmother drawing while the grandmother busied herself with chores. "The First Death in Nova Scotia" relates the death of her cousin Arthur, who is made to resemble a "frosted cake" and supposedly borne off "to be / the smallest page at court." "Sunday, 4 A.M." shows how much later the poet's dreams confuse the memories of people who had deeply impressed her as a child with more recent acquaintances. Only daylight and its bird song restore order. Yet, however minor these poems may seem, the logic of the returns is no different from that of the philosopher who equates man's nature with his origins, and in proposing the returns, Bishop accepts a pattern similar to that which a number of postmodern poets have used. Roethke recurs to such a pattern in *The Lost Son* (1948) and *Praise to the End!* (1951), Lowell in *Life Studies* (1959), Jarrell in *The Lost World* (1965), and Berryman in his own late reconstructions of youth.

Returns continue in *Geography III* (1977) in such poems as "In the Waiting Room," "The Moose," and "Poem." The first pictures the poet on the verge of her seventh birthday in the waiting room of a dentist's office in Worcester, Massachusetts. World War I is in progress, and the poem describes the awareness that she achieves by a growing empathy first with an aunt, then with others in the dentist's waiting room, and finally with everyone on earth. In this move to adult awareness, Bishop chooses an age traditionally linked to the start of moral responsibility, and she tampers with the actual contents of the *National Geographic*, but rather than move the subject toward the often personal and, hence, sentimental lessons of *Questions of Travel*, the tampering broadens the work's appeal. "The Moose" describes what begins as a bus trip from Nova Scotia to Boston—first in terms of the coast, then in terms of farms and the past lives of the passengers. Suddenly the trip out of raw nature is interrupted by the appearance of a moose, and one discovers that man's technical progress in no way defeats his fascination with the primitive. "Poem" details another painting of Nova Scotia. Like that of "Large Bad Picture" it is painted by the poet's great uncle George Hutchinson. The poet identifies the painting's subject by the location's general characteristics and, as the poem gains subjective power, by her own recollection of the precise place and a history of how she came into possession of the work. The poem ends with a coincidence of visions, indicating that places which are personally and deeply felt can be matched by different but equally deeply and personally felt experience.

In this new corollary of personal and collective experience, Bishop's speakers achieve something akin to what Angus Fletcher in *Allegory* (1964) describes as the allegorical protagonist. This protagonist acts "as if possessed," implying "cosmic notions of fate and personal fortune." His actions touch on both "human and divine spheres" and make "an appeal to an almost scientific curiosity about the order of things." He is "a conquistador," arbitrating "order over chaos by confronting a random collection of people and events" and "imposing his own fate upon that random collection." As in medieval allegory, the literal sense of a Bishop poem comes first, "it being the meaning in which the others are contained and without which it would be impossible and irrational to come to an understanding of the others, particularly the allegorical." The literal sense permits the factive sense to border at times on rationalism and at times on surrealism. One may see this allegory, moreover, as a necessary solution to what she describes in her interview as a love of religious poetry and a dislike of didacticism. She told Ashley Brown: "Auden's late poetry is sometimes spoiled for me by his didacticism. I don't like modern religiosity in general: it always seems to lead to a tone of moral superiority. . . . Times have changed since Herbert's day." By means of a corresponding and accessible ideal world at one remove from experience, she can assert a "moral" meaning at the same time that she keeps her narrative from overt moralizing.[25]

Out of this ideal world and the manipulation of "precious objects," Bishop has created a significant poetry; and just as one may say that she in her returns is not so individualistic as Robinson, Frost, or Stevens, and hence different from that generation, one may add that she is never so mystical as Roethke or so involved with gaining reader sympathy as are the "confessional poets." Regardless of their conclusions, her poems are still active; and despite their searches for self and their emphases on dream, her reconstructions are not inspired by Freudian analysis and its wish to have one's direction altered by the conscious. Although Bishop returns mentally to her origins, her returns do not reflect any of the pathological compulsion that Sherman Paul detects in Crane's reveries of childhood nor do they reflect the therapeutic aims that seem to lie behind the returns of Roethke, Jarrell, Plath, and Berryman. One has the sense, particularly in these late poems, that, unlike some of her contemporaries, she has lived the life she imagined—with all its necessary disappointments—and that, despite the narrow range of choice and the pain of disappointment, she is willing to see her past as the only kind of life she could have lived. She is not, as are Ignatow, Plath, and Berryman, trying to fix blame; nor is she necessarily, as are Roethke and Jarrell, trying to be sympathetic. Like Baudelaire's voyagers she seems instead to be accepting the conditions of voyaging as the process of a life which itself will arrive meaninglessly at death with perhaps a few poems as a dividend.

In their consistent pessimism about ultimate purpose, the ranges of Bishop's vision relate her to the views of modernist poets like Robinson, Frost, and Stevens as well as to the major questions asked by their successors. Her work is perhaps more profoundly existential than the poetry of any of her contemporaries, and like Ignatow she questions even the evolutionary thrust on which occasionally a poet like Jarrell relies. She can and does believe in "tradition" and a sense of linear history, but not in a tradition or history that concedes the immortality of art. Her "tradition" with its accumulation and reinforcements of feeling is no different from the cumulative effects of experience. Her use of works which have preceded her functions more to reinforce than, as in Jarrell, to effect a death struggle with a father figure and to supplant his image. Her "precious objects" give the reader the only durability that she has discovered, and in presenting this durability, she never fights for an idiosyncratic idiom. Such an idiom would distort the reality she values and would finally prove immaterial, an exercise in will without regard to environment. She thus opposes the "rarity" that poets of her generation have assumed to promote their own egos and work and which, by its occasionally strident assertions of importance, can be as self-pitying as her denial of will. Nonetheless one may wonder what her poetry would have been like if she, like her man-moth, had relinquished her "one tear." A more militant stoicism like that she admires in O'Connor might have resulted and produced an equally interesting body of work, but one with far less emphasis on detail and inclined even more to allegory.

If Bishop's approach to life by its inclusion of impediments seems less "intellectual" than that of other poets, it is that she is finally given more to necessity than they are. She is more willing to see life as a dialectical process involving man and his environment rather than a process of man's will being imposed upon his surroundings. Although man may not be improving in her view, he will survive, much as other animal life has survived; and he will need whatever beauty may be preservable. To accept this vision she must abandon the superstructures that most critics rely on to cope with poets—those structures of thought which by their very separation from experience seem to define the ego. By minimizing the organizational nature of such separations and by placing her definition of being on specific interactions with objects, she embraces a relativism like that of other postmodernist poets but based on situation rather than on voice. Her diverse "characters," as Southworth points out, lie not in personae but in her manner of selecting subjects, in a tonality, and in her varied ways of massing detail into significant form. She emerges, therefore, as a balance to the tendency of other poets of her generation to overstress will and rarity. She reminds one how narrow the choices of life are and how unimportant rarity is. Erosion takes its toll of that, too. When *The Complete Poems* appeared in 1969, readers were thankful mainly for the convenience of having all her poems under one cover. Her tendency there to keep her subjects isolated, small, and circumscribed, worked toward establishing her as a master of the self-contained anthology piece. The poems she published afterward, however, have brought her as close as any contemporary writer to the scope and to the "one significant, consistent, and developing personality" that Eliot makes requisite to great poets.[26] It is a greatness, moreover, linked intimately to postmodernist methods.

Notes

1. F. Cudworth Flint, "New Leaders in English Poetry," *Virginia Quarterly Review* 14 (1938):510; Anne Stevenson, *Elizabeth Bishop* (New York: Twayne

Publishers, 1966), pp. 13–14; James G. Southworth, "The Poetry of Elizabeth Bishop," *College English* 20 (1959):213.

2. Stevenson, p. 44; Elizabeth Bishop, "As We Like It," *Quarterly Review of Literature* 4 (1948):130–31; Bishop, "It All Depends," in *Mid-Century American Poets*, ed. John Ciardi (New York: Twayne Publishers, 1950), p. 267; John Crowe Ransom, "Poetry: II. The Final Cause," *Kenyon Review* 5 (1947):643.

3. Elizabeth Bishop, "Gregorio Valdes, 1879–1939," *Partisan Review* 6 (summer 1939):95, 92; Bishop, "Flannery O'Connor," *Spirit* 8 (winter 1964):14, 16; Bishop, "An Inadequate Tribute," in *Randall Jarrell: 1914–1965*, ed. Robert Lowell, Peter Taylor, and Robert Penn Warren (New York: Farrar, Straus and Giroux, 1967), pp. 20–21.

4. Robert Lowell, *Life Studies* (New York: Farrar, Straus and Cudahy, 1959), pp. 12–13.

5. Gaston Bachelard, *The Poetics of Reverie*, trans. Daniel Russell (Boston: Beacon Books, 1971), p. 99; Stevenson, pp. 34–35; 26.

6. Elizabeth Bishop, "The Baptism," *Life and Letters To-Day* 16 (spring 1937), 72, 76, 78; Bishop, "Gwendolyn," *New Yorker* 29 (27 June 1963): 26–31.

7. Elizabeth Bishop, "In the Village," *New Yorker* 29 (19 December 1953), 26–34; Stevenson, p. 28.

8. Elizabeth Bishop, "The Sea and Its Shore," *Life and Letters To-Day* 17 (winter 1937):108, 103.

9. "Flannery O'Connor," p. 16; "An Inadequate Tribute," p. 21; Ashley Brown, "An Interview with Elizabeth Bishop," *Shenandoah* 17 (1966):8–9.

10. Roland Barthes, *Writing Degree Zero*, trans. Annette Levers and Colin Smith (New York: Hill & Wang, 1968), p. 4; Prince Modupe, *I Was a Savage* (London: Museum Press, 1958), p. 133.

11. Norman J. W. Thrower, *Maps & Men* (Englewood Cliffs: Prentice-Hall, 1972), p. 60.

12. Stevenson, p. 111; Joseph N. Riddel, "Stevens on Imagination," in *The Quest for Imagination*, ed. O. B. Hardison, Jr. (Cleveland: Case Western Reserve University Press, 1971), p. 55.

13. "The Baptism," p. 72; "In the Village," p. 26.

14. Elizabeth Bishop, "In Prison," *Partisan Review* 4 (1938):3, 7, 9, 10.

15. "In Prison," pp. 3, 8. For a more detailed discussion of "Crusoe in England" and other recent Bishop poems, see my "The Recent Poems of Elizabeth Bishop," *South Carolina Review* 10 (November 1977):99–115, and "Elizabeth Bishop's Particulars," *World Literature Today* 51 (winter 1977):46–49.

16. Robert Lowell, "Thomas, Bishop, and Williams," *Sewanee Review* 55 (1946):497.

17. Randall Jarrell, *Poetry and the Age* (New York: Vintage Books, 1955), p. 213.

18. Ibid., p. 213; Randall Jarrell, "The Year in Poetry," *Harper's* 211 (October 1955):99; Elizabeth Bishop, Introduction, *The Diary of "Helena Morley"* (New York: Farrar, Straus, and Cudahy, 1957), p. xxiv.

19. Stephen Stepanchev, *American Poetry since 1945* (New York: Colophon Book, 1967), p. 74

20. Brown, p. 19.

21. Wallace Fowlie, "Poetry of Silence," *Commonweal* 65 (1957):514.

22. "Flannery O'Connor," p. 16; Stevenson, p. 46.

23. Elizabeth Bishop, "Santarém," *New Yorker* 54 (20 February 1978):40; Howard E. Evans and Mary Jane Eberhart, *The Wasps* (Ann Arbor: University of Michigan Press, 1970), pp. 176, 135.

24. Elizabeth Bishop, "What the Young Man Said to the Psalmist," *Poetry* 79 (1952):213.

25. Angus Fletcher, *Allegory: The Theory of a Symbolic Mode* (Ithaca: Cornell University Press, 1964), pp. 68–69; *The Literary Criticism of Dante Alighieri*, trans. and ed. Robert S. Haller (Lincoln: University of Nebraska Press, 1973), p. 113; Brown, pp. 10–11.

26. Southworth, p. 214; T. S. Eliot, *Selected Essays*, new ed. (London: Faber and Faber, 1951), p. 203.

Index

199

Index

Index

Index

Index